Governance and Society in Colonial Mexico

Chihuahua in the Eighteenth Century

Governance and Society in Colonial Mexico

Chihuahua in the Eighteenth Century

Cheryl English Martin

Stanford University Press
Stanford, California

Stanford University Press
Stanford, California

Printed and bound by CPI Group (UK) Ltd,
Croydon, CR0 4YY

CIP data are at the end of the book

To Charles

Acknowledgments

Many people and organizations provided invaluable material help and moral support while this book was in the making. I am most grateful to all of those associated over the years with the Mexican Microfilming Project at the University of Texas at El Paso. Their efforts made it possible for me to conduct a great deal of my research in the comfort of the UTEP Library. In particular, I would like to thank Wilbert H. Timmons for his contributions to the microfilming project as well as for his energetic promotion of research in Borderlands history.

The University of Texas at El Paso also provided funds to help underwrite various phases of this study. During their respective tenures as director of the Center for Inter-American and Border Studies, Oscar Martínez and Samuel Schmidt authorized grants to cover travel and other research expenses. Additional funds were provided by the UTEP Graduate School, the College of Liberal Arts, and the office of the Vice President for Academic Affairs.

Others at UTEP who deserve a heartfelt *gracias* include my colleagues Sandra McGee Deutsch in the Department of History, Howard Campbell and Alejandro Lugo in the Department of Anthropology, and Kathleen Staudt in the Department of Political Science, all of whom read portions of the manuscript and provided excellent insights and criticisms from a variety of disciplinary perspectives. Vicki Fisher graciously took on the task of printing the final version of the manuscript. Two of my former graduate students also helped with the project. Coreta Justus served as my research assistant for several months, and I gratefully acknowledge her for diligently tracking down obscure references in the Chihuahua parish registers and for sharing my fascination with the remarkable life history of Juana de Cobos. Yolanda Leyva also provided crucial research assistance and citations drawn from her own work. In addition, I would like to thank the hundreds of other graduate and undergraduate students, many of them descendants of Chihuahua's earliest settlers, who have taken my courses in Mexican and Borderlands History at UTEP over the years. Their questions have often inspired me and my colleagues to think about our material in new ways, and thus they have shown us that teaching and research are complementary endeavors. In particular I would like to mention Carlos Chacón, an exceptionally gifted and perceptive student who read portions of this book in manuscript form and whose death in January 1995 cut short a promising future.

A generous fellowship from the National Endowment for the Humanities permitted me to spend an entire year working full-time on the project. For those of us employed at universities that do not provide sabbatical leaves, such grants are a godsend. My thanks also to Anthony Reaza of San Gabriel, California, a descendant of the founders of San Felipe el Real de Chihuahua, who generously shared the results of his own very thorough genealogical study and made detailed comments on the penultimate draft of the manuscript, and to William E. French of the University of British Columbia, who also offered very helpful suggestions.

Finally, I thank my parents, Hal and Helen English, for their continued love and support. To my son Jeff, my very special gratitude for cheerfully putting up with two historian-parents, and for always giving us good reasons to look to the future as well as the past. And to Charles—husband, colleague, demanding but gentle critic, and, after more than a quarter-century of *vida maridable*, still my best friend—this book is fondly dedicated.

Contents

Tables

All tables are located in the Appendix, page 201.

Governance and Society in Colonial Mexico

Chihuahua in the Eighteenth Century

Introduction

IN 1702 prospectors discovered silver at Chihuahua, a remote desert location in the province of Nueva Vizcaya, nearly a thousand miles to the northwest of Mexico City. Though less well known to historians than Zacatecas, Guanajuato, and other more centrally located mining sites, the district of Chihuahua contributed heavily to the economic growth of New Spain in the first half of the eighteenth century. Between 1703 and 1737, the area yielded silver worth an estimated 60 million pesos, or one-fourth of the total output for the entire viceroyalty. For the period from 1705 to 1790, Chihuahua accounted for one-eighth of the colony's production of silver.[1] Not surprisingly, news of the fortunes to be had there spread to Europe and throughout New Spain.[2]

The most important population center in the region was the *villa* or Spanish municipality of San Felipe el Real de Chihuahua (today the city of Chihuahua). Following the discovery of silver in the region, the town flowered almost overnight on a site where no previous permanent settlement had stood, and it was formally constituted as a villa in 1718. Complete with an imposing central plaza and other urban amenities and governed by a municipal council, or *cabildo*, the villa quickly emerged as the foremost administrative and commercial center on the north-central frontier of New Spain. For much of the eighteenth century San Felipe el Real also served as the de facto capital of Nueva Vizcaya, since many of its governors preferred to reside there rather than in Durango, the nominal capital of the province. The jurisdiction of the *corregidor* (royal magistrate) posted at San Felipe covered much of the present-day state of Chihuahua and included a number of other important settlements, such as military garrisons (*presidios*), rural estates of varying sizes, and Indian mission villages.

The villa's economic influence extended even farther than its political reach. Its merchants soon gained control of trade between central New Spain and the Spanish colony of New Mexico. Although the depletion of its silver ores and attacks by hostile Indians blunted the local mining boom after 1740, San Felipe el Real de Chihuahua remained an important governmental and commercial center for many years thereafter. During the final quarter of the eighteenth century, as colonial authorities stepped up their efforts at frontier defense, the villa also became a principal headquarters for military operations.

The men and women who flocked to Chihuahua seeking their fortunes during the eighteenth century represented a microcosm of colonial Mexican society. They included more than 500 Spanish immigrants, the most prominent of whom commanded a virtual monopoly over local government, economic activity, and social precedence. A handful of non-Spanish Europeans plied various trades, while a much larger number of Mexican-born people claimed Spanish descent and therefore styled themselves *españoles*. Though the latter occupied a variety of niches in the social and economic pecking order, they invariably demanded special privileges by virtue of their ethnicity. Slaves of African descent, brought north as domestic servants of the more pretentious settlers, and soldiers assigned to frontier presidios formed other important components of the area's population.

Chihuahua's Indian population included Tarahumaras and others indigenous to the northern frontier, some grudgingly "reduced" to Spanish rule and others still stubbornly defiant. A sizable contingent of Yaquis from Sonora and many Indians from the densely settled communities of central and southern Mexico also made their way to San Felipe el Real. Young Apaches and occasionally Comanches, captured (or, in local parlance, "ransomed" or delivered from heathenism) in New Mexico and sold as servants in Chihuahua, also supplemented the labor force and gradually assimilated into local society. Most numerous of all, however, were the laborers and drifters of every racial classification, especially those described as being of *color quebrado* (literally, broken color). These men and women were summoned from great distances, as one such individual put it, "by the voices of the mines of Chihuahua."[3] One *arriero* (muleteer) of mixed racial ancestry, for example, came from as far away as Guatemala.[4]

My purpose in writing this book is to examine the dynamics of social interaction that emerged as this diverse group of people assembled at San Felipe el Real and at the nearby mining camp of Santa Eulalia. I hope to show how abstract relationships of class, political subordination, ethnicity, and gender took concrete form in the daily routines of ordinary men and women in this newly formed community. I examine the ethos of governance expressed by those who wielded power as local officials, employers, and *padres de familia* (male heads of households), and the ways in which successive generations of Spanish immigrants shaped the evolution of colonial society. My focus thus centers on the process of government, and only incidentally on its institutions, while at the same time extending to such other contexts of governance as the household, the workplace, and the street. To the extent that my sources permit, I also probe the attitudes of people relegated to subordinate positions. Mindful of Robert Darnton's observation that the historian of popular attitudes aims not to "make a philosopher out of the man in the street, but to see how street life called for a strategy," I seek to understand how people adapted, in ways appropriate to their race, class, gender, and political status, to the power realities they encountered in their daily lives.[5]

Finally, I explore the implications of my findings for eighteenth-century Mexico as a whole. Indeed, this book is as much an interpretive essay on the workings of late colonial society as it is a case study of a single community. Historians have often portrayed Chihuahua as an extension of the "Spanish Borderlands" region of the United States and peripheral to the long-term historical development of Mexico, at least until railroads and telegraphs effectively unified the country during the regime of President Porfirio Díaz in the late nineteenth century.[6] Latin Americanists have also distinguished between the "core" areas of the Spanish empire and its outlying "fringes." With their dense, sedentary indigenous populations and high concentrations of mineral wealth, core regions such as central Mexico and highland Peru attracted large numbers of European immigrants from the sixteenth century forward, while the fringes had much less to offer. Over time the cores gradually expanded as more and more Spaniards migrated to the New World, but even in the late colonial period Chihuahua remained part of the fringe, at least according to the historians who have done the most to popularize these concepts.[7]

Certainly conditions unique to the frontier left their mark on colonial Chihuahua. Even in the best of times, drought and distance made life's necessities, let alone its comforts and luxuries, expensive and difficult to obtain. The elaborate bureaucratic apparatus that we have come to associate with colonial society was stripped to the bare essentials of social control and revenue collection, while the military assumed a far more visible presence than in central Mexico. The proximity of hostile Indians who spurned Catholicism and Spanish sovereignty provoked repeated and agonized laments over the precarious nature of life "on the enemy frontier." Those indigenous peoples who accepted Spanish rule lived in artificial communities created when Jesuit and Franciscan missionaries gathered semisedentary groups from their widely dispersed *rancherías* into more compact settlements. They therefore lacked the sense of historical continuity voiced by the articulate and politically sophisticated indigenous caciques of the center and south.

Despite these distinguishing characteristics, Chihuahua provides an instructive laboratory in which to observe features of social organization and interaction that were operative throughout New Spain. Here I will ask readers to think for a moment in terms of science fiction rather than history. A colony established in outer space would not exactly replicate any one community on planet Earth, and the founders of the new settlement might explicitly resolve to avoid some of the less desirable aspects of life back home. Yet we could learn much about this particular group of earthlings, and the society they had left behind, by observing what troubled them most as they went about setting up their colony, who took command as the settlement took shape, what practices and attitudes survived the journey relatively intact, and what forms of social behavior were abandoned.

For residents of eighteenth-century Mexico, and for many in Spain who aspired to better their personal fortunes by venturing to the colonies, the expedition to far-off Chihuahua must have represented a type of intergalactic travel and a chance to escape certain unpleasant features of social reality as they knew it. Moreover, those who made the trip brought with them the specific preoccupations of the historical moment in which they lived. The bonanza of the Santa Eulalia silver mines began at a particularly sensitive juncture in the history of New Spain. In 1680 the Pueblo Indians of New Mexico temporarily rejected Spanish rule and sent several hundred colonists fleeing in terror from Santa Fe to the Franciscan mission at El Paso del Norte some 300 miles to the south—and a little over 200 miles due north of what would soon become the villa of San Felipe el Real de Chihuahua. Over the next two decades other northern Indians tried to follow the Pueblos' example, jeopardizing Spanish sovereignty along much of the frontier.[8] Meanwhile, droughts, epidemics, and crop failures triggered social unrest throughout New Spain. The most spectacular revolt occurred in June of 1692, when an angry mob sacked markets and set fire to the cabildo chambers and the viceroy's palace in Mexico City.[9] Other less serious but still disquieting tumults rocked the city in 1696 and 1715.[10]

At the beginning of the eighteenth century those who commanded power in the viceregal capital or in provincial settlements thus had compelling reasons to doubt the stability of the social order over which they presided. Meanwhile, French incursions into the heartland of North America and the rapid growth of England's colonial empire prompted serious questions about the prospects for continued Spanish hegemony in the north. The builders of Chihuahua carried all of these anxieties with them to the frontier, together with their hopes of carving out new positions of power, wealth, and prestige for themselves. Indeed, Antonio Deza y Ulloa, governor of the province of Nueva Vizcaya from 1708 to 1712, had not only witnessed the Mexico City riot of 1692 but led squads of men who stormed the central plaza in an effort to contain the "enormous irreverence" of the crowd.[11]

In fact, everyone who trekked northward in search of better opportunities in Chihuahua brought aspirations and expectations based on prior experience in New or Old Spain. Those first on the scene may have envisioned a new settlement organized along lines that favored their personal advancement in ways not possible in their communities of origin. Others, perhaps more realistically, may have seen at least the chance to escape social opprobrium by forging new identities among strangers. Those not betrayed by physiognomy could have exploited the opportunity to alter their racial designations. At the same time, preexisting colonial institutions, practices, and attitudes awarded some people a disproportionate share of influence over the collective cultural and sociopolitical choices being made. But virtually everyone in the community had some say in the outcome of these choices, reached through a delicate process of give-and-take, and a close observation of that process can shed further light on the dynamics of colonial society throughout New Spain.

Social Negotiation in Colonial Mexico

A prominent theme in the recent historiography of colonial Mexico is the extent to which social, cultural, and even racial boundaries that may have seemed fixed at the level of law and ideology were in fact subject to constant revision. Spanish colonial authorities in the sixteenth century attempted to protect indigenous peoples from abuse by isolating them in their own communities and forbidding Spaniards and other non-Indians to reside or acquire lands in these *pueblos.* As time passed, however, this supposed division of colonial society into separate "republics" of Indians and Spaniards all but disappeared in many parts of Mexico. Indians took up residence in Spanish cities and became acculturated to European ways, while on occasion persons of mixed racial ancestry, or even españoles, might adopt the guise of Indian in order to gain access to land or office in rural villages that were officially reserved for Indians (but were in fact peopled largely by non-Indians). Whatever their ethnicity, leaders of the pueblos personally adopted many characteristics of Iberian material culture. They also alienated choice community lands to selected españoles and other outsiders while invoking the special legislation designed to protect Indian holdings when it suited their purposes. In some places land-hungry hacendados swallowed up neighboring Indian communities and obliterated their corporate identity. In other cases the resident peons on large estates joined together to replicate the social organization of Indian villages and then sought legal recognition as such.[12]

Throughout the colony other social boundaries proved equally permeable. Most communities included substantial numbers of men and women who had migrated in from somewhere else, and whenever new faces appeared they forced some realignments of existing arrangements.[13] Everywhere wealth, acculturation, and racial mixing enabled some people to pass from one ethnic category to another.[14] Historians have also shown how men and women officially assigned to subordinate positions in colonial society might in fact play pivotal roles in shaping at least the terms of their submission, even if they seldom succeeded in challenging the very fact of that submission. Even those who lacked realistic avenues to upward mobility did not necessarily subscribe to elite notions of racial and social hierarchy; instead, as R. Douglas Cope observes, "Elite-plebeian relations had to be constantly renegotiated, hammered out daily in thousands of implicit contracts with members of the plebe who were not passive, alienated, or crushed by feelings of racial inferiority and worthlessness."[15] Meanwhile, workers in silver mining and other occupations rarely met their employers' demands with regard to punctuality, productivity, or deferential demeanor, and colonial officials charged with handling disturbances in Indian villages often imposed token or symbolic punishments while appeasing rebel communities with land concessions and tax relief.[16] Even the energetic reformers of the late eighteenth century, determined though they were to enact a "revolution in government" that would bind New Spain more closely to the mother country and secure greater revenues for the Bourbon monarchy, found themselves forced at nearly every turn to bargain with recalcitrant colonials of all social ranks.[17]

In most respects, then, colonial Mexican society was marked by negotiation, though rarely in the twentieth-century, legalistic sense of the term, which suggests relatively polite, contractual arbitration conducted at bargaining tables and formalized in written agreements. If, however, we understand the word "negotiation" to mean any process of give-and-take, then we are very justified in using it to describe the day-in, day-out struggle to modify existing social arrangements in New Spain, one in which everyone quite literally took whatever he or she could get and gave away as little as possible.

I shall argue in this book that Chihuahua provides an instructive window through which to glimpse the kind of social negotiation that characterized eighteenth-century Mexico and to assess how much or how little in fact lay open to discussion. The early mining boom attracted people from across the Atlantic and from all over New Spain, and therefore furnished particularly abundant opportunities to strike new bargains in all manner of social interaction. For this reason I place principal emphasis on patterns established in Chihuahua during the first six decades of the eighteenth century, a time when newcomers to the region exercised their greatest control over the evolution of social relations. At first, of course, the adult population of San Felipe and Santa Eulalia consisted almost entirely of migrants. As we shall see, just when the area's first generation of native sons and daughters began reaching maturity in the 1730s, the first perceptible signs of economic decline appeared, and some people left to seek the next bonanza somewhere else. But scores of others continued to enter the region during the 1740s and 1750s, unaware that the best days of silver mining had passed, and migrants continued to have a substantial say in the social bargains being struck.

By the 1760s, however, mining had deteriorated still further, and attacks by enemy Indians intensified, so that people found fewer obvious incentives to make the long trek to San Felipe el Real. As a result, I shall argue, the frequency of social negotiation in Chihuahua declined noticeably during the closing decades of the colonial period. At least among those native to the region, the arrangements made by previous generations remained more securely in place, as collective memory lost track of some of the reasons why a particular modus vivendi had been adopted in the first place. But the process of give-and-take never ended completely, in part because negotiation itself became habit. Moreover, even into the 1790s and beyond, the faint promise of new bonanzas, or the simple attraction of a chance to start over again, proved just strong enough to lure a steady trickle of migrants from Spain and from central Mexico. Meanwhile, Indian hostilities prompted refugees from outlying areas to seek relative safety at San Felipe el Real, and authorities in Mexico City dispatched increasing numbers of military personnel to the area.

The continuous appearance of new faces thus provided fresh occasions for rewriting existing social contracts throughout the eighteenth century. Even if long-time residents eventually had fewer reasons to question the existing order of things, each newcomer might begin the process of social negotiation all over again, often unaware of tentative bargains struck long before his or her arrival in Chihuahua. Similar quarrels over matters weighty and trivial appear over and over in the archival record, with little evident change in form or content from, say, the 1720s to the 1750s and beyond. Thus the examples given in the chapters that follow may seem more like a series of undated snapshots than frames in a movie that documents a clear progression across the years, and part of the reason, paradoxically enough, lies in the very dynamism of social reality in colonial Chihuahua. New actors appeared at every turn, but they could not improvise on the script until they first rehearsed all of the same opening scenes that previous players had performed years or decades before. Moreover, as we shall see, the discourse available to them, namely Spanish concepts of honor, ethnicity, and patriarchy, furnished plot lines that were acceptable to many participants in the drama while offering few alternatives for those who might have wished for other outcomes.

Sources

The principal source used in this study is the microfilm copy of the Chihuahua municipal archives, located in the Library of the University of Texas at El Paso. More than 150 reels of film span the period of this study. Very few historians have utilized these records. In the 1970s Philip Hadley effectively used the original documents to write an excellent overview of Chihuahua's mining economy from its founding to the end of its bonanza days in the 1730s.[18] Throughout his distinguished career, local historian Francisco Almada also consulted these archives in compiling his many studies.[19] Despite these pioneering works, the Chihuahua archives still contain abundant and hitherto untapped sources for social history. In addition to the records of cabildo transactions, civic and religious celebrations, probate records, civil litigation, and military campaigns, they contain a particularly rich run of criminal prosecutions that yielded colorful testimony from men and women of all social ranks. I have also used parish registers from the villa of San Felipe el Real and from Santa Eulalia to obtain biographical data on individuals and indications of general demographic trends. Additional information comes from the municipal archives of Parral, an important mining center founded during the first half of the seventeenth century and located about 120 miles south of Chihuahua. Because the governor of Nueva Vizcaya resided in Parral at the beginning of the eighteenth century, many crucial administrative papers pertaining to the early history of Chihuahua ended up in the Parral archives. In selected other cases information on social relations in Parral helped clarify or qualify my findings for San Felipe.

Like most documentary sources, these materials present problems of interpretation for the social historian. The vast majority of colonial Mexicans were illiterate, and even those able to read and write seldom committed their innermost thoughts and feelings to paper. Very few kept personal diaries, and correspondence, at least that which has been preserved in the archives, focused largely on commercial transactions. Letters seldom conveyed any sentiments more intimate than presumably sincere but relatively unimaginative expressions of affection and concern for the physical and spiritual well-being of distant kin and countrymen. Thus the sources available for my study, abundant though they are, were for the most part generated by local officials as they went about their administrative and judicial duties.

My documentary base is therefore admittedly and unavoidably weighted toward those who held positions of command. The voices of governors, corregidores, and cabildo members come through loud and seemingly clear even at a distance of more than 200 years. They and their social peers routinely articulated their opinions on local issues and wrote lengthy and well-crafted treatises explaining their decisions to superiors and subordinates alike. They staged elaborate ceremonies apparently designed to display their superior positions in local society. Yet more often than they would have openly acknowledged or even tacitly recognized, their public statements and official behavior concentrated on the high ground of moral justifications for their own precedence while obscuring the more tawdry and sometimes brutal underpinnings on which their power rested. Like ruling groups in most other times and places, they seldom allowed more cynical interpretations of their own position to enter the official record.

Still, the self-serving rhetoric of local elites and their carefully orchestrated exhibitions of power offer valuable clues to the social dynamics at work in eighteenth-century Chihuahua. As James Scott has observed, to the extent that elites actually believed their verbal and ritual self-justifications, such exercises contributed to their group solidarity and self-confidence.[20] Proponents of the concept of cultural hegemony would argue that these activities also served to convince subordinates of the legitimacy or at least the inevitability of the existing order of things.[21] On the other hand, as frequently occurred in eighteenth-century Chihuahua, inconsistent or poorly executed displays of power and privilege often revealed the hypocritical and fragile base on which elites built their dominance.

Understanding the attitudes of people in subordinate social positions poses other challenges for the historian. Much of the available information on the activities of ordinary men and women in colonial Chihuahua comes to us from accounts given by officials or by *gente decente* (literally, decent people), respectable individuals whom authorities accepted as creditable witnesses. Even when the written record purports to show people of lower social strata speaking in their own words, we cannot know how faithfully, if at all, the documents reproduce their true feelings and perceptions. The petitions they presented to local officials for redress of grievances were framed by literate notaries who by definition ranked closer in social standing to the officials than to most of the persons they represented. Even if they were utterly sincere in their efforts to secure their clients' demands, the notaries tried to capture the attention of those in authority by embellishing the petitions with pretentious phrases and allusions that hardly sprang from the lips of the humble supplicants who enlisted their services. Nevertheless, the fact that notaries felt it appropriate to voice such sentiments on behalf of people in subordinate positions tells us something about the underlying assumptions of social order. Moreover, over time the petitioners may have absorbed something of the content of the words articulated in their behalf.

We must also consider the fact that when subordinate people testified in civil or criminal proceedings the same notaries recorded and perhaps paraphrased their remarks, and that even a verbatim transcript of their oral testimony or complaint might not tell us everything we would like to know. The court appearances of lower-class men and women brought them face to face with imposing local representatives of the colonial state. Certainly the judge's customary stern warning about the dire penalties for perjury, in this world and the next, might persuade members of the lower classes to tell the truth or at least to fabricate convincing lies.

But they may also have found compelling reasons to withhold crucial portions of the truth. Given the power realities confronting them, prudence suggested that they choose their words carefully and behave in a properly submissive and deferential manner in the presence of authority figures. By acting out the roles prescribed for them by people who commanded power over them, they might win the favor they sought or secure a lighter punishment for misconduct. At most they might insert an oblique editorial comment into their performance—a look, a gesture, or a slight inflection in tone of voice—that belied the outward subservience of their actions without incurring the risks of blatant insubordination. Only later, in the safer company of trusted friends and fellow subordinates, might they act out what Scott calls their "hidden transcripts," perhaps spinning elaborate fantasies of revenge or otherwise venting their anger toward those who dominated them.[22]

Unfortunately, few direct and uninhibited expressions of these hidden transcripts have come down to us from eighteenth-century Chihuahua or any other historical context. In fact, as I hope to demonstrate in the chapters that follow, the particular historical circumstances of Chihuahua limited the opportunities for subordinate people to rehearse and codify their own dissenting rituals and litanies. Ethnic divisions, continued migration into, within, and out of the region, and the relative absence of privileged spaces beyond the control of employers or other authority figures all delayed the growth of working-class organizations or a well-defined subculture among people of lower social standing.

None of these factors prevented subordinates from thinking about the political realities they faced as they went about their daily struggles to provide for themselves and their families, however. Their well-being and even their very survival often depended on their accurate reading of the power structure that surrounded them, and their words and deeds preserved in the historical record provide at least some clues to the conclusions they reached. On rare occasions men and women individually and collectively posed open and unequivocal challenges to existing power relations. Much more often they expressed their discontent less conspicuously in what Scott calls "infrapolitics." They pilfered silver and other valuables, they walked away without much fanfare from jobs they considered disagreeable, they sported elegant finery in defiance of assumptions held by the elite about how subordinates should dress, and they qualified acts of deference with subtle insult.[23] The documentary record of eighteenth-century Chihuahua is replete with references to such expressions of lower-class sentiment.

Colonial documents also show that lower-class men and women exploited elements of the ruling ideology in fashioning their strategies of self-protection and advancement. At times they simply called the elites' bluff by asking them to live up to the self-righteous images that they had painted of themselves. Subordinates might demand, for example, that local officials actually behave as the impartial dispensers of the king's benevolent justice they purported to be. On other occasions the subordinates took advantage of the elites' argument that their own superior moral conduct conferred the right to a greater measure of personal autonomy, dignity, and material comfort. Lower-class people who conformed to the same behavioral codes felt justified in asking for similar rewards. Colonial assumptions about the moral and intellectual superiority of Europeans over other races also provided crucial openings for anyone, no matter how humble in social rank, who dared to claim Spanish descent. Customarily encouraged by officials of church and state, men of all social categories also adopted prevailing notions of patriarchy to justify their dominion over their wives, children, and servants.

These and other tactics of subordinate people constituted in part a pragmatic, self-conscious, and even cynical appropriation of ruling ideology for their own ends. But I will also argue that on occasion lower-class men and women, for reasons quite understandable within their historical context, sincerely internalized parts of the dominant message, though not necessarily the components that local elites intended for them to absorb. In other words, for at least a brief period, local elites in Chihuahua succeeded in creating a limited and fragile but still genuine form of cultural hegemony. It was, however, a hegemony shaped in part by people in subordinate social ranks.

Such are the general contours of social relations in eighteenth-century Chihuahua, at least as they appear to a female historian of the late twentieth century, an Anglo-American reared on the U.S.–Canadian border, who has spent a large segment of her professional career in a binational, multicultural community some 220 miles from the site of San Felipe el Real. Even though I have hazarded some conclusions about the social attitudes of elites and subordinates alike, I will readily concede that my documentary evidence reveals more about their outward poses than about their private thoughts and feelings. At the same time I stress that we should not underestimate the importance of public behavior as a source for social historians. The people we study adopted the guises that they hoped might best serve their interests in specific situations. Sometimes they based their conduct on shrewd and well-informed assessments of the social reality they confronted. Perhaps more often they made their decisions without a full appreciation of the range of choices available to them or the likely consequences of a particular course of action. In any case their public performances reflected their understanding, however imperfect, of the society in which they lived.

My first two chapters are admittedly descriptive rather than analytical, and they are designed to give readers, especially those new to the field of Mexican studies, a brief overview of the book's historical context. Chapter 1 surveys the principal events in Chihuahua's colonial history, while Chapter 2 introduces the reader to the different groups that composed local society. In Chapter 3 I explore the relations between workers and employers that developed in silver mining and other enterprises. I then proceed to look at other facets of social organization. Chapters 4 and 5 focus on those who wielded overt political authority as provincial governors, corregidores, and members of the municipal council. I describe the personnel and customary practices of local government and the publicly articulated ethos that officials used to justify, at least in their own minds, their exercise of power. I then survey the rituals they staged in order to display what they considered the proper order of social precedence, and analyze the extent to which those in subordinate positions accepted the messages conveyed in these ritual performances.

The next two chapters shift to other contexts of subordination and domination. Chapter 6 looks at the day-to-day operation of Chihuahua's local variant of colonial Mexico's multiethnic society, or *sociedad de castas*. I attempt to explain how members of different groups perceived their own positions in this society and how they interacted with other groups as they went about their daily routines. In particular, I seek to discover the extent to which colonial society succeeded in formulating a widely accepted etiquette to govern the interaction of various groups. Chapter 7 turns to an examination of patriarchy as another principle that governed social relations in eighteenth-century Chihuahua. Finally, in the Conclusion I offer my reflections on the importance of my findings for other regions of colonial Mexico and its northern frontier.

Terminology

A word about terminology is in order before we embark upon our journey to northern Nueva Vizcaya. In describing the social groupings to which eighteenth-century men and women assigned themselves and others, I have tried to adopt language that faithfully reproduces colonial categories, without at the same time confusing readers of English in the late twentieth century. The distinction between those of Spanish descent born in the New World and those who had emigrated from Europe was a crucial one throughout colonial Latin America, and I have tried to offer my readers gentle reminders of its importance. Whenever I use the words "Spanish," "Spaniard," or "*peninsular*" (plural, *peninsulares*), I am referring to those people known to colonials as *españoles europeos* (European Spaniards), or in less flattering terms, as *gachupines* (singular, *gachupín*), a word of Nahuatl origin that connoted the habitual arrogance of Europeans toward natives of the New World.

For persons born in the New World but claiming that their ancestors came exclusively from Spain, I have borrowed the term commonly used in colonial Mexico, "españoles" (masculine singular, *español*; feminine singular, *española*; feminine plural, *españolas*). I have avoided the word "Creole" (*criollo* in Spanish), simply because people in eighteenth-century New Spain rarely employed it to designate ethnicity. Instead, they usually used it with the preposition "*de*" ("from" or "of") to denote specific geographical origins. Thus a "criollo de Durango" meant someone from Durango.[24] The term was most often used to describe the native origins of livestock or human chattel. A horse or a slave might thus be described as a "criollo" from a particular hacienda.

I have also tried to replicate colonial usage in describing individuals of mixed racial ancestry who exhibited African physical characteristics. Such a person was called a *mulato* if male, and a *mulata* if female. I have kept the Spanish spelling rather than adopt the English word "mulatto," which at least to Anglophone readers suggests African and white parentage exclusively. In colonial Mexico, mulatos could indeed be part African and part European, but they could also be of African and Indian extraction, or a combination of all three races. There is no satisfactory word in English to connote a person of mixed Indian and European ancestry, so I have simply used the Spanish word "*mestizo*" (feminine, *mestiza*). The word "Indian," of course, poses its own problems, especially the justifiable sensitivity of present-day descendants of those who arrived in this hemisphere long before Christopher Columbus. In the interests of historical accuracy I have substituted the names of specific groups whenever possible. But in other cases I have used the term "Indian" to reflect colonial attitudes, however reprehensible from a twentieth-century standpoint, that collapsed all indigenous peoples into a single category and assigned them to an inferior position within colonial society. Captured Apaches and other indigenous peoples were bought, sold, and held as chattel in eighteenth-century Chihauhua, but unless otherwise indicated the word "slave" will denote unfree Afro-Mexicans.

I employ the word "Mexican," as a noun and as an adjective, to refer collectively to people born in New Spain, regardless of racial classification. Although this term is to some extent anachronistic, I use it in an effort to recreate the impression conveyed when the word "*mexicano*" occasionally appeared in eighteenth-century documents. If people in colonial Chihuahua called a particular individual a "mexicano," they usually meant someone from central or southern New Spain, especially a native of Mexico City or its environs, although a person from as far north as Durango could earn that designation as well.[25] A resident of Santa Eulalia thus described an arriero as "al parecer indio blanco, que se dice ser mexicano o de sus contornos" ("apparently a white Indian [an Indian of light complexion and presumably having some European ancestry], reportedly a mexicano or from thereabouts").[26] The term was often applied to Indians—*indios mexicanos*—like a man named Marcos from the Indian neighborhood of Tlatelolco in the viceregal capital.[27] On the other hand, a mestizo or mulato might also be nicknamed "El Mexicano."[28]

I believe that for the people of eighteenth-century Chihuahua the term "mexicano" signified something more than mere geographical origins, however. Mexicanos arriving in San Felipe or Santa Eulalia might be españoles or mestizos, mulatos or Indians, and they might hail from a big city or a tiny Indian hamlet, from southern New Spain or from Durango in Nueva Vizcaya. In no objective sense were they carriers of any static or essential "Mexican" cultural synthesis, much less the exponents of an embryonic political nationalism. Indeed, as I shall argue, the ethnic and regional diversity of lower-class mexicanos and their limited access to wealth and power made it difficult for them to recreate cultural practices or community traditions they may have known in their places of origin. But to people already on the scene in Chihuahua, whether born there or erstwhile newcomers themselves, mexicanos represented a society more than two centuries in the making, with folkways and mentalities, however fluid and ill-defined, different from those brought in by Spaniards recently disembarked. For their part, too, immigrant gachupines must have viewed the society of colonial New Spain—south, center, and north—with the sense that they had stumbled onto something quite exotic and more than a little frightening. They therefore sought refuge in amenities, routines, and attitudes they had carried with them across the Atlantic, and their generally superior positions in the pecking order of wealth, power, and social prestige helped them to reproduce what was familiar. What baffled them was the fact that their continued success in so doing required the cooperation of "Mexicans" who failed to grasp the substance or refused to accept the legitimacy of such endeavors.

Neither "Spanish" nor "Mexican" identities were stagnant anywhere in New Spain, precisely because social reality demanded continued mutual accommodation between those long in place and those more recently arrived. The social history of colonial Mexico was everywhere marked by the constant renegotiation of social boundaries, but especially so in Chihuahua, where everyone at first was a newcomer, and "Mexican" and "Spaniard" confronted together, albeit with sharply contrasting blueprints and dissimilar tools in hand, the task of creating a new community in the northern reaches of Nueva Vizcaya.

ONE

The Villa of San Felipe el Real de Chihuahua

THE DEVELOPMENT of silver mining at Chihuahua during the first decade of the eighteenth century culminated a long history of northward Spanish colonization along the central plateau of Mexico. That process began in 1546 with the discovery of silver at Zacatecas, where the promise of easy wealth lured many people from the relative comfort of central New Spain to the otherwise uninviting domain of the hostile Chichimecas indigenous to the area. Officially founded in 1548, the city of Zacatecas became a thriving municipality almost overnight.[1]

Zacatecas also served as a springboard for further northward exploration and settlement during the latter half of the sixteenth century. In the early 1560s Francisco de Ibarra, nephew of one of the founders of Zacatecas, established the province of Nueva Vizcaya, became its first governor, and founded its capital at Durango. Within a few years Spanish settlement extended as far north as Santa Bárbara, close to the present Chihuahua-Durango state boundary, and to the agricultural zone of El Valle de San Bartolomé (now known as Valle de Allende), some twenty miles to the northeast.[2] These settlements in turn became starting points for other expeditions. In 1598 Juan de Oñate and several hundred followers set out from Santa Bárbara to establish the Spanish colony of New Mexico, more than 600 miles to the north.[3]

Despite this flurry of settlement activity, the Spanish-Mexican presence in the vast region between Santa Bárbara and Santa Fe remained limited in the early seventeenth century to a handful of prospectors, ranchers, slave-raiders, and missionaries. The indigenous inhabitants of Nueva Vizcaya included Tarahumaras, Tepehuanes, and other groups gathered into loosely organized rancherías scattered along the eastern fringe of the Sierra Madre Occidental. They supported themselves through hunting, gathering, and slash-and-burn agriculture. Other groups, such as the Conchos and Tobosos who inhabited the edges of the arid Bolsón de Mapimí, had not yet adopted fixed places of residence. Their agriculture was more primitive still, and hunting and gathering provided a greater share of their subsistence needs. During the 1590s and the first three decades of the seventeenth century Franciscans and Jesuits operating out of Santa Bárbara began efforts to congregate these people into mission villages, but encountered frequent resistance.[4]

In 1631, the discovery of silver at Parral, located less than 20 miles northeast of Santa Bárbara and about 120 miles south of the present site of San Felipe el Real de Chihuahua, stimulated further Spanish-Mexican settlement in Nueva Vizcaya. Parral quickly prospered as eager prospectors registered over 400 mining claims in the first year alone. Its population reportedly reached 1,000 españoles and 4,000 Indians and Afro-Mexican slaves by 1635. By that time the town had also become the de facto capital of Nueva Vizcaya; for the remainder of the seventeenth century provincial governors customarily resided at Parral. Meanwhile, the development of mining created additional demand for agricultural produce, and haciendas in nearby El Valle de San Bartolomé grew accordingly.[5]

Following the settlement of Parral, missionary activity accelerated in Nueva Vizcaya. By 1648 the Jesuits had established eight missions among the Tarahumara, including one at Satevó, located about 50 miles south of the site where the town of San Felipe would one day stand. The Franciscans continued working among both the Tarahumaras and the Conchos. Meanwhile, owners of mines and haciendas tried to appropriate the Indians' labor through outright enslavement and through the colonial institutions of *encomienda* and *repartimiento*. Indigenous peoples showed little enthusiasm for mission life or the other changes that had resulted from the growing presence of non-Indian settlers in the area. During the 1640s and again on numerous occasions for the remainder of the seventeenth century, they rose in rebellion, forsaking the missions in favor of their original settlements and resisting demands for their labor. Spanish authorities met these threats with their customary combination of military force and appeasement, and Franciscans and Jesuits continued their missionary endeavors.[6] Meanwhile, Captain Diego del Castillo registered the first mining claim in the vicinity of Chihuahua in 1652, but Indian hostilities soon forced him to abandon the site.[7]

The final two decades of the seventeenth century were particularly turbulent throughout the north-central frontier of New Spain. In 1680 the Pueblo peoples of New Mexico rebelled, killing some 400 Spanish-Mexican residents and sending several hundred others fleeing southward to El Paso. Unrest soon spread to other indigenous groups throughout the territory comprising the present state of Chihuahua and beyond. Spanish military operations then took the offensive, showing progressively less inclination to concede peace every time the Indians requested it.[8] Many of the officers who commanded these campaigns remained in the area to become the foremost mining entrepreneurs and political leaders of Chihuahua after the turn of the century. Meanwhile, epidemics and crop failures in the 1690s added to the general sense of crisis; hacendados in El Valle de San Bartolomé, for example, suffered serious financial reverses during these years.[9]

New mining ventures quickened the pace of Spanish-Mexican settlement in the area even in these troubled times. In 1687 the discovery of silver at Cusihuiriachic, located about 60 miles southwest of the eventual site of San Felipe el Real, gave many of Chihuahua's future silver magnates a chance to make their first fortunes. At the same time a number of prominent families were busy securing land grants in the surrounding region, while missionaries redoubled their efforts to pacify the frontier by converting the Indians to Catholicism and a settled existence in the missions. In 1697 Franciscans founded the Concho mission of Nombre de Dios about three miles from the location of the future town of San Felipe; it is now part of the city of Chihuahua.[10]

Silver Mining in Chihuahua: The Bonanza Years

In November of 1702 Bartolomé Gómez, a resident of Cusihuiriachic, registered the first permanent mining claim in the Chihuahua area, and during the next several months many others followed suit. Most of these early strikes were concentrated at a place that soon received the name of Santa Eulalia de Mérida, situated in the rugged terrain fifteen miles east of the eventual site of San Felipe el Real. Santa Eulalia quickly attracted numerous settlers. By 1709 at least 41 men counted themselves as *vecinos* (householders) in the new mining camp, while many others worked in the mines but lacked the economic resources or social standing to claim official status as householders.[11] The rudiments of civil and ecclesiastical administration also took shape. Soon after the first mining claims were staked, the *alcalde mayor* (district magistrate) of Cusihuiriachic appointed a lieutenant to administer justice in Santa Eulalia. By 1708, however, the new settlement had grown sufficiently to warrant an alcalde mayor of its own. A primitive parish church also began operations in Santa Eulalia sometime after 1709.[12]

Meanwhile, another settlement developed on the site of the present-day city of Chihuahua. Known as San Francisco de Cuéllar in honor of the current viceroy, the Marqués de Cuéllar, it was located at the junction of the Sacramento and Chuvíscar Rivers on lands reportedly purchased from the Indians congregated at Nombre de Dios. Though not as close to the silver deposits as Santa Eulalia, San Francisco offered the advantages of level terrain and relatively abundant water for domestic use, agriculture, and the refining of silver ore. The site also lay astride the *camino real* (royal road) linking Nueva Vizcaya with New Mexico. The most prominent mining entrepreneurs soon built their principal residences at San Francisco and established refineries along the banks of the Chuvíscar, although many also maintained homes at Santa Eulalia. By August of 1709, a simple adobe church had already been erected at San Francisco.[13]

With the growth of San Francisco de Cuéllar, local residents began debating which of the two settlements should serve as official headquarters for local agents of the church and state. In the fall of 1709 Nueva Vizcaya Governor Antonio Deza y Ulloa broke the deadlock, siding with the most substantial silver magnates in favor of San Francisco. The alcalde mayor—now designated by the functionally equivalent term of corregidor—promptly took up residence there, appointing a *teniente* (lieutenant) to serve in Santa Eulalia. A few years later, for reasons of political expediency and to advance his own considerable economic interests, Nueva Vizcaya Governor Manuel San Juan y Santa Cruz moved from Parral to the new settlement.[14]

During these years San Francisco de Cuéllar rapidly assumed the guise of a proper Spanish municipality. A grid of streets led to its central plaza, where a more substantial parish church was consecrated in 1715. In contrast, the streets of Santa Eulalia twisted around its hills and *arroyos* (gullies), the random arrangement of its buildings reflecting its more haphazard development as a mining camp.[15]

Chihuahua's mining economy grew steadily during these years. By 1716 there were eleven silver refineries in San Francisco de Cuéllar and seven more in Santa Eulalia. The two settlements boasted a combined population of at least 336 adult males, excluding Afro-Mexican slaves, Indians, and probably a large number of other workers.[16] Meanwhile, in 1718, Viceroy Baltasar de Zúñiga y Guzmán elevated San Francisco de Cuéllar to the status of a villa, with the right to be governed by its own municipal council. The community now became known as San Felipe el Real de Chihuahua, in honor of King Felipe V of Spain.[17] Flattering the royal ego definitely served a useful purpose. Although the king initially protested that the viceroy lacked authority to confer villa status, he eventually relented and allowed the order to stand.[18]

The apparatus of municipal government quickly took shape with the inauguration of the town's first cabildo in December of 1718. The council included permanent members, called *regidores*, who purchased their positions and theoretically served for life. During the course of the eighteenth century their numbers varied from as few as one to as many as six; four were installed in 1718. Some regidores held other official titles, either on a permanent or rotating basis, including the positions of *alguacil mayor* (chief constable), *alférez real* (royal standard bearer), and *fiel ejecutor* (inspector of weights and measures). Each January 1 the regidores chose two local citizens to join them on the cabildo for one-year terms as *alcaldes*. These men assisted the regidores in deciding important matters of town government and oversaw the day-to-day administration of justice in both civil and criminal cases.[19]

By the early 1720s San Felipe el Real had emerged as the premier center of mining, trade, and colonial administration on the northern frontier of New Spain. Following the example of Manuel San Juan y Santa Cruz, subsequent eighteenth-century governors typically maintained a residence there, despite repeated orders from higher authorities that they maintain their headquarters at Durango.[20] With ample justification local residents boasted that their villa was "la más principal de este reino" ("the most important in this kingdom").[21] Bishop Benito Crespo y Monroy of Durango agreed, noting in 1726 that San Felipe was the "most opulent" settlement in his large diocese.[22] By that time work was under way on a parish church much grander in scale than the one built in the previous decade.[23]

The town bustled with activity during these bonanza years. In addition to foodstuffs and other merchandise from all over New Spain, its many shops carried fancy ribbons and lace, fine stockings, buttons of silver and gold, Chinese silks, and other luxury fabrics imported from England, France, Flanders, and Castile.[24] Nor was there any shortage of tailors willing to fashion all of this finery into elegant garments. In January of 1735, no fewer than 106 men claimed that occupation in San Felipe, although many of them were evidently willing to take other jobs that might yield higher earnings.[25] Meanwhile, by the mid-1720s Chihuahua merchants had captured control of the New Mexico trade.[26]

Estimates of the villa's population during these early years vary widely. A muster roll taken in 1724 listed 129 men equipped with horses and arms, while another count for 1725 shows 292 vecinos in San Felipe and 214 in Santa Eulalia.[27] Both of these sources, however, omit large numbers of lower-class workers as well as all women and children. According to an account of Chihuahua's history compiled in the 1790s, San Felipe had a total population of 7,000 in 1720, while another 6,000 lived at Santa Eulalia.[28] The priest of San Felipe estimated in 1723 that his parish served some 9,000 people, while other sources give a total of 2,000 families for 1730.[29] Writing in 1733, the Jesuit José Arlegui probably exaggerated when he claimed a population of 25,000 for San Felipe el Real.[30] In 1742 Antonio Villaseñor y Sánchez reported a much more realistic combined total of 17,850 inhabitants for the two settlements, while still another count shows a total of 2,000 Spanish and mestizo vecinos in 1746.[31]

Though any bonanza was likely to attract a crowd, the special characteristics of local geology stirred hopes of easy fortunes even among those with little capital to invest. Compared to other mining centers in New Spain, Chihuahua's silver lay much closer to the surface, often accessible through large natural caves around Santa Eulalia. Although some shafts reached 90 meters in depth, most of the area's mines active during the early eighteenth century extended less than 45 meters beneath the surface. In contrast, many of Parral's mines were more than 120 meters deep. Those in Real del Monte and Zacatecas often exceeded 300 meters, and the famous La Valenciana in Guanajuato dropped nearly double that distance.[32] Opening a silver mine therefore entailed less cost in Chihuahua than in other mining centers. As a result many people registered claims and dabbled in mining; merchants or others with small amounts of capital often pooled their resources to maintain a few workers in a small mine.[33]

Refining of silver also demanded more modest investments of capital than in other mining centers. The quality of local ore and its high concentrations of lead made smelting by fire (*fundición*), rather than mercury amalgamation, the preferred method of refining, as long as sufficient firewood remained available. Fundición necessitated a smaller initial investment than amalgamation, and the process took only 24 hours from start to finish, while amalgamation required two to three months.[34] Though the largest refineries usually belonged to the most prominent mining magnates, many other individuals also processed silver on a much smaller scale.

Despite the circumstances that seemed to favor a relatively wide participation in mining and refining, a handful of powerful men, most of them peninsulares, soon came to dominate these activities. Those who could quickly marshal large labor forces often extracted the best ores before others got their chance. Their wealth and political influence also helped them drive competitors out of business. Because it was relatively easy to connect several caves with underground passageways, and any particular mine might therefore have several routes of access, legal battles inevitably erupted over conflicting claims. Miners able to make costly appeals to high-ranking officials in Guadalajara or Mexico City held a substantial advantage in these contests. The principal mine owners also achieved substantial vertical integration of their enterprises. Beginning in the 1720s they embarked on a determined if not entirely successful campaign to eliminate the independent refiners.

Economic Decline after 1740

The silver bonanza that nurtured Chihuahua's growth rested on a precarious base. Even in the prosperous decade of the 1720s the community suffered periodic food shortages and epidemics. Christmas of 1724 found hungry people begging from house to house while cabildo officials rationed bread.[35] A measles outbreak spread throughout Nueva Vizcaya in 1728, severely disrupting mining and agriculture.[36] Hostile Indians also threatened the villa in the heyday of its mining boom.[37] By the 1730s it was clear the area's best and most easily accessible ores had been taken, while droughts and epidemics continued. Smelting costs rose as local supplies of firewood became depleted, and few refiners could afford to convert to amalgamation. In 1737 three of the villa's most prominent mining entrepreneurs cited their ruined fortunes when they defaulted on a bond they had posted several years earlier.[38] Civic leaders complained that local citizens no longer contributed generously to finance celebrations in honor of the villa's patron saints and that the resulting divine disfavor had brought further calamity.[39] Meanwhile, workers deserted Chihuahua as they heard of abundant silver strikes in the Pimería of Sonora.[40]

Beginning around 1740 and accelerating after midcentury, the deterioration in mining was further exacerbated by intensified Apache attacks that imperiled Spanish-Mexican settlement throughout the northern frontier. Travel to and from Chihuahua became increasingly unsafe, and hostile Indians carried off livestock used in transporting ore and supplies.[41] From the 1750s forward the parish registers of Chihuahua periodically noted the burials of people killed by Indians.[42] Growing numbers of abandoned haciendas and ranchos dotted the barren landscape of Nueva Vizcaya, especially in El Valle de San Buenaventura and other points north of San Felipe. In 1751 hostilities moved to within a few miles of the town itself, persuading the bishop of Durango to abandon plans to visit portions of his diocese that lay beyond to the north. Meanwhile, 79 merchants in San Felipe and Santa Eulalia contributed over 2,000 pesos to a campaign led by Governor Juan Francisco de la Puerta y Barrera against the Apaches.[43]

Chihuahua's troubles continued over the next several decades. In 1766 Cayetano María Pignatelli Rubí Corbera y San Climent, better known as the Marqués de Rubí, visited the area during his inspection tour of the northern frontier. Nicolás Lafora, cartographer of the Rubí expedition, reported "total decadence of the mines" in Chihuahua.[44] A few years later the administrator of confiscated Jesuit properties in the area had difficulty selling a mine and refinery that had been repossessed after its initial purchaser had failed to pay outstanding debts.[45] In the 1770s and 1780s the town's jail was filled to overflowing with local Indians accused of collaborating with the enemy.[46] Meanwhile, periodic food shortages brought further hardship. Maize from as far away as El Paso del Norte, more than 200 miles to the north, sold at inflated prices in San Felipe el Real.[47]

Economic decline, Indian attacks, and the recurrent ravages of epidemic disease brought noticeable but not catastrophic reductions in the area's population during the second half of the eighteenth century.[48] Though available population estimates are imprecise and tend to underreport groups of lower social status, they nonetheless reveal certain general tendencies. In 1759 local residents estimated a combined total of between 6,000 and 7,000 people for San Felipe and Santa Eulalia. They also calculated that epidemics during the previous three years had reduced the local population by about a third.[49] When Bishop Pedro Tamarón y Romeral conducted his pastoral visit the following year, he counted 692 families, composed of 4,652 persons, in San Felipe el Real and another 733 families, composed of 4,755 persons, in Santa Eulalia. It is impossible to determine how many of these people, especially those living in San Felipe, were refugees who had fled outlying settlements for the comparative safety of a large town. We do know that Bishop Tamarón y Romeral counted an additional 5,395 people living on haciendas and in mission towns in the surrounding area.[50]

In 1765 the population of the entire jurisdiction of Chihuahua was estimated at approximately 13,000.[51] The region experienced further population loss over the next three decades. San Felipe reportedly had a population of 5,678 people in 1779, but a census taken just six years later recorded only 3,739 persons living in the villa and 897 in Santa Eulalia. By 1791 San Felipe had 4,077 residents, with just 518 in Santa Eulalia.[52] Another census compiled on the eve of Mexican independence in 1821 showed that the population of San Felipe el Real had rebounded slightly, to 4,441.[53]

Whatever the discrepancies in available population counts, the numbers of baptisms recorded in the parish church of San Felipe el Real reflect the villa's changing fortunes during the course of the eighteenth century. Table 5 in the Appendix shows annual totals for sample years at five-year intervals from 1715 to 1815. As might be expected, baptisms rose steadily during the early years of the mining boom—from 113 in 1715 to 219 in 1720 and to 329 in 1725. The slight drop (to 307) in 1730 was probably due to lingering effects of the measles epidemic of 1728. The total peaked at 482 in 1735, fell to 391 in 1740, and then fluctuated between 218 and 375 for the remainder of the eighteenth century.

Despite these vicissitudes in its fortunes and population, San Felipe el Real remained a vital economic center in northern New Spain. Silver mining continued, albeit on a more modest scale, so that in 1765 local residents still considered mining to be "the principal nerve of this villa."[54] Philip Hadley has estimated that during the 1760s Santa Eulalia contributed 7.68 percent of the total volume of silver produced in New Spain.[55] Hopes of new bonanzas lingered throughout the eighteenth century; in the 1790s several peninsular Spaniards registered new mining claims in and around Chihuahua.[56] Even as late as 1791, there were 63 refineries operating in San Felipe and Santa Eulalia.[57]

Trade also remained important even after the best of the bonanza years had ended. At least eight merchants were still doing business in Santa Eulalia in 1759, while many others had shops in San Felipe.[58] The following year Bishop Tamarón y Romeral judged the area's trade to be the liveliest of his diocese.[59] In 1783 twelve stores were open for business in San Felipe.[60] Meanwhile, resourceful entrepreneurs diversified their interests into commercial agriculture and other ventures.[61] In 1780, for example, the peninsular merchants Martín de Mariñelarena and Manuel de Urquidi built an *obraje* (textile factory) in San Felipe el Real.[62] Chihuahua merchants also retained control of the lucrative New Mexico trade, which expanded with that colony's remarkable economic and demographic growth during the last two decades of the century.[63]

The expansion of military activity on the northern frontier during the final quarter of the eighteenth century underscored the political and strategic importance of Chihuahua and brought new openings for commercial gain. In 1772 King Carlos III ordered the creation of a unified military command, known after 1776 as the Provincias Internas, to coordinate defense throughout the frontier. Although the town of Arizpe in Sonora served as official headquarters for the commandant and his staff, San Felipe el Real provided a convenient meeting place for high-level military juntas and a starting point for many campaigns. Local merchants thereby found opportunities for substantial profits supplying the troops.[64]

Throughout the eighteenth century men and women of many social ranks found reasons to make the difficult journey to the deserts of Nueva Vizcaya and make new lives in San Felipe el Real de Chihuahua. Spanish immigrants carried dreams of quick fortunes as mine owners and merchants and a cocky self-assurance that their peninsular origins would guarantee them privileged status as principal vecinos of the villa. Mexicans of every racial category hustled north with perhaps more limited ambitions but still the hope of finding fresh opportunities, legitimate or otherwise, for social and economic advancement. Some people undoubtedly migrated for very personal reasons, escaping criminal charges, bad debts, or hapless marriages in their home communities. Still others came to Chihuahua against their will: Apaches "ransomed" in New Mexico, Afro-Mexican slaves, and criminals banished to service in frontier presidios or silver refineries. Chapter 2 offers a more detailed portrait of this remarkable cross-section of colonial Mexican society.

TWO

The People of Colonial Chihuahua

IF TWENTIETH-CENTURY students of Latin American history could transport themselves back two centuries or more in time, a walk through San Felipe el Real de Chihuahua would provide a compact but highly instructive overview of colonial Mexican life. The imposing parish church and spacious central plaza replicated the elegant physical layout of much larger cities throughout the viceroyalty, while the single-story adobe structures lining the villa's dusty streets testified to the simpler lifestyle of the northern frontier. Silver refineries belching noxious fumes offered a sensory reminder of the importance of precious metals to the economy of New Spain, and anyone who tarried in one of the town's many shops could easily grasp the complexity of commerce in the Spanish colonial world. At the height of the mining boom, customers in Chihuahua could purchase luxurious laces and taffetas from France, fine woolens from England, silks from China, more prosaic cloth from obrajes in central Mexico, chocolate and sugar, spices from around the world, and even dried shrimp from the coast of Sonora.

People representing a microcosm of colonial Mexican society jostled one another in the streets and plazas of San Felipe el Real. Itinerant merchants and produce vendors noisily hawked their wares while women scurried about, carrying their laundry to the river or delivering freshly prepared meals to paying customers. Arrieros might be seen unloading fresh merchandise in front of a shop. In secluded alleys mine workers playing hookey from their jobs squandered their previous week's earnings in games of cards and dice. Clusters of vagabonds loitered around, exchanging boisterous toasts over drafts of *aguardiente* (cane alcohol) and making fun of the arrogant Spanish shopkeepers who went about their business. Occasionally an officious magistrate passed by on his way to investigate a domestic disturbance, brandishing his staff of office lest anyone question the gravity of his mission.

Peninsulares

From a twentieth-century vantage point, and in many respects from a colonial perspective as well, the most easily visible of Chihuahua's vecinos were the peninsular Spaniards who resided there. At least 511 of these immigrants found their way to San Felipe el Real and the surrounding area during the eighteenth and early nineteenth centuries.[1] Tables 2 and 3 in the Appendix show the number of peninsulares whose names appear in local documentation for each decade and for selected years from 1710 to 1820. As might be expected, the bonanza years of the 1720s and 1730s attracted the largest numbers of immigrants, but the administrative and military reorganization of the northern frontier and the continued promise of commercial profit in the late colonial period also created new opportunities for ambitious Spaniards in the 1770s and beyond. As the villa's principal miners and merchants, and as cabildo officers, royal appointees, and military leaders, peninsulares wielded disproportionate influence over Chihuahua's civic and economic life. They left a copious paper trail documenting their public activities. Far more often than their Mexican-born neighbors, they also wrote lengthy testaments that provide abundant details on their personal lives.

Despite their high profile, peninsular immigrants comprised a minuscule fraction of the aggregate population. In 1740 at least 93 Spaniards lived in the area, most of them at San Felipe el Real, a few at Santa Eulalia. If the villa's population was about 7,000, then peninsulares constituted approximately 1.3 percent of the total, or perhaps about 0.7 percent of the combined population of San Felipe and Santa Eulalia. Similar percentages can be found in late colonial records for the area. At least 31 peninsulares resided in San Felipe in 1785, accounting for about 0.8 percent of the villa's enumerated population of 3,754.[2] Chihuahua's ratio of peninsular Spaniards to total population is roughly similar to those observed in many other provincial centers in the eighteenth century. In the early 1790s immigrants made up about 0.63 percent of the population in Querétaro, 0.8 percent in Guanajuato, and 1.36 percent in Oaxaca, for example. Even in Mexico City, with its heavy concentration of colonial bureaucrats and high-ranking clergy, only about 1.87 percent of the population was peninsular.[3]

Virtually all of Chihuahua's Spanish immigrants were male; the only exceptions—two in number—appear late in the colonial period. In October of 1779 María de los Reyes Bonilla, a native of Seville and daughter of an army captain, married a Basque named Fernando de la Torre in the villa's church.[4] Ten years later the parish priest recorded the baptism of María Catarina Francisca, daughter of Domingo de Beregaña and his wife (who was probably also his cousin), Micaela García y Beregaña. All four of the child's grandparents were listed as natives of the villa of Ugarte in Navarre. Though it is possible that Micaela was born to Spanish parents elsewhere in Mexico, she was probably a peninsular immigrant.[5]

Like their counterparts who emigrated to other parts of Latin America in the eighteenth century, a large percentage of the peninsulares who settled in Chihuahua hailed from small towns and rural hamlets in the increasingly crowded provinces of northern Spain.[6] Birthplaces have been determined for more than half of Chihuahua's peninsular immigrants. Table 4 in the Appendix shows their regions of origin. Just over two-thirds (194, or 66.9 percent) of the 290 Spaniards whose birthplaces are known came from the northern provinces of Galicia, Asturias, Cantabria, Burgos, Alava, Navarre, Vizcaya, and Guipúzcoa; 47.5 percent (138) came from Galicia, Burgos, Vizcaya, or Guipúzcoa.

Despite the wealth of available detail on these men's careers in Chihuahua, we know very little about their social origins in Spain. Most mentioned their early lives only when they wrote their wills, and these documents give only terse notations of their home towns and their parents' names, usually accompanied by a perfunctory assertion that their families were all honorable and free of any taint associated with Moorish or Jewish ancestry. Juan de Bonilla, a physician by training who served as scribe of the cabildo in the 1720s and 1730s, was one of the few immigrants to reveal any additional detail on his prior life. He had left behind a house on the central plaza of his home villa of Provencio in the diocese of Cuenca.[7] Ignacio Alfonso de

Riaza, originally from Guadalajara in Castile, may have descended from a corregidor who served in a villa near Guadalajara in the 1630s. Another relative, one Francisco de Riaza, served as treasurer of the royal council of Castile at precisely the time Ignacio Alfonso was helping found San Felipe el Real on the frontier of Nueva Vizcaya.[8]

The educational attainments of Chihuahua's peninsulares suggest that they did not come from the poorest strata of Spanish society. At a time when the majority of Spain's rural population and urban lower classes were illiterate, virtually all of the immigrants to Chihuahua were able to read and write. Most, in fact, signed their names with elaborate rubrics that suggested more than passing familiarity with pen and ink. A few had attended *colegios* in Spain, where boys between the ages of nine and fifteen learned the rudiments of Latin grammar and the classics. Pedro Soler Pardo, one of the villa's two elected alcaldes for the year 1735, and Francisco Xavier de Armenta, who served briefly as the cabildo's scribe in the late 1730s, had studied together at the Colegio de Santo Tomás in Seville, for example.[9] Late colonial creoles in the viceregal capital may have belittled the intellectual accomplishments of many immigrant gachupines, but the peninsulares who made their way to Chihuahua easily ranked among the best educated vecinos in San Felipe el Real.[10]

Many Spanish immigrants to the New World evidently dreamed of making their fortunes and returning to positions of enhanced power and prestige in their native communities.[11] Some of those who settled in Chihuahua may have nurtured similar aspirations. In 1735 Antonio Valerio de Andrade, who managed a store for the Portuguese merchant Domingo Carvallo, announced his intent to return to his wife and daughter in Burgos after his employer died.[12] Another shopkeeper from Burgos, Juan Gómez Cajiga, wrote his brothers promising to return home, but died before realizing his ambition.[13]

Once they had made the grueling trek to the deserts of Nueva Vizcaya, however, few other immigrants expressed any serious intent of returning to Spain. Many married local women and settled down for the rest of their lives. We know that more than 170 immigrants, and probably many others, lived in Chihuahua for a decade or more, founding families and businesses. One immigrant who made the return voyage to Europe ultimately decided that his destiny lay in Chihuahua. Santiago Gómez de Escontría, a successful merchant and mine owner who arrived in San Francisco de Cuéllar as early as 1716 and later served on the cabildo, visited Spain sometime before 1748 but then returned to Chihuahua.[14] Most others limited their ties to the old country, corresponding occasionally with relatives and leaving modest bequests to family members or religious institutions in their home communities.

Many peninsulares stayed because they found significant opportunities for upward social and economic mobility in Chihuahua. Throughout the eighteenth century the most successful immigrants dominated silver mining, refining, and local commerce in the villa. Moreover, they achieved a virtual monopoly of political office. Most governors of Nueva Vizcaya and corregidores appointed to serve in Chihuahua were Spaniards.[15] Peninsulares also constituted an overwhelming majority of those who served on the cabildo, both as regidores who occupied permanent seats they had purchased and as annually elected alcaldes who were entrusted with the administration of justice in civil and criminal cases.[16]

Peninsulares also dominated civic affairs in less formal ways. At least 24 of the 129 men listed on the militia muster compiled in 1724 were peninsulares, for example.[17] In 1725, thirteen principal citizens met to discuss questions of local defense; ten of them were peninsular Spaniards.[18] Six years later a much larger group generated a petition protesting the conduct of Corregidor Juan Sánchez Camacho; of the 63 vecinos who signed the document, at least 24 were from Spain.[19] At a town meeting or *cabildo abierto* (open cabildo) held in 1759, fifteen men were present in addition to the municipal council members. At least eight, and probably several others, were peninsulares. Six other men, four of them definitely peninsulares, were summoned to the meeting but did not attend.[20]

The most successful of Chihuahua's peninsular immigrants achieved a level of economic and political influence that far surpassed their numerical importance in the villa's population. These individuals formed a tightly woven circle, linked by kinship, business partnerships, and sentimental ties to mutual home provinces in Spain. They served as godparents for one another's children and executors of one another's estates. Most important, ambitious immigrants who arrived as bachelors enhanced their prospects for upward mobility by marrying daughters of peninsulares already established in the villa.

The career of Ignacio Alfonso de Riaza, a regidor who also served as alcalde in 1724 and again in 1735, illustrates the close ties that bound members of the Chihuahua elite. Born in Guadalajara, Castile, about 1682, he was living in Durango, Nueva Vizcaya, in 1712 but had established himself as a merchant in San Francisco de Cuéllar sometime before 1717. In that year he married María Dorotea Velarde Cosío, a native of Sombrerete in Nueva Galicia who was evidently related to a number of prominent men in Chihuahua. She died shortly after the marriage, and in 1726 Ignacio wed Catalina de Orio y Zubiate, daughter of the late General José de Orio y Zubiate, who had been a member of the villa's first cabildo and corregidor from 1720 to 1723. Ignacio and Catalina had several children, for whom other leading peninsulares served as godfathers.[21] In 1749 their daughter María Josefa married Manuel García, a peninsular who was elected alcalde in 1756 and again four years later.[22]

Often this kind of pattern continued over several generations. Born in Oviedo, Asturias, about 1662, Juan Antonio Trasviña y Retes was one of the founders of San Felipe el Real. His wife, María Rosa Ortiz de Campos, was the only daughter of Bartolomé Ortiz de Campos, an immigrant from the Spanish region of Extremadura and one of the area's first successful miners.[23] Micaela Trasviña, daughter of Juan Antonio and María Rosa, married José Antonio de Uranga, who was elected alcalde in 1734, while another daughter, Manuela, wed Eugenio Ramírez Calderón, native of Toledo, prominent mining entrepreneur, and regidor of the cabildo for many years.[24] In 1740 their daughter, Rita Ramírez Calderón, in turn married Domingo del Valle, a miner from Asturias who had served as alcalde four years earlier and was elected to the cabildo again in 1753.[25]

In some cases later immigrants were able to secure political office without first forming kinship ties with members of the local elite. Nonetheless, they preferred to marry the daughters of other preeminent peninsulares and to perpetuate their influence through succeeding generations. Francisco Duro, born about 1721 in Galicia, arrived in Chihuahua with his younger brother Jacobo in the 1740s. The two established a *tienda* (shop), and by 1747 Francisco had been elected alcalde. Twenty years later he married, evidently for the first time. His bride was Catalina Gómez de Barreda, daughter of José Gómez de Barreda, a peninsular merchant who had settled in San Felipe el Real in 1736 and served as alcalde on three separate occasions in the 1740s. Following Catalina's death, Francisco married her sister, María Guadalupe. Meanwhile, until his death in 1779, Francisco remained a principal member of the villa's elite, serving again as alcalde in 1769 and 1775. In February 1782 his daughter, María Josefa, wed Andrés Martínez de Alballe, a merchant in his twenties and a Galician like his deceased father-in-law. By 1786 Martínez de Alballe had secured a position as a regidor, and he was also elected alcalde in 1787, 1801, and 1804. He too succeeded in extending the family's political prominence into the following generation. In 1804 María Leocadia Martínez, daughter of Andrés Martínez de Alballe and María Josefa Duro, married Eugenio Vizoso, yet another Galician who in turn served on the cabildo on various occasions during the final decade of Spanish colonial rule. María Leocadia Martínez was thus the wife, daughter, granddaughter, and great-granddaughter of peninsular immigrants who served on the cabildo of San Felipe el Real.[26]

Not all immigrants belonged to this select coterie, however; peninsulares occupied a number of less prestigious socioeconomic niches as well. Many started out as modest clerks or shopkeepers whose diligence afforded them a certain level of respectability. A fortunate few even rose to positions of prominence despite their failure to form close ties of kinship with upper echelons of the villa's elite. Pedro Antonio Cadrecha, for example, was in his twenties when he migrated to Chihuahua from his native Asturias in the late 1730s. He worked first as a cashier for his fellow countryman Juan Cacho de Herrera, a lifelong bachelor and merchant who had settled in the area as early as 1716. Cadrecha married outside the local elite; his wife was Micaela Alcaraz y Rentería, from a family of bakers originally from Nuestra Señora del Rosario in Nueva Galicia. Cadrecha then set up his own bakery and soon came to dominate the local bread trade. By the late 1740s the cabildo named him to coordinate the bakers' guild's participation in local civic celebrations. A decade later he had been elected alcalde and spokesman for the Chihuahua guild of merchants. He served as alcalde again in 1766 and later as head of the villa's most prestigious religious confraternity, the Archicofradía del Santo Sacramento. In 1772 his son, Pedro Nicolás, became an alcalde.[27]

Other peninsular merchants failed to achieve distinction equal to that of Pedro Antonio Cadrecha. At most they might serve as active participants in juntas convoked by the town's merchants to discuss matters of mutual concern. A few of these men married considerably beneath themselves in social rank. For example, shopkeeper Francisco de Angulo wed a free black woman in 1730, and the following year Antonio de Moreno, also a small-scale merchant and in his late sixties, married a seventeen-year-old Apache woman who had been his servant.[28] An even greater number of such peninsulares remained bachelors and therefore missed a crucial opportunity to bond with other members of the town's peninsular elite. Still, even some bachelors earned positions of respect in the community. The unmarried Basque Manuel de Garaygorta, for example, operated a tienda with his nephew and cousin; in 1724 his fellow merchants selected him to be their official spokesman.[29]

Nineteenth-century writers such as Lucas Alamán and Lorenzo de Zavala vividly depicted the frugal austerity of the Spanish shopkeepers and *cajeros* (cashiers) who became familiar figures in the cities and towns of late colonial New Spain.[30] Many of Chihuahua's peninsular immigrants closely conformed to this image, sleeping in cramped quarters at the back of their shops and often eating at their counters. They suffered the indignity of personally attending to customers who ranked far beneath them in social prestige. Others even peddled their merchandise in the villa's streets or in nearby Indian villages. Antonio Amor, for example, was a Spanish shopkeeper who found that sales improved if he went out personally to sell his merchandise about town while leaving his wife in charge of the store.[31]

Some small-scale entrepreneurs also endured great personal risks in the performance of their duties. Manuel Gutiérrez de la Rasilla, a native of Burgos, was in his late teens when he arrived in San Felipe with his father, brother, and brother-in-law shortly after the villa's founding. The foursome established a small retail business, with Manuel serving as cashier and night watchman. One evening in 1722 thieves entered the shop and shot him in the thigh.[32] Juan Gómez Cajiga, also from Burgos, was even less fortunate. A bachelor, he operated a small store that specialized in retail foodstuffs. Many of his customers were persons of color quebrado who traded scraps of silver ore for merchandise or pawned personal treasures with him. In 1731 intruders entered Gómez Cajiga's store and murdered him, ending his dreams of one day returning to Spain.[33]

Other would-be merchants lacked the capital to establish their own shops or the connections to secure a position managing someone else's business. Simón Rojas Taboada typified the itinerant peddler who made the rounds of cities, villages, and mining camps throughout colonial Latin America. Immigrating to the New World in 1740 at the age of twenty, he went first to Mexico City and then to Guanajuato. Evidently his hopes of quick wealth failed to materialize in either of those locations, so in 1748 he headed north toward New Mexico. En route he stopped in Chihuahua, but soon fled after being implicated in a murder and suspected of other mischief.[34]

Other Spanish immigrants were skilled artisans. The villa's guild of silversmiths, for example, included a few peninsulares.[35] Diego de Lira y Sayas was a master tailor from Valladolid in Castile who settled in San Felipe during the boom times of the 1720s and remained there for the next several decades. He married at least twice; evidently his second wife was a mestiza.[36] Other Spaniards pursued even less prestigious occupations. Juan José Molina, for example, was a native of Cádiz who had worked as a cook in Zacatecas before proceeding northward in hope of reaching Sonora. In 1772, however, he was detained in Chihuahua because an arriero had stolen his livestock and money.[37]

Some impoverished immigrants became troublesome vagabonds or charity cases. José Real, a 38-year-old native of San Cipriano de Paredes in the kingdom of León, had evidently circulated among several mining communities in northern New Spain after abandoning his wife in Guanajuato. In Chihuahua he held occasional odd jobs for shopkeepers in Santa Eulalia, but was described as a vagabond "without any employment or occupation whatsoever" when he was jailed for robbery in 1736.[38] Juan Francisco del Castillo was one of the few illiterate peninsulares to settle in the area. The 28-year-old bachelor worked as an itinerant merchant and as a mine laborer, and in the mid-1730s he was jailed for stealing 160 pesos from his employer.[39]

Other Europeans

Peninsular Spaniards were not the only European residents of Chihuahua. At least 23 non-Spanish Europeans, some of them subjects of the Spanish crown from outside the Iberian peninsula, also migrated to the area during the eighteenth century.[40] All of these immigrants were male, many were merchants, and most occupied social ranks comparable to those of the less pretentious Spanish shopkeepers, excluded from office holding but sometimes included in the ranks of substantial vecinos. Perhaps the most distinguished foreigner was

Juan de Majalca, a Spanish subject but a native of Ghent in Flanders. His wife was Gregoria de Anza, originally from Sonora, and he formed ties of *compadrazgo*, or ritual kinship, with at least one peninsular immigrant who served on the cabildo. Captain of the local militia in the 1720s, Majalca was often present when the town's citizens gathered to discuss matters of civic concern. In 1726 he was nominated, but not elected, to serve as an alcalde.[41]

Chihuahua's foreign community also included several Frenchmen, a number of whom were placed under temporary arrest after the French assault on Mobile in 1719.[42] Among those detained was Bernardo Perches, who operated a bakery in San Felipe el Real and also dabbled in mining. He too participated in civic affairs, joining his fellow vecinos in demanding the ouster of Corregidor Juan Sánchez Camacho in 1731. His son-in-law, Juan Gregorio Suárez, was a foreman for Manuel San Juan y Santa Cruz, former governor of Nueva Vizcaya and the area's most powerful entrepreneur in the 1730s.[43] Andrés Fourzán was another French baker, and he played an active role in staging comedies and other diversions presented at local civic celebrations. Though he died in 1776, he and his family left their mark on the city of Chihuahua; a census taken in 1785 referred to the "street that they call 'of Fourzán.' "[44]

There were several Italians also, including surgeon José Marioni and Domingo Cuarón Leyva y Santa Bárbara, a veteran of the Philippine galleons known informally as "El Romano," even though he hailed in fact from Milan.[45] Cuarón's nephews Félix and Melchor accompanied him to San Felipe in the early 1720s and remained active members of the town's merchant community over the next two decades.[46] A few Portuguese subjects also settled in the villa. Domingo Carvallo, originally from the province of Entreduero, was a prominent merchant during the heyday of the mining boom. When he died in 1735, a prominent peninsular and former alcalde served as executor of his estate.[47] At least one Irishman, a petty merchant and basketmaker whose hispanicized name was Manuel Hermundo, also made his way to Chihuahua.[48] During the final years of the colonial period a few immigrants from the United States, usually called *angloamericanos*, took up residence in the villa. Louisiana native Simon McCoy arrived around 1800 and eventually found work assisting the manager of the municipal obraje. Documents also mention a Juan Finch, who settled in Chihuahua in 1805. He was a tailor who also participated in the New Mexico trade. Both Finch and McCoy married local women in the parish church of San Felipe.[49]

Españoles

Far more numerous, though often less conspicuous, than the Spaniards or other immigrants were those known as españoles—people born in New Spain who claimed Spanish ancestry. In the census of 1785 españoles numbered 1,307, or 34.8 percent of the villa's population. They accounted for an even greater share of those considered to have a stake in local society; 322, or 46.8 percent, of the 688 heads of households listed in the census were españoles.[50] Many españoles were quite likely mestizos or other racial mixtures whose physiognomies favored their European ancestors and whose social prestige enabled them to "pass," especially in a new environment where few of their neighbors might know their true antecedents. As time passed, growing numbers of españoles garnered sufficient standing to warrant the honorific titles *Don* and *Doña*. In 1785, 179 heads of households—113 men and 66 women—enjoyed that distinction.[51]

Españoles occupied such a wide range of positions in the social and economic hierarchy of the villa that they defy easy description as a group. Toward the end of the colonial period a select few achieved municipal office, though most of these enjoyed close associations with influential peninsulares. In 1772 Pedro Nicolás Cadrecha, son of immigrant and former alcalde Pedro Antonio Cadrecha, evidently became the first Chihuahua native elected to the cabildo.[52] José Félix Trespalacios, active in local politics during the first two decades of the nineteenth century, was the son of Francisco Antonio Trespalacios, an immigrant, bureaucrat, and former alcalde who had begun his career serving as a cajero for the elder Cadrecha.[53] Mariano Orcasitas, a member of Chihuahua's cabildo on three separate occasions between 1816 and 1821, was a third-generation resident of New Spain's northern frontier. His father Ramón was born in El Paso del Norte in 1743, the son of a peninsular immigrant from Vizcaya.[54] Only Pedro Sandoval y Moscoso, a native of Nochistán in Nueva Galicia who settled in Chihuahua in 1764 and became an alcalde in 1783, seems to have lacked obvious links with the villa's peninsular elite.[55]

Other relatively successful españoles occupied social positions comparable to those of the more distinguished non-Spanish Europeans. Municipal office generally remained closed to them, and seldom were they asked to become *compadres* of peninsular immigrants by serving as godparents for the immigrants' children. Nevertheless, they figured among the wider circle of those accorded a say in local affairs. Tomás Durán y Chávez, for example, was a native of New Mexico who had established himself as a merchant in Chihuahua as early as 1716. Though he never sat on the cabildo, he was the only known native of the colonies among the thirteen principal vecinos summoned to discuss local defense in 1725. When he died in 1750, he was buried "de cruz alta," which signified that he was given the more lavish, and more expensive, form of funeral rites.[56] Some españoles were active participants in civic fiestas, often serving as "captains" of Moors and Christians in the mock reenactments of the medieval Spanish Reconquest. Vicente Vargas sometimes played the "Gran Turco" ("Great Turk") in these rituals. Evidently he ranked somewhat lower in social status than Tomás Durán y Chávez; the priest who recorded his simple burial ("de cruz baja") in 1756 did not list him as "Don."[57]

Mateo de Olague was another typical español. A native of Zacatecas, he appeared on a militia muster roll compiled at Cusihuiriachic in 1716 and married Josefa de Salas in Santa Eulalia the following year. There he registered several mining claims and eventually established a refinery, but never entered the inner circle of San Felipe's elite. His signature lacks the elaborate flourishes affected by local peninsulares, suggesting that his literacy was tenuous at best. Finally, in the early 1740s Olague retired to the jurisdiction of Julimes, about 40 miles southeast of San Felipe, where he held a minor political office but also had his goods embargoed when he failed to pay his many debts.[58]

The Muñoz de Olvera family provides another good example of the social position of people reputed to be españoles. Sometime in the 1730s Juan Muñoz de Olvera, his wife Juana de Cobos, and several of their children migrated to San Felipe from El Valle de San Bartolomé, where their families had resided for several generations. Their fathers and grandfathers had held military titles and haciendas in the valley. Juan, born in 1698, was the son of Captain Juan Muñoz de Olvera and Margarita Ponce de León, who was in turn the daughter of an officer named Juan Ponce de León. In 1712 the elder Juan Muñoz de Olvera owned a flour mill and a hacienda, with some 500 head of cattle and 100 horses, located about one league from the pueblo of San Bartolomé.[59] Juana's father was Ignacio de Cobos, born in 1677. Her mother, Catalina de Olguín, was listed as illegitimate and of unknown parents in the parish records of El Valle de San Bartolomé.[60]

Surviving documents show little trace of the younger Juan Muñoz de Olvera after the family settled in San Felipe el Real. He was reportedly still living in the villa in 1752, but by that time maintained a residence apart from his wife and children; documents give no clue as to his occupation. Juana de Cobos, however, was a highly visible resident of the town. Unable to read or write, she nevertheless established a bakery in the early 1740s and used its proceeds to support herself, her children, and grandchildren for the next several decades. Though occasionally her detractors disparaged her social standing by calling her a mulata, and the census of 1785 lists her as a mestiza, most documents consistently refer to her and her children as españoles, and her neighbors often addressed her as "Doña Juana."[61] Juana's son, Gregorio Antonio Muñoz de Olvera, was a typical español of modest social standing. He somehow acquired sufficient literacy to sign documents and manage the financial affairs of his mother's bakery.[62] In 1766 he formed a partnership with Juan Antonio Mariño de Cadaval, a scribe who was probably a peninsular Spaniard, to grow maize and beans at a site eight leagues from Chihuahua.[63]

Other españoles worked as skilled artisans. Of the 106 tailors who resided in San Felipe in 1735, at least 36 declared themselves to be españoles.[64] Others held supervisory positions in mines, refineries, and rural estates. Cayetano Jáquez, for example, was an illiterate español who served as a *mayordomo* (majordomo or supervisor) of a silver refinery in the 1730s.[65] Many others performed manual labor in various enterprises. Manuel Morales was a 23-year-old pickman, born at the presidio of Conchos, who worked in the mines of Manuel San Juan y Santa Cruz.[66] Early parish registers listed many others like him, españoles who were employees of the great mining entrepreneurs.[67] A few persons listed as españoles even lacked surnames, like Juan Bautista and María Gertrudis, who married in Santa Eulalia in 1720.[68]

Indians

A variety of Indians formed another important component of society in colonial Chihuahua. Throughout the eighteenth century forced labor drafts, known locally as *mandamientos*, brought Tarahumaras from nearby Franciscan and Jesuit mission-pueblos to labor in temporary shifts in San Felipe and Santa Eulalia. Indians recruited through mandamientos worked at mines, refineries, bakeries, haciendas, and public works projects. Beginning in the 1750s Tarahumaras built the famous aqueduct that brought water into the villa of San Felipe.[69] Mission Indians also came into town to play ceremonial roles on special occasions. Festivities held in 1761 to honor the coronation of King Carlos III featured buglers from the Tarahumara village of Satevó, for example.[70]

Some Tarahumaras, ignoring official efforts to keep them "reduced" to residence in their pueblos, settled permanently in the villa or on rural estates in the surrounding area, while others sought temporary, paid jobs in various enterprises.[71] A census taken of the mission of Santa Isabel in 1750 revealed that the majority of the pueblo's Indian men worked as hired hands in mines, haciendas, and silver refineries.[72] Meanwhile, growing numbers of non-Indians settled in the Tarahumara villages, cultivating lands rented from the missions or setting up small retail shops.[73] As the eighteenth century advanced many "Indian" pueblos gradually evolved into racially mixed farming communities. An occasional mulato even appeared among "Indians" sent out to work in forced labor drafts.[74] By 1785 Santa Isabel had 491 residents, of whom only 58 were Indians.[75]

Throughout the eighteenth century Yaqui Indians from Sonora worked as wage laborers in Chihuahua's mines and refineries. Like other workers, they often ran up huge debts and then fled without paying.[76] Some joined the celebrated workers' strikes that disrupted local mining in the 1730s, although others assisted law enforcement officials in surrounding a mine seized by dissident workers.[77] The Yaquis formed a distinct community of their own that antedated the foundation of San Francisco de Cuéllar.[78] When Durango Bishop Pedro Tamarón y Romeral visited San Felipe el Real in 1760, he found about 100 Yaquis living near the sanctuary of Nuestra Señora de Guadalupe on the villa's outskirts.[79] Six years later Nicolás Lafora reported 30 Yaqui families at the same location.[80] By the 1760s the Yaquis had become well-acculturated members of the local community. Occasionally one of their number served as the town's official crier, or *pregonero*, and in 1762 a contingent of Yaquis accompanied the cabildo in a solemn procession honoring the Immaculate Conception.[81]

Male and female Apaches captured in New Mexico also blended into local society. Known as *indios de rescate* (ransomed Indians) because their captors argued that they had been rescued from a life of paganism, they were shipped southward along with salt, hides, piñón nuts, and other staples of the New Mexico trade. Somewhere along the way they were received into the Catholic church, and they account for the bulk of the adult baptisms noted in Table 5 in the Appendix. On May 31, 1725, for example, the priest at Santa Eulalia baptized eight adult Apaches, two males and six females.[82] Buyers then paid the Indians' "ransom" and in return received a claim on their labor, theoretically for a limited term but often in fact for life. Sometimes people in Chihuahua contracted for future delivery of captives. In 1729 Gaspar Macías asked a soldier from New Mexico to procure him two young Indians, promising two well-trained horses and an elegant saddle in return.[83] Apaches were regularly bought and sold as chattel in eighteenth-century Chihuahua. In the 1730s and 1740s young adults cost between 70 and 100 pesos, about one-third the price of Afro-Mexican slaves.[84] These Apaches became the frequent objects of litigation among those who bought and sold them, and they sometimes appeared along with black slaves in the inventories of estates.[85]

Because many of these Apaches were "ransomed" as young children and reared as *criados* (servants) in their masters' households, they became fluent in Spanish, adopted Spanish surnames, and married black slaves or other members of the underclass. Some managed to escape their bondage and became paid workers in mines and refineries. A lucky few became apprenticed in skilled trades, while others mastered a variety of hustles in an effort to improve their situation.[86] The life story of the Apache José de la Cruz Enríquez was typical. He worked first in a bakery owned by a rather disagreeable peninsular Spaniard. Later he turned to gathering and reselling scraps of silver ore. His luck in gambling apparently brought additional income, enabling him to assist his mulata slave wife in purchasing her freedom.[87] María Rosa Serrano was also an Apache; 50 years of age in 1762, she supported herself by selling fruit in the central plaza of San Felipe el Real.[88]

Other Indians, known locally as "indios mexicanos," migrated to Chihuahua from all over New Spain.[89] Most accepted menial, unskilled positions wherever they could find them, but a few tried to gain special distinction by claiming to have been caciques in their home communities. Dionisio Torres del Castillo, for example, said that he was a cacique from San Miguel el Grande. Whatever the truth of his assertion, he achieved a higher social status than many other Indians in Chihuahua. He became a master weaver with his own shop, in which he employed a number of people, including even some españoles. He was also able to sign his name, albeit rather crudely.[90] Other Indians advanced themselves through luck and initiative. An *indio ladino* (Indian fluent in Spanish) originally from Cusihuiriachic, Francisco de la Cruz operated a simple silver refinery in the 1730s.[91]

People of "Color Quebrado"

Even more numerous than the españoles or Indians were mestizos and others of mixed ancestry, known in local parlance as *castas* or people of "*color quebrado*." Mestizos, numbering 1,715, accounted for 45.7 percent of San Felipe's population in 1785, while the villa's 484 mulatos comprised another 12.9 percent of the total.[92] The occupational profile of mestizos and mulatos was very diverse. An enterprising few, many of them mestizos, became owners of simple refineries or practiced skilled trades, and some were literate. José Alexo Juárez, for example, was a mestizo saddlemaker originally from San Miguel el Grande who affixed a rather graceful signature to a document in 1734.[93]

Many mulatos and mestizos were muleteers and cowboys, while others toiled in mines, refineries, and bakeries. There were 24 mestizos and 21 mulatos listed among San Felipe's 106 tailors in 1735.[94] A small and steadily declining percentage of Chihuahua's Afro-Mexicans were slaves; just 21 slaves remained in the villa by 1785.[95] Most slaves were well-acculturated mulatos used as domestic servants, though a few worked in mining or other occupations. José de Aguirre left a slave force of 21 (13 males and 8 females) when he died in 1728. One or two of the men worked in Aguirre's mines, while others were carpenters, arrieros, or coachmen.[96] When Diego González de la Herrán died in 1747, an inventory of his assets showed seven adult male slaves working at his rural hacienda and his silver refinery.[97]

Many of Chihuahua's mestizos and free mulatos had drifted from one mining center to another across the northern frontier of New Spain, stopping to work at "whatever presented itself" and quickly departing in the face of bad debts, criminal charges, or simple wanderlust. José Lorenzo Graciano, alias Chico, and his friend Juan de Dios de los Reyes, nicknamed Angolita, were typical members of Chihuahua's working class. Chico was a mine worker by trade, born in Zacatecas about 1712—he himself did not know his exact age. His parents had come originally from Sombrerete. Though others identified him as a mulato, he classified himself as a *coyote*, a term that in some parts of colonial Mexico meant mestizo and in other places connoted both African and Indian ancestry. The early 1730s found Chico working in San Juan del Río. He was soon "summoned by the voices of the mines of Chihuahua," as he put it, though the prospect of escaping a 38-peso debt to his employer probably strengthened the attraction of those voices. In Chihuahua he worked at various odd jobs before departing for El Paso del Norte, where he remained a few months. Finally in the spring of 1733 he returned to San Felipe and obtained employment with a local innkeeper. Like Chico, Angolita was a native of Zacatecas, born around 1710. Described as a *lobo* and therefore presumably of mixed African and Indian ancestry, he worked for a local tailor and in construction and mining. In April of 1733 he and Chico hit the road again, this time fleeing criminal charges. They headed south but soldiers apprehended them at the Florido River and escorted them back to San Felipe, where they were tried, convicted, and eventually executed for the murder of Spanish shopkeeper Benito Godoy (see Chapter 6).[98]

Social Negotiation

With the exception of the Tarahumaras and other Indians native to the region, none of these people would have settled in northern Nueva Vizcaya without the discovery of silver at Santa Eulalia at the beginning of the eighteenth century. The first settlers included Spanish army officers tired of fighting Indians and now ready to make the kind of fortunes that had lured them to the New World in the first place, as well as workers from all over New Spain, some more or less coerced into the journey and others who came of their own volition. Word of the bonanza soon spread, and other newcomers made their way to Chihuahua—enterprising Spaniards and españoles hoping to stake their own belated claims to mineral wealth or strike it rich through trade, and many others with objectives less clearly defined but nonetheless convinced that the long trek to the north was worth the effort.

All of these men and women fell under the jurisdiction of the colonial state, subject to laws, edicts, and precedents emanating from Madrid, Mexico City, Guadalajara, Durango, and Parral. Those dicta delineated all manner of right and proper conduct, imposing unequivocal punishments for murder and treason while at the same time stipulating such trivia as the proper attire to be worn by each of the many groups comprising New Spain's sociedad de castas. In theory, then, a coherent set of governing principles awaited the first settlers in Chihuahua and those who followed in their wake. In fact, however, much lay open to negotiation as they began setting up their new community. Those hoping to gain for themselves the right to interpret and enforce the canons of the colonial state had to create viable and credible institutions of local government, but little in their own education or experience prepared them for the job of governance. Moreover, even if they had in fact mastered all of the minutiae of Spanish jurisprudence, they would soon have learned that the law could not cover every social situation. Legal regulations might specify the formal relationships among Indians, Spaniards, and castas in colonial society, but no rules prescribed in detail what should happen when a Spanish shopkeeper newly arrived from the mountains of Burgos met a mulato customer with money to spend.

Before the founders of Chihuahua could even deal with these kinds of questions, however, they first had to set the ground rules for the enterprise that had drawn such a diverse population together in the first place—the mining of silver. Those who staked claims to silver mines faced the practical challenge of extracting the ore, converting it to refined silver, and shipping it overland to places where it might fetch them the necessities and luxuries of life. The more socially pretentious of these miners shunned the task of working the mines themselves, and all of them knew that they needed more than their own efforts to make their dreams a reality. Chihuahua's primordial social negotiations, then, centered on how, and under what conditions, some individuals could command the muscle power of others. The bargains struck in this arena in turn affected other aspects of social relations. Chapter 3 examines the social relations of production that governed the mining industry and other enterprises in eighteenth-century Chihuahua.

THREE

Labor Relations

WORD OF THE discovery of silver at Santa Eulalia spread rapidly throughout the northern frontier of New Spain during the first two decades of the eighteenth century. Would-be mining magnates easily grasped the urgency of prompt action. Whoever arrived first on the scene with a large, tractable labor force could quickly extract a sizable portion of the area's relatively accessible silver deposits. In theory, employers needed to have at least four workers in place to maintain their claim to a particular mine, but a profitable enterprise demanded a much larger crew. Mine operators needed *barreteros* or pickmen to loosen the silver-bearing rocks, *tenateros* to carry the heavy sacks of ore to the surface without benefit of pulleys or other mechanical devices, and a host of transport workers to ferry it to refineries in Santa Eulalia or San Felipe.[1] Owners of refineries also required large numbers of skilled and unskilled workers.

Forms of Labor Recruitment

Ambitious entrepreneurs arriving in Chihuahua early in the silver bonanza moved quickly to exploit the area's indigenous population as a source of labor. During the first two decades of the eighteenth century, political authorities issued decrees or mandamientos ordering Tarahumaras and other recently subdued Indians from nearby missions to perform periodic service in newly developed mines and refineries, and these officials used military force to ensure that many of those drafted actually showed up for work. Although employers in

Chihuahua continued to rely on this local variant of the repartimiento system for more than two generations to come, they never regarded these workers as more than incidental, stopgap, and generally inferior components of their labor force.[2] Indians supplied through mandamientos seldom served willingly and rarely worked long enough to develop any skill. Other forced labor mechanisms proved equally unsatisfactory in filling the pressing labor needs of this burgeoning mining center. Afro-Mexican slaves were scarce and usually too valuable to risk in dangerous activities such as mining, and captured Apaches never constituted more than a small fraction of the area's work force.

Some of Chihuahua's most successful early mining entrepreneurs attempted to surmount these difficulties by importing their own labor supply. Colonel Juan Felipe de Orozco y Molina, one of San Felipe's most ambitious and politically influential miners, secured a large contingent of convicts sentenced by the Inquisition and criminal courts in Mexico City.[3] Other entrepreneurs came accompanied by *cuadrillas* (work crews) that they had assembled in other mining centers. When José de Aguirre arrived from Sonora about 1716, he brought over 100 workers, many of them Yaquis, and set them to work in the mines of his father-in-law, General José de Orio y Zubiate.[4]

In the early days of Chihuahua's mining boom employers and local authorities envisioned a stable labor force, with each worker clearly attached to a particular enterprise in some kind of proprietary relationship. Those who wrote documents recording the transfer of a mine, refinery, or rural estate to a new owner routinely assumed that the property came equipped with an organized work crew.[5] Parish registers from the first few decades of the eighteenth century designated many individuals as *sirvientes* (literally, servants, but in practice a generic term applied to most employees) of one of the great mining magnates. All but 10 of the 42 men who married in Chihuahua in 1716 were listed as sirvientes of a particular master, for example.[6] Workers themselves thought in similar terms, referring, for example, to the servants of General Orio y Zubiate as "los Zubiateños."[7]

In fact, however, the stability of the labor force and the proprietary control of employers over their workers often proved illusory. Workers frequently fled in search of better opportunities, while epidemics and other hazards took their toll. In 1731 Juan de Bonilla entered a bid for the rancho El Sacramento, which had belonged to the late General Orio y Zubiate, assuming that it came with "gente bastante" (enough people) along with its livestock and other assets. He was later dismayed to find that only a single peon was available to work.[8]

Therefore employers regularly had to replenish their work forces from among the floating population who drifted in and out of San Felipe and Santa Eulalia. Many of these people reportedly showed little enthusiasm for the arduous and often dangerous work of mines or refineries, preferring instead to enrich themselves through gambling or theft. Political authorities, many of whom had invested heavily in the silver industry themselves, accordingly used their positions to compel these "vagabonds" to work. In 1715 Nueva Vizcaya Governor Manuel San Juan y Santa Cruz ordered all employers to give their workers written proof of employment, complete with a physical description of the worker. Any individual caught without this documentation could then be forced to work.[9] As a result Miguel de la Meda, a tailor by trade who earned a reputation as a gambler and general troublemaker, received a stern warning that people like himself were customarily placed in mines and refineries so that they could occupy themselves "not in games but in work."[10] Authorities soon conceded that such coercive measures had little effect, however. By the early 1730s, exile of habitual vagabonds had become standard policy.[11]

Employers therefore had no choice but to offer economic incentives to attract workers. Many mine owners solved this problem by adopting a practice common in other Mexican mining centers from the sixteenth century forward. Workers delivered a stipulated quota of ore to their employers each day and then were free to keep some or all of the rest of what they mined for themselves. Known variously as *partidos* or *pepenas*, these bonuses proved very attractive to workers, making them the virtual partners of their employers.[12] In Chihuahua the pepena system appealed especially to the large numbers of petty merchants and other small-scale entrepreneurs who dabbled in mining. They could recruit the number of workers they needed without having to expend great quantities for wages, rations, or supplies.[13] The area's principal mine operators also conceded this benefit, sometimes allowing workers to retain as much as half of the ore they extracted.[14]

Employers in Chihuahua soon found these pepenas to be expensive nuisances, however. Workers shunned any task other than the extraction of ore, and they often tore down mine supports in their improvident haste to gather rich deposits for themselves. For their part, administrators of mines sent workers to less productive parts of a mine after the daily quotas had been delivered, but workers still found ways to take the best ore for themselves and sell it to *cendradilleros* (independent refiners). Pepenas also gave workers a certain independence; they could exchange their bonuses for commodities supplied by local merchants rather depend on their employers to sell them food and other necessities. Finally, their legal access to abundant quantities of ore gave workers a convenient cover to use in selling stolen ore to independent refiners.[15]

Abolition of the Pepenas

During the 1720s mine owners made sporadic, unsuccessful attempts to terminate the pepenas, but workers routinely responded by walking off their jobs until the customary benefits were restored. General José de Orio y Zubiate and other miners also tried requiring their workers to sell the pepenas back to them, presumably at prices less attractive than those offered by independent refiners. Again the workers simply threatened to go elsewhere unless their employers allowed them to sell the bonuses to whomever they wished.[16] Meanwhile, economic forces undermined mine owners' efforts to do away with the independent refiners, because the refineries owned by the villa's principal miners lacked the capacity to process all of the ore being gathered in Santa Eulalia during the boom times of the 1720s.[17]

In March of 1730 Manuel San Juan y Santa Cruz spearheaded a much more concerted effort to eliminate the pepenas and the independent refiners who purchased them. More than any other miner, San Juan y Santa Cruz possessed the economic and political power to accomplish this objective. A Basque and a member of Spain's prestigious Order of Santiago, he had extensive military experience throughout the empire, having served in His Majesty's Armada de Barlovento, at the presidio of Santo Domingo, and in the Philippine Islands. Upon assuming the governorship of Nueva Vizcaya in 1714, he determined to exploit his political position to build his fortunes. He allegedly imported 100,000 pesos' worth of merchandise, hoping to become a principal supplier for all mines, presidios, and haciendas in his jurisdiction. By 1719 his lavishly stocked tiendas in

Chihuahua, Parral, and Cusihuiriachic had made him, in the words of one local resident, "the absolute lord of all commerce" in Nueva Vizcaya. Troops assigned to the Conchos presidio worked his silver refinery, while generous grants of repartimiento Indians labored at his hacienda of San Pedro de Alcantará, near San Felipe el Real. Meanwhile, he established a reputation for hostility toward mine workers, reportedly using his influence to crush the use of the pepenas in Parral.[18]

Following his retirement from the governorship in 1720, San Juan y Santa Cruz remained one of Chihuahua's foremost mine owners until his death in 1749. By March of 1730 he had managed to have himself named *diputado* or spokesman for the area's mine owners, despite opposition from some other entrepreneurs. With the help of his political protégé Juan Sánchez Camacho, a controversial figure who served intermittently as corregidor from 1726 to 1734, San Juan y Santa Cruz proceeded to execute his plan.[19] He prevailed upon Sánchez Camacho to convoke a meeting of mine owners who shared his antipathy to the pepenas, pointedly excluding all others. Those in attendance quickly drafted new mining ordinances that abolished the bonuses, and Sánchez Camacho ordered the immediate publication of the revised regulations. Although the scribe charged with posting the ordinances balked, fearing an upheaval, several mine owners simply stopped giving pepenas to their workers.[20]

Word of the new measures spread rapidly, and workers lost no time in manifesting their anger. At least 300, and by some accounts as many as 600, quickly armed themselves and gathered in the hills some five leagues from Santa Eulalia. There they built a makeshift stone parapet, unfurled a banner proclaiming their defiance, and vowed to storm the villa of San Felipe, kill San Juan y Santa Cruz, and burn his house to the ground. For the next several weeks they refused to budge from their mountain redoubt, where they passed time by composing and singing songs of protest. The lyrics of one of these early Mexican *corridos* addressed Ignacio Francisco de Barrutia, governor of Nueva Vizcaya, confidently informing him that "Señor, Captain General, you will give us our pepena, or if not, the head of San Juan." Meanwhile, they also sent emissaries to the governor to explain their grievances in detail.

The upheaval provoked a severe crisis in San Felipe and Santa Eulalia. Mining stopped for several weeks during what one observer called "the most opportune season of the year." Local residents later predicted that it would take several years of bonanza to remedy the strike's effects. Frightened townspeople huddled in their homes in San Felipe, expecting an angry mob of workers to descend upon the villa at any moment. Meanwhile, rumors circulated that rebellious Indians from nearby Tarahumara settlements and from as far away as the Río del Norte (the Río Grande) had allied with the strikers.

Governor Barrutia hastened from Parral to Chihuahua as soon as he learned of the disturbance. He then summarily suspended Corregidor Sánchez Camacho from office and sent messages to the workers in an attempt to calm them. On April 14 he met with mine owners. Reportedly rejecting a handsome bribe of 10,000 pesos offered by San Juan y Santa Cruz, he ordered all employers to retain the pepenas. Meanwhile, Bishop Benito Crespo y Monroy of Durango, who happened to be in Chihuahua for his pastoral visit, also attempted to mediate the dispute.[21] The combined efforts of the governor and bishop apparently succeeded in persuading the mine owners, with the crucial and utterly predictable exception of San Juan y Santa Cruz, to agree to restore the pepenas for a month, during which time workers could settle accounts with their employers and agree on the terms under which they would return to work.

Bishop Crespo y Monroy then commissioned Father Miguel de la Sierra, the priest assigned to Santa Eulalia, to convey word of this compromise to the workers. Sierra saddled his horse and rode up the rugged slopes to the workers' camp. There he read them a letter from the bishop, promising them immunity from prosecution for their roles in the strike and at least a temporary restoration of the pepenas if they would return to their jobs without further incident. Reportedly the workers remained completely unconvinced until Sierra added his own assurances that the mine owners would respect the terms of the bishop's conciliatory proposal.

Although still somewhat reluctant to accept these conditions, the workers returned to Santa Eulalia within a few days. There they found little to substantiate the bishop's promises. Mine overseers beat them and called them *perros alzados* (rebellious dogs) and other insulting epithets, while several employers denied them the expected restoration of the pepenas. Worse yet, the workers' own families ridiculed them for having given in so easily to the perverse designs of San Juan y Santa Cruz. Their wives questioned their masculinity by calling them *maricas mantillones* (loosely translated as effeminate old women; more literally, homosexuals draped in shawls), *gallinas cobardes* (cowardly hens), *cocineros* (cooks), and *pendejos* (literally, pubic hairs; figuratively, a scornful insult directed at men). Humiliated and disheartened, the workers trudged back to the hills and renewed their strike, reportedly vowing this time to die rather than submit.

Surviving documents do not reveal precisely what happened next, but evidently the workers gradually drifted back to work over the next several weeks. Meanwhile, tensions continued to smolder, and local officials pondered measures to avert further unrest. Governor Barrutia spent the entire summer of 1730 personally inspecting the mines in Santa Eulalia and conducting a thorough investigation of the events that had provoked the walkout. He listened patiently while leading citizens offered vivid testimony documenting the corruption of Sánchez Camacho and the despotic power wielded by San Juan y Santa Cruz. For their part, the cabildo members decided to inform the *audiencia* (court of appeals) in Guadalajara of their complaints against the deposed corregidor, citing in particular his role in precipitating the strike.[22] San Juan y Santa Cruz had little to fear when the matter reached the audiencia. One of his key allies during the strike, the miner Juan José de Urrutia, was the brother of Fernando de Urrutia, an *oidor* (audiencia judge) who had served in Guadalajara since 1710. The court accordingly ignored the cabildo's concerns and ordered Sánchez Camacho's reinstatement.[23] However, Governor Barrutia in turn delayed executing the order because he feared further unrest. Instead he forwarded the matter to Viceroy Juan de Acuña, who issued a decree upholding the audiencia's decision in June of 1731.[24]

Word of the viceroy's action spread quickly in San Felipe and Santa Eulalia. Workers then joined Sánchez Camacho's political opponents in voicing their displeasure, and copies of seditious verses threatening further violence circulated freely in the mining camp. On July 19, 1731, Governor Barrutia therefore dispatched six soldiers from his personal guard to assist the teniente of Santa Eulalia in maintaining order. Back in San Felipe, a tumultuous cabildo meeting took place on July 20. While the alcaldes and regidores were discussing the decree ordering the corregidor's restoration, a delegation of angry townsmen stormed into the room and demanded that the council consider their concerns. They presented a petition, bearing the names of 63 leading citizens, calling for the permanent ouster of Sánchez Camacho. They even offered to pay the corregidor 2,000 pesos if he would renounce all claims to the office. In support of their position they recounted events of the last few days, including the mounting discontent in Santa Eulalia. They therefore asked that Governor Barrutia be persuaded to set aside the viceroy's directive. Although the cabildo endorsed the citizens' proposal, the governor decided that he had little choice but to obey the mandate from Mexico City. Sánchez Camacho did not actually resume his duties for another three years, however, and the summer of 1731 evidently passed without any further walkouts in Santa Eulalia.[25]

Conditions for workers showed little improvement during the next few years, however. According to a report prepared by the cabildo in 1735, workers were beaten, underpaid, and asked to deliver more ore each day. As a result, their morale progressively deteriorated and they degenerated into gambling and drunkenness, pastimes to which, in the cabildo's opinion, they were all too inclined by nature. The council members further observed that although the "continuous complaints of these miserable ones" had only embittered the "fresh tears of this kingdom," the workers remained as obstinate as ever, so insolent that no authority could subdue them.[26]

Meanwhile, however, Manuel San Juan y Santa Cruz utilized his wealth and political connections in his continued campaign to end the practice of granting pepenas to workers in Chihuahua. A critical turning point in these efforts came in 1735, when the audiencia awarded him control over a disputed portion of a particularly lucrative mine. The rival contenders were the Arrieta brothers, Sebastián and Antonio, who enjoyed a reputation for relatively favorable treatment of their workers.[27] They were also avowed enemies of San Juan y Santa Cruz and Sánchez Camacho, having led efforts to secure signatures on the petition demanding the corregidor's ouster during the summer of 1731.

The audiencia's decision to award the disputed claim to San Juan y Santa Cruz therefore provoked another workers' uprising. In late September or early October 1735, Santa Eulalia's newly appointed teniente, José de Acevedo, received orders to close the mine in preparation for turning it over to San Juan y Santa Cruz. He decided to temporize, fearing that workers gathered in San Felipe for the week-long fiesta of San Francisco, held each year in early October, would revolt if he enforced the order immediately. San Juan y Santa Cruz then belittled the teniente and complained of his "despotism."[28]

When Acevedo finally bowed to pressure and complied with the audiencia's ruling in mid-November, his worst fears were confirmed. Some twenty workers immediately declared their opposition. Shouting "Long live the King and death to San Juan and bad government," they occupied the mine themselves in an early version of the sit-down strike. They then set about recruiting workers from other mines to join them, so that within a few days their numbers had grown to more than 40 men and boys. Without explicitly mentioning the pepena, they nonetheless complained that San Juan had repeatedly refused to grant his workers a just share in the fruits of their labor.

Rejecting suggestions that he crush the strike summarily "by fire and blood," Acevedo sought a peaceful resolution to the conflict. He offered the workers a full pardon if they would surrender without further incident, but they replied that they would rather have money than advice. The teniente then surrounded the mine with 50 armed men, half of them Yaquis equipped with bows and arrows. Hoping to starve the striking workers into submission, he forbade anyone to deliver food or drink to them. Meanwhile, employees loyal to San Juan y Santa Cruz aggravated tensions by taunting the strikers. By February of 1736, more than three months after the walkout had begun, the workers still had not capitulated; rather, they reportedly displayed "más orgullosa resolución" ("more arrogant determination") with each passing day. For reasons that remain unclear, their bravado collapsed abruptly in early March, however, and San Juan y Santa Cruz finally took effective possession of the disputed mine.[29]

Evidently San Juan y Santa Cruz's victory seriously weakened the practice of granting pepenas in Chihuahua.[30] Although some workers continued to exact the bonuses for a few more years, employers gradually deprived workers of this benefit after San Juan's legal triumph. From the early 1740s forward there are no further mentions of the pepenas, even in documents that might be expected to yield such references. For example, employers regularly complained that their workers were lazy, ill-disciplined, and unappreciative of the many benefits they received. Had pepenas still been common practice, at least a few employers would surely have touted their generosity in conceding this coveted perquisite to their workers. Also absent from the documents are suggestions from creditors that workers use profits from their pepenas to pay off their many debts. Particularly revealing is a set of documents from 1751, when cabildo officers interrogated local shopkeepers accused of purchasing stolen ore and refinery workers suspected of stealing it. Not a single respondent implied that he had obtained his ore from a worker who had received it as a pepena. If pepenas had still been common, such an alibi would surely have suggested itself. The best the suspects could offer was that employers allowed workers to scrape up residue from around the furnaces in which ore was heated or to collect small quantities from the mines.[31] We are left, then, with the conclusion that by this time the giving of pepenas was no longer common practice.

Workers' Credits and Other Compensation

The evident elimination of the pepenas did not represent as radical a departure in labor relations as might appear, however. From the earliest days of mining in Chihuahua, it is probable that a substantial portion of mine workers did not receive this benefit. In the 1720s many evidently worked at night and on holidays for the independent refineries, reportedly because they received so little in payment for their labor in the mines.[32] Moreover, Chihuahua employers quickly adopted a practice long observed in Zacatecas and other mining centers, that of using advances in cash or merchandise to attract workers.[33] The size of these advances, often amounting to a year's salary or more, suggests that, even before the victory of San Juan's legal maneuvers, credit had replaced the pepenas as the principal incentive used to attract workers to jobs in mining.

Although provision of credit to workers presented obvious drawbacks for employers, it held definite advantages over reliance on pepenas. In theory if not in practice, workers were obliged to remain at their jobs until they paid their debts. Without pepenas they had fewer opportunities for legitimate acquisition of ore, and employers could therefore monitor theft more efficiently. At the same time, the creative juggling of accounts gave employers new opportunities to cheat illiterate and uneducated workers. Abolition of pepenas may also have facilitated the recruitment of labor into refining and other jobs that lacked such customary fringe benefits. Since owners of the largest mines usually operated refineries as well, the use of credit enabled them to hire workers for mining and refining on the same basis and perhaps to rotate workers as the need arose. A final bonus lay in the opportunity to strike a major blow to the independent refiners by cutting off one of their most important sources of raw material.

Credit evidently became far more important than nominal wages in the total package of compensation used to attract workers. Salaries for mine and refinery workers in Chihuahua ranked substantially below those adopted some decades later in Guanajuato, where employers compensated for the elimination of the partido by raising wages to eight or even ten reales per day. Even if he worked only four twelve-hour shifts per week, as was evidently common in many mining centers, a Guanajuato worker still would have received sixteen to twenty pesos (128 to 160 reales) per month in wages.[34] In Chihuahua, the typical barretero earned between eight and twelve pesos monthly, while tenateros and other unskilled mine workers usually received between six and eight pesos. Wages in refining and other occupations were comparable: unskilled refinery workers earned six pesos per month, while a skilled *fundidor* (smelter) could expect a salary of ten or sometimes twelve pesos.[35] Thus workers in Chihuahua earned nominal wages only marginally higher than those of unskilled agricultural peons in central Mexico, who typically received two reales per day, or six pesos for a month of 24 workdays.[36]

The slight differential paid to workers in Chihuahua was more than offset by the higher cost of living on the northern frontier. Maize offers a well-documented example of the inflated prices people in Chihuahua paid for basic commodities. At the Mexico City municipal granary, maize prices fluctuated between ten and sixteen reales per *fanega* (a measure equal to about 1.5 bushels) in good years, and never cost more than 26 reales during the first half of the eighteenth century.[37] Chihuahua prices far exceeded these levels even in the best of times. Only an exceptionally good harvest brought prices below 20 reales per fanega; normally they ranged between 20 and 30 reales.[38] Bad years brought even higher prices. In December of 1724, for example, the governor issued an order restricting the amount of grain that could be shipped from Parral and El Valle de San Bartolomé to Chihuahua. As a result, food prices soared, with maize reaching eight pesos (64 reales) per fanega in San Felipe, and a reported peso per *almud* (one-twelfth of a fanega, about 4.5 liters) in Santa Eulalia.[39]

In 1739 prices climbed to 80 and even 90 reales per fanega, almost twice the record set in Mexico City during the terrible famine of 1786.[40] At the end of the 1740s Chihuahua prices again climbed above 50 reales for one fanega.[41] Even other mining centers of northern Mexico boasted lower prices than did Chihuahua. In the 1750s, a period of generally good harvests in central Mexico, a fanega of maize sold in Zacatecas for between eleven and fifteen reales.[42] In Chihuahua, I have found only one occasion during that decade when prices dropped *below* sixteen reales.[43]

Although most regular employees received rations of maize, meat, and chocolate in addition to their salaries, many of them probably had to buy additional food for their families. In Chihuahua the customary weekly allotment of two *almudes* (about nine liters) of maize for a married worker was exactly the same as that given to agricultural peons in central Mexico. According to Charles Gibson's calculations, two almudes per week barely sufficed for two persons. Therefore workers with more than one or two dependents probably had to buy maize or other foodstuffs at the inflated prices posted in the Chihuahua market.[44] Mineworkers reportedly exhausted their weekly meat rations by Tuesday, so that they had to buy any meat that they ate during the remainder of the week.[45] On the other hand, workers sometimes sold their rations, thereby taking advantage of high prices.[46]

Only by obtaining substantial cash advances and merchandise on credit, and then evading payment, could workers offset the effects of low wages and high prices. Despite local authorities' sporadic attempts to force payment of their debts, workers were often able to flee without paying or even working for any significant length of time. In 1728, for example, a mestizo named Diego Andrés Armendáriz left his job on a hacienda in El Valle de San Bartolomé without paying the 122 pesos his boss had furnished him. He then went to work for the Jesuit hacienda of Tabalaopa. Within less than a year he also owed 80 pesos to his new employer.[47] From the late 1720s onward virtually every inventory of a mine, refinery, or rural property listed substantial debts owed by employees, many of whom were designated as absent from their jobs. When an employer died, the heirs and executors seldom succeeded in collecting debts from workers.[48] In 1729 administrators of General José de Orio y Zubiate's estate noted that 23 workers owed a total of 3,293 pesos, not counting the debts of slaves or of workers who had died.[49]

Rather than wages it was the opportunity to obtain cash and merchandise, theoretically on credit but in fact for free, that proved to be the most powerful incentive for luring workers to jobs in mining, refining, and many other endeavors. By the 1730s credit had become so crucial in recruiting labor that employers spoke readily of the need to furnish their workers with *avío*, a word that in other contexts denoted working capital for the operation of a hacienda or other enterprise, but which was also used throughout colonial Mexico to indicate advances extended to workers.[50] When hiring a new worker an employer could expect to pay off a substantial debt, often as much as a year's salary, to the worker's former boss. The employer then had to supply cash, clothing, and other goods before the individual actually began his job. Once employed, workers continued to obtain additional advances from week to week. In late December most owners of mines and refineries totaled up their employees' accounts for the previous year. On this occasion many workers, although they were already heavily in debt, received 100 pesos or more before agreeing to return to their jobs after the Christmas and New Year's holidays. Some employees evidently demanded new supplies of avío after Easter as well. Anyone unable to provide these advances risked losing his or her labor force.[51] Competition among employers only heightened workers' leverage. Although local authorities tried to prevent workers from taking a new job unless they had satisfied any previous debts, in practice they found it difficult to enforce such provisions. Moreover, an employer could legally lure away another's workers by paying their debts and offering new advances.[52]

So pervasive was the system of credit that its principles even extended to the institution of Afro-Mexican slavery. A dissatisfied slave could seek legal permission to change masters by locating someone willing to pay his or her "market value." Often slaves were able to persuade a new employer to let them work off the purchase price over a period of time. These amounts often equaled the sums paid to clear free workers from debt, and employers evidently saw little difference between the two kinds of transactions.[53] Free workers in turn cited the experience of slaves to argue that they should not be required to work off a debt if they could liquidate it in cash or find another employer willing to do so. If slaves had the privilege of buying their freedom, then surely the same privilege extended to free workers, they reasoned.[54]

There is little evidence that debts served very effectively to bind workers to their jobs. As one employer grudgingly put it, he extended credit in hope of obliging his workers to stay until the debts were paid, but they treated these credits as simple loans or even gifts.[55] Employers often maintained single accounts for entire families and tried to hold relatives accountable for one another's debts. In theory a boss could thus fire a recalcitrant worker and still receive compensation for advances the worker had received.[56] On some occasions employers succeeded in forcing children to pay burial fees and other debts left by their deceased parents, and some workers carried this burden with them if they changed jobs.[57]

On the other hand, parents or guardians frequently "pawned" their children's labor to satisfy their own debts, and orphans became the objects of "custody battles" in which various relatives accused one another of trying to exploit the children's labor in this manner.[58] In these instances, however, an employer might be required to prove that the arrangement had been concluded with the youngsters' knowledge and consent.[59] In 1743 local authorities accordingly relieved two young boys of a debt contracted in their name but then turned them over to a new employer, who immediately supplied them with 125 pesos' worth of clothing and debited their account.[60]

Regardless of how much time elapsed, workers rarely made significant progress in paying off their debts. Typical was the case of a man hired to work the mines of Martín de Tovar in 1732. Tovar paid 30 pesos to the man's former boss and then provided his new employee with goods valued at 57 pesos, including silk and linen cloth, imported stockings, and a pair of cordovan shoes. Soon thereafter the worker received a horse, worth 12 pesos, and 24 pesos in silver, which he used to buy back clothing he had lost in a game of chance. When the worker ran away, Tovar spent an additional ten pesos seeking his apprehension. After two years the worker's debts amounted to over 133 pesos, more than fourteen times his monthly salary of nine pesos.[61]

Juan Antonio Jáquez, a mine worker hired by Juan Conde in June 1735, offers another example. Jáquez began his employment with a debt of over 250 pesos, or more than twice his annual salary, calculated at eight pesos per month. By May of 1736 he had worked a total of 108 days, and his total debt stood at 232 pesos. At this rate, Jáquez would have needed more than a decade to work off his initial debt, had he not fled his job. His brother Tomás was similarly unable or unwilling to change his debt status. After having worked for Conde more than two years, Tomás still owed 207 pesos, over twenty times his monthly salary.[62]

Cristóbal de Salazar offers another example. He signed on to work as a peon at Nicolás de Padilla's refinery in January of 1748 at a salary of seven pesos per month, plus one peso's worth of rations each week. He began his employment with a debt of 77 pesos, which Padilla paid to his former boss. When the time came to total his accounts the following December, Salazar's debt had reached 168 pesos, including charges for rations received during two months and thirteen days in which he had not worked and for numerous amounts of cash and commodities he had received. Despite his absences, he received a raise in salary to seven pesos, four reales. During the following year Salazar accumulated additional debts, so that he owed 254 pesos by the end of 1749. A year later his debt had risen to 347 pesos, and by March of 1752 it stood at 420 pesos, more than four times his annual salary.[63]

Workers sometimes used their advances to obtain goods that their employers considered to be luxuries scarcely appropriate for working-class people. In the 1730s José Victoriano Leal signed on to work as a *cargador de mulas*, loading freight on mules, at a salary of ten pesos per month. Immediately his employer advanced him the lavish sum of 400 pesos for expenses related to his forthcoming marriage. Leal used the money to outfit his bride with fine stockings, two linen blouses adorned with Flanders lace, blue serge undergarments, a shawl from Seville, fabrics imported from France, and fancy ribbons. For himself, he selected four pairs of *calzones* (trousers), a shirt with linen sleeves, a handkerchief trimmed in fine lace, and blue silk stockings. Five months later Leal reportedly left his job without paying the debt, but he evidently continued to live in Chihuahua. Parish registers from San Felipe show that in 1739 a son was born to him and his wife Francisca Antonia Jiménez.[64]

Credit enabled workers to exploit the scarcity of labor by demanding liberal advances from their employers. Moreover, abolition of the pepenas did not end workers' access to silver. Despite laws forbidding the purchase of ore from youngsters, slaves, or other "suspicious persons," stolen ore found a ready market among people known as *rescatadores*, petty entrepreneurs of varying social ranks who either scavenged ore for themselves or purchased it from others, with no questions asked.[65] In 1734 Santiago Gómez de Escontría charged his muleteers with habitually pilfering small quantities of ore en route from his mines in Santa Eulalia to his refinery in San Felipe.[66] During the strike of 1735, a large number of rescatadores set up huts near the disputed mine and bought ore directly from the strikers.[67] In addition, workers freely traded stolen silver in the shops of Santa Eulalia and San Felipe. In 1758 one shopkeeper told authorities that men and women called at all hours of the day and night, offering to sell him small quantities of ore.[68]

Anyone possessing stolen ore had little difficulty selling it in turn to small-scale refiners. According to one prominent miner in San Felipe, many of these cendradilleros were in fact former peons who made common cause with workers to defraud the more prosperous entrepreneurs.[69] Vicente Romero, a worker who had argued with his employer over the abolition of the pepena in the late 1730s, decided to strike out on his own and set up a refinery. Though he failed to make a profit, other workers tried their luck at similar ventures.[70] Into the nineteenth century people maintained these simple smelters, where they would sometimes melt down objects made of silver.[71]

The Politics of Labor Relations

Thus employers in eighteenth-century Chihuahua failed to establish the regimen of labor relations that they had initially envisioned. Workers exercised considerable autonomy in negotiating the terms of their employment even if they lost access to the customary pepenas. They broke explicit or implicit contracts at will and exacted liberal advances that far exceeded their nominal salaries. Workers also refused to behave "properly." In day-to-day contacts with their employers or supervisors, workers displayed thinly veiled hostility rather than the abject servility, or "obedience and courtesy," that employers expected.[72]

In return employers and local authorities disdained workers and felt that only coercion would get them to work. Despite his reluctance to use violence in crushing the 1735 labor disturbance, Santa Eulalia teniente José de Acevedo held little sympathy for the strikers. In his opinion, they were far too easily swayed by unnamed villains, and, "not knowing God, much less fearing the king," they showed little respect for His Majesty's ministers.[73] Employers frequently voiced similar sentiments. In 1724 Juan Antonio Tarín, owner of a charcoal-producing property near the rural community of Babanoyaba, observed that "the workers of this land are all men of little dependability, precision, or care in the fulfillment of their obligations."[74] Relations between employers and domestic servants were particularly tense. Lorenzo Gutiérrez, a Spanish-born baker, used the phrase "domestic enemies" to describe his relationship with a troublesome female slave.[75] The vecinos who wrote the petition asking for the permanent removal of Corregidor Juan Sánchez Camacho voiced the general opinion that leading citizens of Chihuahua held toward the working class; such people were "vulgar, and without distinction, due to their limited capacities."[76] All evidently agreed that it took considerable energy and skill to supervise workers. In 1727 Diego González de la Herrán asked the cabildo to relieve him of his duties as alguacil mayor because the burden of managing the large, unruly work force in his mines demanded his undivided attention.[77]

Local officials assumed that masters had the duty to police and supervise potentially troublesome workers, and workers sometimes cited this presumption in an effort to excuse their own misconduct. A slave jailed along with fellow bakery workers on charges of theft convinced the authorities that his master bore some of the responsibility because he had failed to secure a responsible overseer, leaving the bakery's day-to-day operations in the hands of this slave.[78]

Though many of them paid lip service to the importance of controlling workers without resorting to physical force, employers and their representatives routinely administered corporal punishment in an effort to maintain labor discipline. In 1738 José Velarde Cosío brought charges against Juan Bernardo Apolo, a worker at his refinery, for assaulting his overseer, José Gutiérrez. Velarde Cosío matter-of-factly explained that Gutiérrez had caught Apolo stealing ore, and had given him the customary four or five blows as punishment.[79]

Local authorities usually supported employers' dominion over their workers and used the powers of state to secure workers' docility. In 1773 cabildo officials apprehended an Indian bakery worker accused of verbally insulting and then stabbing his employer. Before the case even received a formal hearing, they bound him to the public pillory in San Felipe's central plaza, with the knife he had allegedly used in the attack suspended around his neck. The culprit then received 50 lashes while the town crier announced his crime so that all could hear, adding the stern warning that "he who so behaves shall so pay." Later, at the official inquiry into the incident, the employer admitted that before the assault he had given the worker several blows "so that he would mend his ways." Cabildo officers tacitly supported the bakery owner's right to discipline his workers in this manner by sentencing the Indian to five years' labor in an obraje.[80]

In some cases, however, local officials protested if employers' efforts to discipline workers encroached on their own prerogatives as guarantors of public order. In 1723 a master tailor cited his obligation to "teach, correct, and punish" the apprentices entrusted to him and complained when one young man failed to show him due respect and obedience. A *letrado* or legal scholar supported the tailor's argument, noting that the apprentice should have displayed "reverential respect," and that his "demasiadas altiveces" ("excessive insolence") had provoked his master to administer physical correction. While certainly agreeing that people in subordinate positions ought to defer to those in command, José Blanco de Sandoval, teniente of Santa Eulalia, reminded the tailor to seek support from the authorities rather than dispense justice privately to his employees.[81] In a similar case in 1775, a refinery owner asked for permission to put shackles on workers who shirked their duty. The cabildo rejected his petition, pointing out that the employer had access to the royal justice to assist him in disciplining his workers.[82]

A more serious case occurred in rural Babanoyaba in 1736. Simón Solorio, an illiterate ranchero, explained that he had accidentally killed an employee because the worker had provoked him by ignoring the fact that Solorio was his *amo* (master) and "as such enjoys the privilege of reprimanding and punishing, when necessary, any sirviente who performs poorly." The local teniente declared Solorio at fault, however, and sentenced him to ten years' service in the Janos presidio.[83]

Despite these occasional constraints, employers still claimed the right to supervise many aspects of their workers' lives. A mayordomo at General Orio y Zubiate's refinery noted in 1722 that his job gave him occasion to enter the houses of his workers regularly. He rose before dawn to summon the peons to work, calling at each hut at five o'clock in the morning.[84] Pedro Antonio Cadrecha, owner of San Felipe's most prosperous bakery and an active participant in the villa's civic affairs in the mid-eighteenth century, articulated the ethos that he shared with his fellow employers. Cadrecha explained that he required his workers to live within his household, "de puertas adentro" ("behind closed doors"), so that he could fulfill his obligation not only to supervise their work but to watch over their behavior and to "prevent offenses to God."[85]

Local officials regarded employers as their allies and indeed their virtual surrogates in subduing unruly workers and maintaining public tranquility. In some cases authorities also conceded employers a role in upholding norms of sexual conduct, which, as we shall see at greater length in Chapter 7, they deemed extremely important in guaranteeing general social order. In 1725 cabildo officers ordered a woman accused of adultery confined to her employer's home until her husband returned from Sonora. They instructed the employer to "be careful of her and not permit her to live in liberty."[86] On other occasions officials enlisted the help of employers in maintaining peace between husbands and wives and reporting cases of marital infidelity among their workers.[87]

Despite occasional jurisdictional disputes, employers and local authorities viewed one another as virtual partners in controlling the unstable aggregate of workers who staffed the area's silver mines and refineries. Because many officials themselves commanded sizable labor forces, and most successful silver magnates aspired to municipal office, it is hardly surprising that they all cast labor relations in political terms. A slave who did not perform as expected was thus guilty of *traición* (treason) against his master.[88] In 1729 one employer secured his own release from house arrest by citing his responsibility to "govern" the men working his mine in Santa Eulalia, who would refuse to work or flee to other jobs without constant supervision.[89] Explaining his daily routine, a mayordomo commented that as he went about distributing rations he carried "the club [*palo*] with which he governed his people."[90]

Paternalism

As we shall see in later chapters, local officials often employed patriarchal rhetoric, styling themselves "fathers of the republic," for example, in describing their political roles and duties. In similar fashion employers invoked the rights and obligations of father figures when they asserted their quasi-governmental power and obligation to discipline workers and supervise their conduct. Did their invocation of such images imply any kind of genuinely paternalistic attitude toward their workers, however? R. Douglas Cope has recently argued that well-defined patron-client relationships frequently developed in the workplaces of colonial Mexico City, where elite employers not only "bore the brunt of the day-in, day-out task of social control" but also shielded Indian workers from tribute collectors, remembered employees in their wills, and often served as godparents for their workers' children. In addition, employers in the capital supplied their workers with food, shelter, and other nonmonetary compensation, to the point that workers were willing to stay on even when their wage payments had fallen into arrears. In short, writes Cope, "what began as a simply economic connection evolved by degrees into a patron-client relationship."[91]

Relatively few traces of this kind of paternalism surfaced in Chihuahua, however. Some employers reportedly gave their workers small quantities of silver at fiesta times, but it would have been completely in character for them to have debited their workers' accounts for these amounts.[92] Slaves, especially female domestic servants, sometimes received their freedom, but little else, when their owners died.[93] On his death in 1722, for example, Pedro Pérez Carrasco emancipated the elderly woman who had attended him in his last illness, but he left her no assets.[94]

Occasionally workers or their families tried to imply that it was customary for employers to supply rations and other benefits for workers who were ill. During the epidemics of 1764, Martín de Echaquibel set aside quarters in his refinery to serve as an infirmary for sick workers. Later, however, the physician called in to treat the patients complained that Echaquibel had failed to pay for his services or for the medicines he had dispensed.[95] Many other sick workers got no benefits at all. In 1748, for example, María Rosa de Montiel complained that during her late husband's terminal illness his employer had not given him "even a real's worth of cigars," or anything else.[96] Even powerful political figures declined to extend paternalistic benefits to their servants. In November of 1753 a mulato who had worked as a coachman for Governor Alonso de Gastesi got into an altercation with another man, who ended up shooting him in the knee. A few months later, when his efforts to secure compensation from his assailant had failed, he claimed that he was utterly destitute, "sin amparo humano" ("without human support").[97]

Whatever occasional tokens of paternalism they might have conceded to slaves or other workers, employers' testaments never provided for the cancellation of debts owed by free workers. Instead they assuaged their consciences with generalized bequests to help "the poor" of the villa, or to establish pious works in San Felipe, Mexico City, or their home towns in Spain.[98] A few also left sums of money for civic purposes. Manuel San Juan y Santa Cruz, for example, provided for the foundation of a primary school in San Felipe, although the terms of this bequest had still not been carried out as of 1786, more than 30 years after his death.[99]

The will of Diego González de la Herrán, an ambitious entrepreneur who served as the cabildo's alguacil mayor for several years during the mining boom, reflects the mix of altruism and miserliness typical of San Felipe's ruling elite. A widower, he left no children other than a young woman for whom he had served as guardian. On his death in 1747 he freed some of his slaves, including a husband and wife named Juan José de la Torreblanca and María Josefa de la Encarnación. More generous than some masters, González de la Herrán left them eight mules, asking that in return they pray for the salvation of his soul. Four years after his death, however, his executors still had not turned the mules over to the emancipated couple. In the meantime they had had little choice but to sign on to work in Pedro Antonio Cadrecha's bakery. Cadrecha then advanced them more than 200 pesos to cover various expenses they had incurred, and they in turn pledged their bequest to reimburse him. Meanwhile, according to the terms of González de la Herrán's will, the couple's four daughters were to remain as slaves of his adopted daughter until her death. González de la Herrán also left 1,000 pesos to be distributed among "the poor of this villa," and provided for a silver lamp and other adornments to be placed in the church of his home town in the mountains of Burgos. Additional bequests benefited pious foundations in Mexico City and his five surviving sisters in Spain. When it came to the debts of workers on his rural hacienda, his silver refinery, and his mine in Santa Eulalia, however, he instructed his executors to treat these sums as accounts receivable and therefore as assets of his estate.[100]

In other words, the extension of credit to workers was a contractual arrangement, no more and no less. It represented employers' grudging concessions to economic reality rather than any inclination to establish paternalistic bonds with their workers. All perquisites given to workers and all gestures of deference tendered to employers remained subject to negotiation, on a strictly quid pro quo basis. Even when arguing for special concessions in times of sickness and other emergencies, workers spoke of these benefits as part of a contractual package rather than any kind of paternalistic gesture. In 1738, for example, a worker complained that during a recent illness he had received neither food nor medicine. He argued that this help was "very much part of [his employer's] obligation," and that by failing to provide it his boss risked losing all dominion or control over him.[101]

Local parish registers also demonstrate the absence of paternalistic ties between workers and employers. Evidently few workers in Chihuahua chose their employers or other powerful entrepreneurs as godparents for their children. Although baptismal records rarely indicate parents' occupations, it is safe to say that many of those who lacked Spanish surnames were probably workers of low social status. Judging from the names of the godparents, and particularly their lack of the honorific titles Don and Doña, it is evident that workers selected *compadres* from among their social peers. Even Afro-Mexican slaves seldom designated their masters as godparents for their children.

Why did so little paternalism appear in the labor relations that developed in eighteenth-century Chihuahua? As we have seen, many of the area's elites had spent time in Mexico City before traveling to the northern frontier, and many workers must also have had some exposure to the kind of paternalism that Cope describes. Certainly from time to time workers phrased their complaints in terms of their employers' failure to offer them paternalistic benefits when they were sick or otherwise in special need, but, as we have seen, employers rarely heeded such requests. In explaining why paternalism failed to take much hold during the best days of Chihuahua's mining boom, we might consider first the importance of the physical distance that separated workers from employers. The types of enterprises that Cope examined for Mexico City had small work forces; in the late seventeenth and early eighteenth centuries most bakeries and artisan shops employed fewer than 10 workers, and even the textile obrajes in the

Valley of Mexico averaged about 40 workers. Paternalistic labor relations flourished best, he argues, in workplaces where workers and employers had protracted, direct contact with one another, and particularly within the in loco parentis relationship between master and apprentice.[102]

Certainly many of those who staked the first mining claims in Chihuahua worked alongside their employees, scraping bits of silver ore from the easily accessible deposits close to the earth's surface. But the region's most ambitious miners envisioned much larger operations, and in time they managed to squeeze out their smaller competitors. Surviving documents give only occasional references to the size of any particular work force—the 100 workers that José de Aguirre brought with him from Sonora, or the 20 men who occupied the Arrieta brothers' mine to impede its takeover by Manuel San Juan y Santa Cruz, for example. Accounts of workers' debts often list dozens of individuals, but we cannot know for certain how many of them were actually available for work at any given time. It is safe to say, however, that the most successful and socially pretentious mining entrepreneurs eschewed the dishonorable "dirty work" of digging silver from the ground, so that personal contact between workers and employers rarely happened in the workplace itself. Meanwhile, with so many potential employers ready to bid for their services, workers had sufficient bargaining power to demand satisfactory compensation, whether in the form of wages or advances in cash and commodities, and little incentive to stay on if their employers were unable to pay them. As a result, rapid worker turnover further diminished the possibility that paternalism might develop. Nor could strong patron-client relationships materialize in the artisan shops of San Felipe, for the villa's guilds were loosely organized and traditional apprenticeship arrangements were rarely observed.[103] I shall argue in later chapters that Chihuahua's elites and its laboring classes in fact had more face-to-face encounters than either might have wished, but seldom under conditions conducive to the growth of paternalistic bonds between them.

The relative absence of paternalism in Chihuahua invites comparison with conditions in eighteenth-century England, where E. P. Thompson notes a shift away from "half-free forms of labor" and toward free and mobile wage labor—exactly the opposite of the transition Cope describes for Mexico City. English workers found increasing freedom to choose among employers or to opt not to work at all. In Thompson's evocative words, nonmonetary compensation declined as "economic rationalization nibbled (and had long been nibbling) through the bonds of paternalism," and employers gradually lost control over aspects of workers' lives not directly related to their jobs. Meanwhile, despite the glaring social and economic inequalities that separated workers from employers, subordination of workers' lives to employers' wishes gradually gave way to negotiation in labor relations. Employers, however, still viewed workers as "servants," linked to their jobs in some kind of bondage to their "masters." They expected workers to show them deference and respect, but at the same time they shunned the paternalistic responsibilities that such relationships implied. In other words, writes Thompson, employers in eighteenth-century England wanted the "best of the old world and the new, without the disadvantages of either."[104]

Labor relations in eighteenth-century Chihuahua bore many similarities to the situation that Thompson describes. Certainly workers often left their jobs without giving notice. Despite employers' propensity to supervise the conduct of bakery workers and domestic servants, many other workers escaped any such scrutiny. Mine workers, for example, typically maintained their homes in San Felipe while spending the week in temporary quarters at Santa Eulalia. On Friday or Saturday they headed for the villa and its attractions, often failing to return promptly to their jobs on Monday.[105] Moreover, as we have seen, a substantial element of negotiation colored labor relations, and employers in Chihuahua wholeheartedly shared their English counterparts' disdain for workers and their desire to have it both ways.

Other parallels between England and Chihuahua are less clear. It is difficult to argue that paternalism was declining in Chihuahua when there is scant evidence that such a notion had ever in fact characterized labor relations in colonial Mexican mining. Under paternalism, argues Thompson, customary perquisites granted to workers "appeared simultaneously as economic and as social relations, as relations between men, not as payments for services or things."[106] Though shrouded in self-justifying, paternalistic rhetoric emphasizing the moral value of labor and the duty of employers to guide and protect their workers, Spanish colonial mechanisms of forced labor recruitment such as the encomienda and repartimiento in practice rarely entailed even superficially benevolent personal contact between workers and employers. Meanwhile, the partido system that arose in most mining communities carried too much implicit equality to qualify as paternalism, because workers became something akin to partners of their employers, sharing the risks and profits of mining.

The system of worker remuneration that evolved in Chihuahua resembles neither the "old" paternalism of eighteenth-century England, nor the patron-client relationships that Cope finds in Mexico City enterprises, nor the "new" economic rationalization Thompson describes. Nonmonetary compensation was the norm in Chihuahua, but it hardly represented vestigial or emergent traces of paternalism. Quite simply, the scarcity of coinage—paradoxical, given the abundance of silver, yet very real—made it impossible for workers to receive more than a small fraction of their earnings in cash. Moreover, when Thompson refers to nonmonetary rewards he is speaking primarily of live-in servants' bed and board, which obviously involves the power of employers to supervise the personal conduct of their workers in quasi-paternalistic fashion. In Chihuahua, however, employers followed established custom in allocating weekly rations of maize, meat, and chocolate, but dispensed these commodities in a way that gave them little chance to intrude into their workers' lives. In most cases workers or their wives simply picked up the rations from the overseer and carried them off to their homes. Most importantly, as we have seen, the credits that employers extended to workers were the products of negotiation, nothing more and nothing less, and their amounts reflected the respective bargaining power of the parties involved. Yet these credits did not quite represent economic rationalization, because the quantities advanced often bore no direct relationship to the amount of labor performed.

Labor Discipline and Cultural Hegemony

Other differences also distinguished social relations in Chihuahua from those of England. Thompson notes that even though employers still routinely referred to their workers as "servants," workers showed a growing reluctance to reciprocate by using the word "master."[107] In Chihuahua workers certainly failed to display the level of respect that their employers expected, but throughout the eighteenth century no one questioned the continued use of the term "amo," and workers of virtually every occupational classification were called sirvientes.

Although they would clearly have preferred for their workers to continue addressing them in customary terms of respect, employers and authorities in eighteenth-century England could evidently tolerate a certain amount of symbolic and rhetorical defiance on the part of workers, as long as these gestures did not question the fundamental principles of subordination and domination at work in English society. Though workers might resist deferring to their "master," all was well as long as they displayed "calculated obsequiousness" toward magistrates and other social superiors. The English upper classes used force only when workers challenged the outer limits of their dominion. Meanwhile, they cultivated "a studied and elaborate hegemonic style" that maintained the appearances of paternalistic social relations even as economic changes transformed the workplace: "Their appearances have much of the studied self-consciousness of public theater. The sword was discarded, except for ceremonial purposes; but the elaboration of wig and powder, ornamented clothing and canes, and even the rehearsed patrician gestures and the hauteur of bearing and expression, all were designed to exhibit authority to the plebs and to exact from them deference. And with this went certain significant ritual appearances."[108] In short, concludes Thompson, the English gentry had achieved a high degree of cultural hegemony. Though workers might try to "struggle free from the immediate, daily humiliations of dependency," they were powerless to change the social order as a whole; "the larger outlines of power, station in life, political authority, appear[ed] to be as inevitable and irreversible as the earth and the sky."[109]

In similar fashion upper classes in eighteenth-century Chihuahua took considerable interest in the paraphernalia and rituals that supposedly validated their own positions of social precedence. They also devised detailed rules of deferential etiquette that they expected their social inferiors to observe. The wealth they derived directly or indirectly from silver mining, and the group solidarity they forged through networks of kinship and compadrazgo, gave them decided advantages in imposing these expectations on others. Moreover, colonial society afforded them other powerful tools to assist them in creating a mental and physical cosmos where their claims to power and privilege commanded respect. Ideology and custom—already almost two centuries in the making by the time silver first surfaced at Santa Eulalia—sanctioned a social hierarchy in which people of European ancestry, especially those born in Spain itself, occupied the top ranks. Meanwhile, prevailing notions of patriarchy not only served to define expected behavior for men and women, but also provided a handy, comprehensible paradigm of subordination and domination that elites could use in explaining and enforcing all other rules of conduct they wished to implement.

Whatever effects the tangible trappings of power and accompanying attitudes and practices might have had on lower-class audiences, local elites in Chihuahua seldom shared their English counterparts' apparent confidence in the relative stability of the social order over which they presided. Many of San Felipe's leading citizens were newcomers to New Spain, and the struggle to comprehend and manipulate the social realities of their adopted homeland often seemed overwhelming. They sought to establish and maintain a new polity in a location far from civilization as they knew it and among a bewildering array of unfamiliar peoples. However secure their positions appear from the vantage point of a twentieth-century historian examining the copious trail of documents they left, elites in colonial Chihuahua always felt that their exalted positions in local society rested on a precarious base. Chapters 4 and 5 examine the real and symbolic power of local elites, while Chapters 6 and 7 explore the ways they drew upon prevailing attitudes of ethnicity and gender in fashioning their own brand of cultural hegemony.

FOUR

The Ethos of Governance

ON MAY 25, 1720, Corregidor José de Orio y Zubiate and the six members of Chihuahua's recently constituted cabildo gathered at the home of Ignacio Alfonso de Riaza. They had come together to render formal assent to a decree in which the Audiencia of Guadalajara authorized the incorporation of the villa of San Felipe el Real. The document in question was no mere piece of paper, however. It was a *real provisión* (royal decree), bearing King Felipe V's seal and worded as if it had come from the monarch himself instead of from the audiencia. Accordingly, the assembled dignitaries doffed their hats and stood at attention, showing "due reverence" while each in turn solemnly kissed the document and placed it over his head as a gesture of submission to His Majesty.[1]

Such ritual acts of deference to royal authority afforded the cabildo members a tangible reminder of their own importance in a chain of command that reached from the dusty streets of San Felipe directly back to the king himself. In the performance of their duties they frequently invoked this connection, asking local citizens to cooperate with them "in the name of the king." Together with the governor of Nueva Vizcaya and a handful of royal tax collectors and military officers from Mexico City, the men summoned to Riaza's home that day constituted the "colonial state" for the people of San Felipe and Santa Eulalia. To grasp the dynamics of power relationships at work in this society, then, we must understand these men. We must know something about the backgrounds and expectations they brought with them to Chihuahua, observe them in the execution of their official duties, and explain how they defined their roles and justified their own positions.

Backgrounds of Political Leaders

Many of the individuals responsible for the founding of Santa Eulalia, San Francisco de Cuéllar, and San Felipe el Real de Chihuahua came from military backgrounds, having served in a variety of posts throughout Spain's vast empire. Governor Manuel San Juan y Santa Cruz, as we have seen, had seen tours of duty in Santo Domingo and the Philippine Islands before making his way to Nueva Vizcaya. Others had assumed administrative responsibilities in addition to their military duties. Martín de Alday, who succeeded San Juan y Santa Cruz as governor from 1720 to 1723, had served in the Armada de Barlovento before becoming the lieutenant captain at the Conchos presidio around 1690. He then participated in the reconquest of New Mexico, served briefly as alcalde mayor of Cusihuiriachic, and led troops in suppressing the Tarahumara rebellion of the 1690s. In 1703 he was named captain of the presidio of El Pasaje and later became alcalde mayor of Cuencamé.[2]

Others prominent in the early history of Chihuahua had also experienced the rough-and-tumble of the Indian wars on New Spain's northern frontier and had acquired political experience along the way. Sargento Mayor Juan Antonio Trasviña y Retes was born in the Spanish town of Oviedo in 1662. He came to the New World as a young man and fought Indians in Nueva Vizcaya. He then settled in Parral and later in Cusihuiriachic, where he amassed a fortune in silver mining and served briefly as alcalde mayor. In 1694 he again took up arms against hostile Indians, helping to suppress the Tarahumara revolt. He went on to become one of San Felipe's leading citizens and held the office of alcalde on the city's cabildo at the time of his death in 1724.[3]

A Basque born in 1659 in the village of Escoriaza in the province of Guipúzcoa, General José de Orio y Zubiate had also fought Indians, serving as a captain from 1680 to 1694. He then became a miner at several sites in Sonora, with a stint as alcalde mayor in Ostimuri, before locating in Santa Eulalia in 1713. He served briefly as alcalde mayor at San Francisco de Cuéllar during the last few months before the foundation of San Felipe. He was chosen for the position of alcalde on San Felipe's first cabildo in 1718 and then held the post of corregidor from 1720 until he died in 1723.[4]

Other early cabildo leaders also had military records. Juan Bautista de Ibave, for example, was a peninsular Spaniard in his early twenties when he was stationed at the Conchos presidio in the early eighteenth century. By 1716 he had established himself as a merchant in San Francisco de Cuéllar. In 1720 he was elected alcalde of San Felipe, and in that capacity he attended the meeting at Ignacio de Riaza's home. Five years later his fellow merchants selected him as their spokesman, or diputado, and in 1731 he served another term as alcalde.[5] Even those with prior service in the colonial bureaucracy also had substantial military experience. Juan Felipe de Orozco had held an important treasury post in Durango before heading north to San Francisco de Cuéllar, but he was also a colonel in the royal armies.[6] A few cabildo officers and other members of the local elite continued to exercise occasional military functions during the 1720s. Alférez Real José de Aguirre conducted a month-long campaign against restive Indians in the area of the Río del Norte (Río Grande) in 1726.[7]

As the years passed, however, progressively fewer cabildo members had prior military experience, as individuals who had devoted their energies exclusively to mining and commerce came to dominate civic affairs in San Felipe. For the most part, these men opted to leave the fighting to professionals. In 1725 the cabildo received word that the Cholomes Indians of the nearby mission of San Pedro had risen in revolt. After consulting with other leading citizens of the villa, they expressed their loyalty to His Majesty and their willingness to help in the present emergency, but voted to rely on troops led by the governor to quell the disturbance.[8]

Urban Pretensions

Indeed, all of Chihuahua's leaders clearly preferred the settled amenities of city existence to the rigors of frontier life. Like their medieval forebears who had reconquered Iberia from the Moors, the people who ventured to the frontiers of colonial Spanish America viewed towns as synonymous with a "civilized" Christian polity. Local officials repeatedly expressed the belief that people from the surrounding countryside were so lacking in sophistication and moral sensibilities that they could not be held fully accountable for their actions.[9] The officials surely shared the sentiments voiced by their contemporaries in Parral, who described an Indian woman accused of sexual impropriety as having "poca urbanidad" ("little urbanity"), and used the phrase "palabras urbanas" ("urbane words") to connote polite interpersonal exchanges.[10]

Like other Spaniards who settled in the New World, Chihuahua's founders also borrowed Renaissance concepts of urban planning, which called for rectilinear streets leading to a central plaza. Although most towns in Spain reflected their haphazard growth over the course of many centuries, the colonies offered an opportunity to create new communities whose layout conformed to these ideals. In Spanish America the grid pattern became the norm, codified in King Felipe II's regulations of 1573, to the point that occasionally a town's leaders might report back to superior authorities that they had followed this convention even when they had not. In major cities and small towns throughout the hemisphere, the central plaza assumed even greater importance in local civic affairs than it had at home.[11]

For the most part Chihuahua's founders eagerly embraced these notions of proper city design. They chose to build their principal settlement on the level site of San Francisco de Cuéllar—ideal for the construction of straight streets and an imposing municipal plaza—instead of the hilly, rugged terrain of Santa Eulalia. From personal experience they had also formulated very precise notions of how a city should be governed. Though most of the Spanish immigrants who controlled local affairs hailed from rural hamlets, many of them had spent time in much larger urban centers before venturing to the rugged frontiers of Nueva Vizcaya.[12] Evidently most of those who left the impoverished villages of northern Spain in the eighteenth century migrated first to a larger city within the peninsula and then to the New World.[13] Those who traveled legally passed through Seville and Cádiz, cities with populations estimated at 72,400 and 40,000, respectively, at the beginning of the eighteenth century, and any who passed through Madrid saw a bustling metropolis of 150,000.[14]

Furthermore, all of Chihuahua's leaders had spent at least some time in Mexico City before heading northward. The capital of New Spain easily ranked as the foremost city of the Western Hemisphere in the eighteenth century. Its population had reached 100,000 as early as 1620, and climbed to over 130,000 by the 1790s.[15] Mexico City boasted a fine park known as the Alameda, lavish fountains, sumptuous churches, the oldest university on the North American continent, and several theaters. A stroll through the city provided abundant opportunities to view the comfortable sophistication enjoyed by its upper social strata. The elegant mansions of the wealthy occupied choice locations in the heart of town, and even in the seventeenth century some 15,000 coaches reportedly crowded its busy streets, alongside the sedan chairs favored by some members of the elite.[16]

Residents and visitors in the capital also received constant reminders of their city's premier status in Spain's overseas dominions. They went about their daily business in the shadow of architectural marvels that amply testified to the might and splendor of the empire. The magnificent viceregal palace, the cathedral, and the Mexico City cabildo headquarters framed the city's majestic central *zócalo*—a plaza that is still impressive even when clogged with twentieth-century traffic and crowds. On the accession of a new viceroy or archbishop and on other special occasions, the people of Mexico City witnessed lavish symbolic displays carefully orchestrated to impress them anew with the grandeur and power of their monarch, the solemnity of their faith, and the rectitude of the hierarchical society to which they belonged.[17]

Passing through Mexico City en route to their destinations in Nueva Vizcaya, the leaders of San Felipe el Real de Chihuahua had a chance to savor the amenities of urban society and to refine their own ideas of proper civic culture. Moreover, they did not abandon their ties to the viceregal capital when they headed north to seek their fortunes. Many Chihuahua merchants described themselves as vecinos of Mexico City even after having established residence on the frontier, and most of them depended on business partners—often their own kinfolk—in the capital.[18] When Domingo Cuarón Leyva y Santa Bárbara died in San Felipe in 1735, local merchants acted on behalf of partners and relatives in Mexico City and Cádiz to place claims on his estate.[19] Other prominent citizens of Chihuahua remembered Mexico City religious institutions in their wills.[20] Juan Antonio Trasviña y Retes, for example, was a major benefactor of the Jesuit Colegio de San Pedro y San Pablo in the capital.[21]

Periodic visits also strengthened ties to Mexico City for some members of Chihuahua's elite. On January 1, 1723, the cabildo nullified the election of Manuel de Hermosino as alcalde for the coming year when they learned that he had departed the previous day for the viceregal capital. By the following year, however, he was back in Chihuahua, and his fellow merchants chose him as their diputado in 1729.[22] While serving as an alcalde in 1747, José Fernández de Hinojosa was busy planning a trip to attend to commercial affairs in Mexico City. In September he informed the cabildo that he intended to leave in mid-November, some six weeks before the completion of his term of office. A native of Seville, Fernández de Hinojosa belonged to at least two pious societies in the capital.[23]

Other members of the Chihuahua elite maintained close ties with Guadalajara, the population of which probably surpassed 10,000 by the late 1730s and reached 22,000 by 1770.[24] Local leaders often traveled there to plead personal or civic questions before the audiencia or to handle other kinds of business.[25] Long-time civic leader Domingo del Valle, who served as alcalde in 1736 and again in 1753, for example, did business with his nephew, a merchant in Guadalajara.[26] When Ignacio Alfonso de Riaza died in 1741, he named Eusebio Antonio de Riaza, a prebendary of the Guadalajara cathedral and probably his cousin, as one of the executors of his estate.[27]

Throughout the eighteenth century Chihuahua's elites did their best to emulate the amenities they had witnessed in the great cities of the Spanish empire. Exotic merchandise from Europe and Asia filled local shops during the halcyon days of the mining boom, while delicate laces and fine silks graced the wardrobes of men and women alike.[28] Despite oppressive summertime heat, both Juan Felipe de Orozco and Corregidor Juan de Paniagua often donned elaborate wigs of the type then fashionable in Europe.[29] As early as the 1720s and continuing thereafter, at least a few prominent members of the local elite had coaches to carry them about the dusty, unpaved streets of San Felipe.[30]

The early leaders of Chihuahua also revealed their urban predilections in the rectilinear layout they envisioned for their community and the elegant plaza they established facing their parish church. In actual practice, however, San Felipe deviated from the model of perfectly perpendicular and parallel streets, because most new vecinos claimed spots along the river and the camino real to Santa Fe. Even before the villa's founding, Juan Antonio Trasviña y Retes appropriated the most propitiously situated terrain along the banks of the Chuvíscar for his own orchard and silver refinery, and for several crucial years he blocked others from settling to the south and west of the parish church. Meanwhile, too, the Jesuit colegio, located a few blocks north of the church, straddled the villa's main street and prevented its further extension. Still, the founders of San Francisco de Cuéllar followed Renaissance concepts of urban planning to the extent that these practical realities permitted.[31]

Most indicative of the founders' urban leanings was the parish church, built over the course of several decades beginning at the height of the mining boom in the 1720s. At the time some people had anticipated the creation of a separate diocese with San Felipe as its seat. With this goal in mind the church's principal architect, José de la Cruz, began drafting a structure worthy of serving as a cathedral. De la Cruz drew on his prior experience as designer of Durango's cathedral, and he made sure that his work conformed to accepted European standards of church construction, sending copies of the building plans to Spain for royal approval. His efforts clearly paid off, for in 1732 the newspaper *Gaceta de México* informed sophisticated readers in Mexico City that the church's design was among "the best that are found in Europe."[32] Even in the late twentieth century it still dominates the city skyline, despite the presence of newer but far less architecturally distinguished high-rise buildings on the plaza.

Those who governed Chihuahua continued their efforts to provide their community with all of the trappings of a proper urban polity even after the collapse of the mining boom. Despite intensified Indian attacks in the 1750s, for example, they initiated construction on an aqueduct to bring water to the villa's plazas, although the project was not completed for several decades.[33] Early in the following decade work proceeded on an enlargement of the local jail, and Governor José Carlos Agüero inaugurated regular postal service between Chihuahua and Durango.[34] Work on the parish church also continued during these difficult years, although sometimes funds collected for its adornment had to be used to pay Indian auxiliaries who assisted in defending San Felipe and its environs.[35] In the early 1770s cabildo officers proposed the construction of *portales* (covered arcades) on their council building and on the municipal *alhóndiga* (granary) in order to provide retail food vendors with shelter from the sun and rain. Although lack of funds stalled the project for several years, by 1783 these portales had apparently been completed.[36]

Frontier Realities

Nevertheless, the rigors of life on the northern frontier prevented Chihuahua's leaders from recreating all of the institutions and amenities that we have come to associate with urban life in colonial Latin America. As we have seen, the town's population probably never exceeded 10,000 and usually fell far below that mark; by the eighteenth century many other towns in New Spain were much larger.[37] As a result, San Felipe el Real remained a villa, never achieving the more prestigious official rank of *ciudad* (city). It remained subject to the ecclesiastical jurisdiction of the bishop of Durango, and only in the late nineteenth century did it become the seat of a separate diocese.[38] The town also lacked the large cadres of professional bureaucrats who assumed such prominent roles in cities throughout the empire. Perhaps the most telling indicator of the absence of an elaborate governmental infrastructure can be found in scattered references to shortages of paper bearing the official stamp of the government, the requisite staple of the colonial bureaucracy.

Nor were San Felipe's ecclesiastical and educational establishments comparable to those of larger towns. Though a Jesuit college had been founded as early as 1718, it evidently provided limited instruction.[39] Indeed, surviving documents suggest that for much of the eighteenth century it served more as a refuge for criminals seeking sanctuary from civil justice than as a center of learning.[40] Until the last few decades of colonial rule, the villa's only other educational institution was a small school that operated for a time in the 1740s, teaching children (presumably boys) "letters and good customs."[41] Whatever the formal educational opportunities available to them and their children, the villa's elite evidently devoted little time to intellectual pursuits. Inventories of their estates show that they maintained copious written records of their financial affairs and accumulated impressive collections of jewelry, silver ornaments, and religious images, but apparently very few owned any books. Chihuahua had no printing press until 1825.[42]

Other institutions and comforts commonly associated with urban life in colonial Latin America were also absent from San Felipe. Its streets remained unlit until the 1830s and for the most part unpaved until well into the twentieth century.[43] An attempt to establish a theater in the 1760s failed because local people could not afford to buy tickets.[44] Like both Durango and Parral, the villa of San Felipe lacked nunneries.[45] The town's various craft guilds, though often mentioned in cabildo documents, were in fact very loosely organized, with no carefully enforced entrance requirements.[46] San Felipe el Real also went for long periods without the services of trained physicians or well-stocked apothecary shops. In the final decades of colonial rule a hospital was founded in the building that had served as the Jesuit colegio prior to the order's expulsion in 1767, but the facility catered primarily to military patients.[47]

Despite the frequent privations and inconveniences of their frontier existence, San Felipe's eighteenth-century leaders saw their aspirations for their community more accurately symbolized by the majestic towers of the parish church than by the single-story adobe structures that surrounded it. These men harbored few doubts about their town's potential as one of the great cities of the Spanish empire. Moreover, despite their relative lack of formal education, legal training, or governmental experience, they also shared a surprisingly well-articulated vision on the kind of social organization that should prevail in their community.

The "Republic" of San Felipe el Real

In the course of executing their duties or deliberating on their responsibilities, those who served on Spanish colonial cabildos and in other governmental posts invariably referred to their community as a "republic." Derived from political theories of classical antiquity, this notion was embodied in the self-governing municipalities of medieval Iberia, in Italian city-states of the Renaissance and towns throughout early modern Europe, and finally on the frontiers of Spanish America.[48] Thus, when San Felipe's corregidores and alcaldes justified measures designed to maintain order and tranquility in their community, they cited their obligation to "cleanse the republic of people who are troublesome and rebellious."[49] The leading citizens who drafted the petition demanding the ouster of Corregidor Juan Sánchez Camacho in 1731 similarly voiced their concern for the stability of the republic.[50]

What did the concept of a republic mean to the men who dominated civic life in eighteenth-century Chihuahua? Their public pronouncements suggest that their notions of polity were remarkably secular in nature, even though religious rites, including a solemn promise to defend the doctrine of the Immaculate Conception, always accompanied the installation of new officials. Authorities spoke readily of the need to inspire the fear of God in their subjects, especially those summoned to testify under oath, but they rarely resorted to more elaborate biblical or theological allusions in explaining their decisions or exhorting people to behave properly.[51] Of course, very few of these officials had opportunities for advanced study in theology or any other discipline, but if the published texts of eighteenth-century sermons at all reflect customary ecclesiastical discourse, the leaders of San Felipe must have been exposed to fairly generous doses of biblical rhetoric when they attended liturgical functions in Mexico City, Guadalajara, or even in Chihuahua itself. Such references seldom colored the speech of local officials, however.

Certainly not all of the town's inhabitants qualified as members of the republic. In 1736 the cabildo discussed the possibility of establishing a hospital to serve the needs of "la plebe" ("the common people") as well as those of the villa's "republicans."[52] Not even all of those commonly designated as vecinos merited inclusion within this relatively select group of republicans, for those who penned petitions on behalf of people of very humble status routinely called their clients vecinos if they were long-time residents of Chihuahua.[53]

Although they failed to stipulate precise prerequisites for active membership in their republic, Chihuahua's leaders usually had little difficulty determining which individuals qualified. Certainly all those eligible by wealth and status for election to the cabildo merited inclusion, but a broader range of male residents—disproportionately composed of peninsulares but also including many prominent españoles—participated less formally in civic affairs. A wide circle of individuals served in the local militia, for example. Until the Indian attacks intensified after 1740, the principal duty of these other "republicans" was to assist law enforcement officials in preventing prisoners from escaping.[54]

Moreover, corregidores and cabildo officers often consulted leading townsmen on matters of importance, sometimes formally designating the gatherings as cabildos abiertos.[55] In 1759 cabildo member Domingo Antonio González de Novoa explained that the 21 men recently summoned to one such meeting had been selected not only because they were married but also because they owned substantial real estate in the villa or its jurisdiction. Following these criteria, he had pointedly excluded itinerant merchants who neither were married nor maintained a permanent residence in San Felipe. According to González de Novoa, those invited qualified as the individuals "most solidly rooted who live and reside in this villa." As further testimony to the right of these men to speak on local concerns, González de Novoa asked one of the alcaldes to certify that those assembled included all persons who held any position of trust in the republic.[56]

The villa's most economically influential citizens also played an active role in local civic affairs through their participation in periodic juntas of mine owners and merchants. Each of these unofficial guilds typically included a dozen or more members, who designated one of their number to act as their spokesman or diputado. Indeed, the governor of Nueva Vizcaya authorized the practice of electing such representatives several years before the establishment of the cabildo of San Felipe.[57] Although the governor or corregidor convoked the meetings at which these officials were selected, and their formal role was purely advisory, the diputados regularly spoke out on issues of interest to their constituencies. In 1719, for example, the two diputados appeared before the cabildo to protest a proposed tax on foodstuffs brought into San Felipe and Santa Eulalia.[58] In the 1740s the merchants' representative tried in vain to block introduction of the *alcabala*, or imperial sales tax, but did succeed in gaining permission to supervise its collection.[59] From time to time the diputados also complained of abuses committed by governors and other officials.

Certainly some of those chosen as diputados also served on the cabildo at some point in their careers, but not all of those who attended the meetings of miners and merchants could aspire to municipal office. The active voice conceded by local custom to the juntas and their spokesmen served to widen the base of effective political influence in San Felipe. As a result, those who governed the villa felt some obligation to represent the concerns of a broader spectrum of the public rather than always catering exclusively to their own personal interests. Thus at least some of Nueva Vizcaya's governors sought to balance conflicting demands in a statesmanlike manner. As we have seen, Governer Ignacio Francisco de Barrutia refused to pander to his fellow Basque Manuel San Juan y Santa Cruz during the strike of 1730, even temporarily defying orders from the viceroy and audiencia in the interests of maintaining public tranquility in Chihuahua.

Moreover, the events of 1730 and 1731 demonstrate that even the cabildo members could set aside their narrow interests as employers in favor of a more conciliatory settlement that would appeal to the entire constituency they represented. They knew that the body of responsible vecinos to whom they answered included not only the villa's major mining entrepreneurs but also its principal merchants, who reaped considerable profits trading workers' pepenas for merchandise. To some degree the council members also understood, perhaps grudgingly but with conviction nonetheless, that certain concessions to workers were necessary in order to guarantee a stable labor force and the continued prosperity of their community.

The very rhetoric that governors and cabildo officers used to justify their actions conveyed an implicit promise of equitable and farsighted governance in the best interests of the "republic" as a whole. Time and again they invoked familial images to describe their own positions of power. Like the monarch whose authority they self-consciously represented on this remote fringe of empire, they cast themselves as paternal figures over those whom they governed. Cabildo members thus became the "fathers of these republicans."[60]

Self-Interest and Civic Duty

Expressions of paternalistic feeling extended beyond the relatively closed circle of active participants in the "republic," however. They also embraced the lowly supplicants, both male and female, who placed their grievances at the feet of those who claimed to dispense justice in His Majesty's name. Though it is perhaps difficult to imagine Manuel San Juan y Santa Cruz taking time from his other pursuits to attend to the concerns of lower-class men and women, other governors entertained literally dozens, and perhaps hundreds, of such petitions from workers, destitute widows, and even slaves. In 1738, for example, a mulata slave named Cecilia Dorotea de Lugo protested to the governor that her master had broken into her home and ransacked all of her belongings in search of goods that she had allegedly stolen. As part of the final settlement of the dispute, she won her freedom.[61]

In the exercise of their quasi-paternal obligations, governors and cabildo officers routinely mediated disputes between workers and their employers. As we have seen in Chapter 3, local officials viewed workers as morally deficient and easily incited to insurrection. Therefore they usually endorsed employers' attempts to discipline workers, including the use of corporal punishment, as long as such measures did not infringe upon their own jurisdictions. At the same time governors and alcaldes often tried to temper at least the worst abuses. Throughout the controversy of 1730 and 1731 the cabildo deplored the "tyranny" that many mine operators exercised over their workers.[62] In 1742 the governor acknowledged the need to "reduce" or pacify the workers, but also stressed the importance of using the gentlest possible means in doing so.[63] Similarly, when local officials sentenced a young man to two years' forced labor in a refinery, they cautioned that if during that time he proved remiss in his duties his master could "punish him in the regular manner but no more."[64]

Although many cabildo members were employers themselves, on numerous occasions they prevented workers from being cheated by ordering employers to make public the workers' accounts, and assisted dissatisfied workers in finding new masters.[65] In 1724, for example, Juan Antonio Tarín had a dispute with the mayordomo of his charcoal-producing estate and a number of other workers. Authorities permitted the men to seek other employers, provided they made provision for paying off what they owed Tarín, who in turn was ordered to have nothing further to do with them.[66] Because they understood that the authorities might offer recourse to disgruntled laborers, employers sometimes attempted to impede their workers' access to local tribunals. In 1748 Florencio de la Cruz explained why he had taken refuge in the parish church. He feared that his boss, a peninsular named Juan de la Maza, might forcibly send him to a rural estate in order to prevent him from presenting his complaint to the justices in Chihuahua.[67]

There is evidence, then, to suggest that, when they acted as a group, cabildo members in Chihuahua displayed at least some sense of civic responsibility for the welfare of the community as a whole. Certainly they were quite capable of setting aside these broader concerns when administering their own enterprises, however. Throughout the best years of Chihuahua's mining boom, Eugenio Ramírez Calderón had been a principal mine owner and a regidor on the cabildo. Sometime after 1740, however, he left San Felipe and settled in Cusihuiriachic, where he evidently showed little mercy toward his workers, allowing his mayordomos to beat them routinely. He also charged exorbitant prices for the goods he supplied to them on credit and refused to let them inspect their accounts. Because local authorities in Cusihuiriachic refused to entertain any protests against these abuses, workers occasionally sought help from officials in San Felipe.[68]

Self-interest surely motivated the ambitions of those who seized control of local office during the first two decades following the discovery of silver at Santa Eulalia, and throughout the eighteenth century local officials often used their offices to advance their personal fortunes. Nevertheless, they readily internalized the rhetorical flourishes they used to articulate and justify their exercise of power. Both their self-definition as virtuous "fathers of the republic" and their sober realization of the need to guarantee public peace by balancing the conflicting demands of their constituents shaped the mental universe of local officials in Chihuahua. In that world, twentieth-century concepts of conflict of interest make little sense. In 1735, after being elected to serve as alcalde, Ignacio Alfonso de Riaza tried to decline the position, citing his responsibilities as the merchants' diputado. The cabildo rejected his request on the grounds that his own personal rectitude would overcome any potential conflict of interest.[69] In a similar manner, in 1753 cabildo members saw no reason to bar Domingo del Valle from serving simultaneously in the same two capacities.[70]

The Sale of Office and Municipal Corruption

Even the fact that the cabildo's permanent regidores and many other officials had purchased their positions posed no challenge to the local elite's belief in its own fitness to exercise power. Beginning in the late sixteenth century, public offices throughout the Spanish empire had gone on sale, with the proceeds diverted to the bankrupt royal treasury. Those awarded positions acquired a vested interest in exploiting their offices in order to recoup their "investments." According to most historians, the sale of office and associated abuses in municipal government peaked in many parts of the empire during the first half of the eighteenth century. On many cabildos the regidores had become a hereditary oligarchy more interested in the perquisites than the responsibilities of office. As descendants of the original purchasers, they had simply assumed office on payment of an additional fee to the crown. On the rare occasions when they even bothered to attend council meetings they wasted time and city resources on trivial matters, seldom displaying any sense of civic responsibility.[71]

San Felipe el Real de Chihuahua presents something of a contrast with this picture of generalized atrophy and corruption in municipal government. The sale of office was definitely practiced; vacancies were advertised first in Guadalajara and then in San Felipe, and candidates were invited to submit their bids. Leaders in Chihuahua saw positive benefits for their republic in this system, however. For them the sale of office served less as an inducement to corruption than a guarantee that the best men, those with a genuine stake in society, would come to occupy positions of command. In the mid-1730s longtime civic leader José Velarde Cosío expressed alarm when the post of fiel ejecutor, or inspector of weights and measures, sold for a mere 400 pesos; the job yielded an income far in excess of that amount. For Velarde Cosío, such developments seemed sure to attract officials of inferior *calidad*—a term that connoted not only racial and social status, but moral virtue as well.[72]

Another factor that helped local leaders to maintain—in their own minds, at least—their own image of civic responsibility was the fact that interest in public affairs did not decline as thoroughly in San Felipe as it evidently did in other municipalities. It is true that enthusiasm for public office peaked in the years surrounding the villa's founding. Seldom did the cabildo have as many regidores as it did in 1718. Most members of the first cabildo had died or left the area by the end of the 1720s, while those who remained on the scene gradually lost interest in cabildo business as the mining economy deteriorated in the 1730s. Eugenio Ramírez Calderón, for example, spent more and more time on his rural estates, some four leagues from San Felipe, and showed increasing reluctance to attend cabildo meetings.[73] Finally, as we have seen, he moved to Cusihuiriachic. By the late 1730s Colonel Juan Felipe de Orozco had become so notorious for his absence from council sessions that his colleagues tried unsuccessfully to oust him from his position as regidor. A few years later he too left Chihuahua and settled in Durango.[74] Meanwhile, Domingo Basoco, a Basque who had played an active role in community affairs in the 1720s and 1730s, fled mounting financial difficulties and took up residence in Guadalajara.[75]

Other signs of declining interest in civic affairs were also evident. After Alférez Real José de Aguirre died in 1729, several individuals entered bids to replace him, but in fact no one again occupied the position on a permanent basis. Instead, it sometimes rotated annually among the regidores, and at other times remained vacant unless a special occasion such as the coronation of a new monarch required the ad hoc appointment of a regidor to bear the royal standard.[76] Meanwhile cabildo members abdicated their positions with increasing frequency. For unexplained reasons both alcaldes elected for 1742 had resigned by early October.[77] Even regidores quit the cabildo; Domingo del Valle became a regidor in 1738 but abandoned the post seven years later.[78] At the same time, few individuals came forward to bid for permanent seats on the council, and for a variety of reasons no sons of the first generation of local leaders stood ready to inherit their fathers' places. By the end of the 1740s Alexandro García de Bustamante was the cabildo's sole regidor.

García de Bustamante's death in 1749 threatened to bring municipal politics to a standstill, for without regidores there was no one to choose the alcaldes for the coming year. Leading citizens in the villa therefore moved quickly to fill the vacuum. The incumbent alcaldes notified the Audiencia of Guadalajara, which advised them to continue in their posts for 1750. Meanwhile, the alcaldes joined other concerned vecinos in securing the help of the viceroy in reconstituting the cabildo. Six men—Francisco Antonio Martínez, José Antonio de Uranga, Antonio Gutiérrez del Castillo, Antonio de Echaquibel, Manuel Gómez del Pinar, and Domingo Antonio González de Novoa—promptly received titles as interim regidores and took over management of town government. In 1754 the viceroy issued permanent titles for these same six individuals.[79]

The continued arrival of successive waves of Spanish immigrants also helped sustain the vitality of local government in San Felipe el Real. As members of the founding generation died or lost interest in civic affairs without leaving sons willing or able to succeed them, new immigrants stood ready to assume positions in local government. Few of these later cabildo members matched the founding generation in wealth. Indeed, when the council gathered in 1760 to debate whether or not an upcoming civic celebration would have an adverse effect on mining, one member noted that only one of their number knew anything about the industry.[80]

Some of those who became alcaldes and regidores after the end of the mining boom had occupied posts in the imperial bureaucracy.

José de la Borbolla received an appointment as Chihuahua's *ensayador*, or assayer, in the early 1740s. In 1757 he served as an alcalde, and two years later he became a regidor, all the while continuing to function as assayer.[81] Juan José Barrándegui had held the playing-card monopoly in the 1740s and served as teniente of Santa Eulalia in the 1750s. In 1762 and again in 1770, he was elected alcalde on the San Felipe cabildo.[82]

In other cases individuals who lacked either prior governmental experience or substantial economic success managed to gain membership on the cabildo. In 1737 Juan de Gálvez was the sole bidder for the office of fiel ejecutor, which carried with it a position as a regidor. Although he had been born in Spain, some members of the town's elite found him notoriously unfit to join their ranks. They cited his alleged gypsy origins, his marriage to a woman reported to be a mulata, and his prior career as a cooper at the haciendas of the Marqués de San Miguel de Aguayo near Parras in present-day Coahuila. Following his arrival in San Felipe, sometime between 1716 and 1720, he had further sullied his reputation by operating a tavern, personally dispensing wine, brandy, and other beverages to customers. Moreover, several witnesses testified that he had a brother who worked as a shoemaker in Mexico City. Despite all of these obstacles, he attained his position on the cabildo, only to endure occasional snubs from his colleagues.[83]

Others who had more "respectable" antecedents but whose economic status was still modest also gained election as alcaldes. As we saw in Chapter 2, Pedro Antonio Cadrecha began his career as a cashier for a fellow Asturian, then established a bakery, and gradually worked his way into positions of community leadership, first as a spokesman for his fellow tradesmen and later as an alcalde, merchants' diputado, and mayordomo of the villa's most prestigious *cofradía*, or religious brotherhood. Other peninsular Spaniards followed Cadrecha's example. Baker Alonso de la Cadena became an alcalde in 1762, and the career of Miguel Ruiz Galdeano demonstrated how one could rise to civic prominence through persistence and hard work. Arriving in Chihuahua in the 1730s, this native of Navarre began his commercial career rather modestly, managing a shop for another merchant and sending consignments of goods to Indian settlements in surrounding areas. Within a few years he had opened his own store in the mission pueblo of Santa Isabel, and in

1748 he declared himself to be a resident in San Felipe and a vecino of Cusihuiriachic. By the 1760s, however, he had become one of the villa's leading bakers, and in 1772 he was elected alcalde.[84]

Thanks to the initiative of the six individuals who reconstituted the cabildo after 1750 and the ambitions of men like Gálvez, Cadrecha, and Ruiz Galdeano, the cabildo of San Felipe el Real remained reasonably vibrant even after the villa fell on hard economic times. Still, the circle of politically active vecinos remained smaller after midcentury than it had been during the best of the mining boom. With increasing frequency past alcaldes were reelected, and the regidores often ignored royal orders forbidding the selection of alcaldes from within their own number.[85] In 1758 Antonio de Echaquibel simultaneously held the positions of regidor, alcalde, and alférez real.[86]

Civic Responsibility

Even though their numbers thinned and the unofficial qualifications for cabildo membership shifted slightly in order to accommodate new aspirants for public office, the men who controlled local government in Chihuahua maintained a solid commitment to civic responsibility as they defined it. They took seriously their duty to guarantee public order and employed a variety of means to achieve this end. Alcaldes patrolled the streets at night, policing *fandangos* (dances) and gambling tables and knocking on doors of reputed sexual offenders.[87] Local authorities resorted to sheer intimidation whenever they thought it would work. They showed little hesitation in sentencing wrongdoers to forced service in silver refineries, obrajes, or presidios. In many instances, however, they sought the more prudent middle ground of conciliation. Meanwhile, they attended to the routine business of urban housekeeping, regulating the sale of maize and wheat at the municipal granary, setting prices for bread and other staples, investigating the health hazards posed by toxic fumes from refineries located near the center of town, and checking complaints of medical malpractice.[88]

Those who served on the cabildo or otherwise participated in the civic life of San Felipe el Real would take exception to twentieth-century Anglo-Saxon critics who emphasize the corruption and virtual atrophy of local government in Spanish America. The men who governed colonial Chihuahua certainly acknowledged that people in positions of command were quite capable of egregious disregard for the public interest. The vecinos who came forward to denounce Manuel San Juan y Santa Cruz and his henchman Juan Sánchez Camacho possessed a clear understanding of the behavior incumbent on officials who wished to discharge their duties in a responsible and honorable manner. Not only did they fault San Juan y Santa Cruz in general terms for exploiting the power of his office to advance his personal fortunes, they cited very specific instances to prove their point. In addition to monopolizing local commerce, demonstrating extreme favoritism in awarding repartimientos of Indian labor and other benefits, and effectively ending customary perquisites for workers in Parral and later in Chihuahua, he had neglected many of his official duties as governor of Nueva Vizcaya. He had failed to make required military inspections of frontier posts, instead visiting the presidios only to collect debts owed him by captains and soldiers. He had likewise disregarded his obligation to make periodic visits to the Indian missions in his jurisdiction. Notoriously vulnerable whenever offered a bribe, he reportedly spent his leisure time gambling, inviting friends to join him in games that lasted far into the night.[89]

The complaints voiced against Corregidor Juan Sánchez Camacho were equally detailed. He allegedly committed gross abuses in the administration of justice, sheltering criminals who enjoyed the favor of his protector San Juan y Santa Cruz. Meanwhile, he reportedly jailed innocent people and released them in exchange for bribes. His personal life was hardly exemplary, either. He too was a habitual gambler, and his flagrant sexual improprieties scandalized the community.[90]

Without question San Juan y Santa Cruz, Sánchez Camacho, and countless other officials in colonial Chihuahua betrayed the public trust and placed personal considerations ahead of civic responsibilities. Moreover, the members of the town's cabildo and its other politically active vecinos were no paragons of personal or civic virtue. Even the cabildo records, which certainly and not surprisingly minimize the shortcomings of council members and their close associates, reveal many examples in which local officials shamelessly jockeyed for real and symbolic tokens of power while openly violating the norms they so frequently cited in their denunciations of others. Scattered references allude also to the bribery of cabildo officials or their connivance with those who trafficked in stolen silver.[91]

Factional turmoil, much of it rooted in the personal ambitions of local officials, repeatedly disrupted the peace of San Felipe during the first decade following the creation of its cabildo. Colonel Juan Felipe de Orozco, who had used his connections in Mexico City to secure the town's designation as a villa, stood at the center of many of these controversies. His contention that the viceroy had named him corregidor of Chihuahua in 1718 brought him into direct conflict with Governor Martín de Alday, who asserted his own right to appoint someone to the post. For several years, therefore, two rival corregidores simultaneously claimed jurisdiction in the villa.[92] Meanwhile, Orozco also competed with José de Aguirre for power and prestige. In 1722 and 1723 both entered bids and counterbids for the office of alférez real (which carried with it a position as a regidor on the cabildo), with Aguirre finally obtaining the post in exchange for a payment of 8,000 pesos to the royal treasury.[93] For his part, Orozco quickly obtained appointment as an alcalde of the Santa Hermandad, an organization supposedly entrusted with the administration of justice in rural areas. That position also provided him with a permanent seat on the cabildo.[94]

After assuming his position as alférez, Aguirre did little to quell the factional troubles that divided the villa. In 1724 he supported his brother-in-law, Ignacio de Zubiate, and future alcalde Pedro Ruiz de Azua in an attempt to depose Corregidor Juan de Paniagua.[95] Meanwhile, Aguirre flaunted the special prerogatives attached to his office, provoking bitter resentment among his colleagues in local government. Among the privileges he claimed was the right to nominate four candidates from whom the other regidores would select the two alcaldes for the coming year. In 1728 his rival Orozco in turn excluded him from the meeting at which the election was scheduled to be held. Aguirre also claimed preferential seating at all gatherings of the cabildo and other official events. Furthermore, he stepped in as acting alcalde if an incumbent died or was otherwise unable to serve, in effect becoming what one contemporary critic called "almost a perpetual alcalde."[96] After Aguirre's death in 1729, the remaining regidores quarreled over their respective seating arrangements at ceremonial functions, while Juan Felipe de Orozco followed Aguirre's example and claimed the right to assume the duties of an alcalde upon the death of the incumbent. In turn Eugenio Ramírez Calderón protested Orozco's action, arguing that he had served as a regidor longer than Orozco and should therefore be permitted to finish the alcalde's term.[97]

In their personal conduct leading local citizens sometimes failed to live up to the standards they attempted to impose on others. While serving as regidor in the early 1720s Francisco de Salcido openly carried on an affair with María Rosa Gómez, a married mestiza from Santa Eulalia. He bought her fancy finery and publicly escorted her and her sisters to the fiesta of San Francisco in the central plaza of San Felipe.[98] In 1782 Ventura do Porto, a native of the town of La Coruña in Galicia, bowed to pressure from the parish priest and married Josefa Aguirre, who had given birth to their son three years earlier. In the meantime do Porto had served a term as alcalde in 1781.[99]

Other politically prominent vecinos were evidently no less given to gambling than Manuel San Juan y Santa Cruz and Juan Sánchez Camacho. In October 1724, during the annual fiesta of San Francisco, leading townsmen began drafting a letter protesting Governor José Sebastián López de Carvajal's recent removal of Corregidor Juan de Paniagua from office. Partisans of López de Carvajal pointed out, however, that the vecinos' dissatisfaction more likely stemmed from the governor's decision the previous year to bar gambling during the festivities that traditionally accompanied receptions honoring visiting dignitaries.[100] In 1752 the cabildo ordered Salvador de Lemus to suspend the games of chance that he conducted in his corral, but three years later the regidores elected him to serve as alcalde.[101]

When disciplining their own workers, leading local vecinos sometimes failed to exercise the restraint they recommended to other employers. As we have seen, long-time community leader Eugenio Ramírez Calderón exercised virtual tyranny over his workers once he had established himself at Cusihuiriachic, beyond the effective reach of his former colleagues in Chihuahua.

Whatever their personal failings, the men who managed the cabildo of San Felipe el Real employed rhetoric that embodied a reasonably coherent vision of their civic duties. There is even evidence to suggest that those who assumed positions of governance after 1740 behaved somewhat more responsibly than their predecessors. Sobered by the economic downturn and the heightened dangers of attacks by hostile Indians, they indulged in far fewer intraelite squabbles. Although on occasion they still quarreled over the order of precedence to be followed in public ritual observances, they seemed to understand that the excessive ambitions of some early cabildo leaders had gravely threatened the peace and stability of their "republic." A major reason why no one ever permanently occupied the position of alférez real after José de Aguirre's death was that leading citizens of the villa had observed the divisive influence of concentrating so much power, and so many visible perquisites, in one individual. When the office went on sale in the mid-1730s, several members of the cabildo threatened to resign if anyone were allowed to assume the post.[102]

The men who served as Chihuahua's alcaldes and regidores in the years after 1740 would certainly disagree with Clarence Haring's dictum that "community spirit, as we interpret the term today, was scarcely to be looked for in a Spanish colonial town."[103] While it is true that substantial segments of the villa's population remained excluded from active participation in local affairs, those within the governing body manifested a genuine sense of civic pride and responsibility. At least on some occasions cabildo members were capable of seeing beyond the narrow confines of self interest, and even down to the troubled years surrounding Mexican independence, they continued to display concern for the maintenance and improvement of public works to the extent that limited municipal finances would permit. Meanwhile, with active encouragement from the commandant of the Provincias Internas, they also began setting aside funds for public schools.[104]

Those who controlled local government in eighteenth-century Chihuahua not only understood the norms of conduct and responsibility incumbent upon them, they also possessed a clear picture of the kind of "republic" they wished to create. This ideal community was a sharply hierarchical society, in which every man and woman fulfilled the obligations appropriate to his or her social standing and gender without questioning the rightful precedence accorded those of higher status. The rhetoric adopted by local elites allowed for no doubt that certain individuals, by virtue of their inherent moral superiority, ought to assume positions of command over others. In other words, they saw little room for negotiation with regard to the distribution of power and privilege in their society. Persuading others to accept their vision posed something of a challenge, but, as we shall see in later chapters, pervasive notions of ethnicity and patriarchy not only reinforced their own belief in the rectitude of social hierarchy but also provided them with powerful instruments to use in convincing at least some of their subordinates to behave as proper inhabitants of their republic.

Chihuahua's leaders would also take exception to Haring's portrayal of civic fiestas as reckless wastes of municipal funds.[105] Such occasions provided opportunities for justifiable expressions of civic pride, as town officials strove to recreate observances they had witnessed in larger cities throughout the empire. Moreover, public rituals featured visual representations of the hierarchy they viewed as essential to social order, as local dignitaries marched in solemn procession through the streets of San Felipe for the presumed edification of the assembled crowds. At the same time these fiestas conveyed a message of community solidarity that supposedly transcended barriers of class, ethnicity, and gender.

Therefore, like elites in most other times and places, the leaders of colonial Chihuahua invested considerable effort in staging theatrical displays of their own hegemony. Although they carefully weighed the costs of local celebrations and their possible effects on labor discipline, they viewed these performances not as frivolous expenditures of town resources but rather as effective tools in carrying out their solemn responsibility of maintaining peace, order, and prosperity in their republic. At times, however, they forgot to ask whether the intended audience grasped the lessons being directed at them, or whether workers and other lower-class people instead simply used festive occasions for their own purposes. Chapter 5 examines colonial Chihuahua's public fiestas and other rituals of governance in greater detail.

FIVE

The Rituals of Governance

AS WE HAVE SEEN in Chapter 4, the individuals who controlled local government in San Felipe el Real de Chihuahua understood quite clearly that they, as the final links in a chain of command that extended directly back to the king himself, embodied the colonial state in the eyes of their constituents. They also believed that they could effectively carry out their responsibilities as His Majesty's representatives and guarantee the tranquility of their community only if they successfully impressed the power and righteousness of their position on the socially inferior and unenlightened people in their midst. They therefore lavished great attention on everyday rituals and periodic public celebrations designed to teach even the most dim-witted of their subordinates the attitudes and demeanor required of those who lived in a civilized republic.

Deference to Authority

Officials in colonial Chihuahua shared well-defined notions of the kind of ritual deference they should receive as the personifications of His Majesty's power and justice. Lest anyone forget to show them proper regard, they usually went about their duties equipped with visual reminders of their positions. When the governor of Nueva Vizcaya ventured out, an escort of soldiers often accompanied him. En route to administer justice somewhere in the villa, the alcaldes carried their *varas*, or batons of office. Often more than a meter in length and topped by a cross, the vara symbolized the royal scepter. To dispossess a justice of his baton was to deprive him of his office.[1]

Authorities were especially concerned that any public display of disrespect might disrupt the fragile balance of social order in general and labor discipline in particular. One foreman who refused to attend an official measurement of his employer's mine therefore received a few blows because officials feared that his action might spark a tumult among the mine workers.[2] In 1734 Alcalde José Antonio de Uranga prosecuted a peninsular merchant who had insulted him in full view of many people of color quebrado, who presumably might infer dangerous ideas if such insubordination went unpunished.[3] Indeed, anyone who neglected to show due respect toward an alcalde or other official risked prosecution.[4] Lucas de Ayllón, for example, faced expulsion from Nueva Vizcaya not only because he was known for his "depraved tongue and bad customs," but also because he had shown disrespect toward alcalde Juan Antonio Trasviña y Retes.[5]

Local officials self-consciously phrased their demands for deference in terms of their roles as His Majesty's representatives on the northern frontier of New Spain. An alcalde summoned to quell a disturbance at a fandango therefore chided a Spanish silversmith for failing to doff his hat in the presence of a representative of His Majesty's justice.[6] In 1772 Pedro Macías resisted arrest for failure to pay his debts and openly mocked the royal justice. In response authorities called upon local citizens to help apprehend him "in the name of the king."[7]

Officials in Chihuahua distinguished between the courtesy they deserved as individuals and the special respect attached to their positions. Assaulted by an irate citizen while discharging his duties as alcalde, Andrés Calles explained that he was prepared to pardon the offense to his person but not the insult to his office. Though of relatively high social status and reportedly insane, the offender spent two years in exile at the Hacienda de Encinillas.[8]

Others of fairly high social standing were also expected to pay proper respect to those in authority. In 1781 the cabildo members severely reprimanded their scribe, Francisco Briceño, when, for reasons that remain unclear, he locked them out of their official chambers following the town's annual procession honoring the feast of San Andrés. They also complained that he had disrespected them verbally; on one occasion he had publicly remarked that all of the council members were nothing but statues and that only he among them knew how to speak.[9]

Local authorities routinely chastised offenders for showing "little fear of God and of royal justice." Following established practice in many eighteenth-century societies, they often meted out punishments for all to see, in the hope of deterring others from wrongdoing. A standard fixture in the central plaza of San Felipe and most towns throughout the Spanish empire was the *picota*, or pillory, where those who violated the law endured public humiliation and corporal punishment. A man who had resisted arrest and stabbed a bailiff thus received 50 lashes at the pillory while wearing his weapon around his neck.[10] A mulato found guilty of repeatedly stealing livestock also went on public display along with the hide of his latest booty.[11] Even people of relatively high social rank sometimes suffered public humiliation for unacceptable conduct.[12]

On a few occasions local officials staged even more dramatic representations of state power in the form of public executions. On October 10, 1733, for example, two young workers were put to death for the murder of a Spanish shopkeeper six months before. At 10:30 in the morning the chief bailiff and the captain of an outlying presidio led a detachment of soldiers and prominent vecinos, who mounted the captives on burros and escorted them through the streets of San Felipe, while over and over the town crier announced their deed and impending punishment. After passing by the scene of the crime, the procession moved to the outskirts of the villa, where a firing squad performed the actual execution. Officials then placed the bodies on display in the plaza for the remainder of the day—except for the culprits' severed right hands, which they placed above the victim's doorstep. Anyone who walked the streets of San Felipe that Saturday, including the many workers who customarily came down from Santa Eulalia for the weekend, could not fail to have been impressed by the awesome weight of His Majesty's justice.[13]

Town officials did not wait for such extraordinary occasions to display the power of the Spanish state or to provide visual lessons in proper social precedence, however. Several times each year they found opportunities to flaunt their wealth and position, buttress their own self-confidence, and foster a sense of civic pride in their fellow vecinos. Each January 1, for example, they staged elaborate rituals, modeled after those held in larger cities, to mark the installation of two leading citizens to serve as alcaldes for the coming year. At 9:00 A.M., the cabildo members gathered to make their selection. A delegation then summoned the new alcaldes from their homes and ordered them to appear in the council's chambers, where they received their staffs of office. After the alcaldes solemnly promised to fulfill their duties faithfully and to defend the doctrine of the Immaculate Conception, the newly constituted cabildo proceeded to the home of the governor, who toasted the new alcaldes with wine imported from Spain. From there they went to the parish church for a mass of thanksgiving. Finally, the regidores escorted the new alcaldes through the streets of the villa back to their homes.[14]

Public Holidays

Public festivals staged at various times in the year provided other chances to dramatize the town's social and political hierarchies in official processions. Local leaders also understood that a certain amount of festivity was essential to labor discipline, because workers expected periodic diversions from their routines. The importance of public celebrations in creating a civilized "republic" on the northern frontier of New Spain was so readily apparent to the men who founded the cabildo of San Felipe el Real that one of the council's first acts was to establish a regular cycle of civic observances, emulating whenever possible the rich ceremonial life they had observed in Mexico City, Guadalajara, or back in Spain.[15]

From the earliest days of Spanish settlement at Chihuahua through the remainder of the colonial period, the most important local fiesta was that held in honor of Saint Francis of Assisi, patron of San Felipe's parent settlement of San Francisco de Cuéllar. This week-long celebration, held each year in early October, began with a religious observance that featured music and a sermon. A full round of secular amusements followed, including fireworks, horse races, comedies, and mock reenactments of the medieval battles between Moors and Christians. Most exciting of all, however, were the bullfights held in the central plaza, which was specially fenced for the occasion. People traveled to San Felipe from great distances to observe these spectacles and to enjoy the gambling, dancing, and other entertainment that also marked the San Francisco celebration.[16]

From the feast of San Francisco it was less than two months to that of San Andrés on November 30, when the city council and other dignitaries marched in solemn procession and bonfires and fireworks illuminated the streets at night.[17] By the late 1750s city officials had added the fiesta of Nuestra Señora de Guadalupe, on December 12, to the round of local observances, again marking the day with religious ritual and fireworks.[18] In the early nineteenth century, horse races also took place on December 12.[19]

The Christmas season soon followed, offering a full two weeks of dancing, singing, card playing, and other amusements in the central plaza of San Felipe. Only after the feast of the Three Kings on January 6 did mines reopen and other economic activities resume.[20] *Semana Santa* (Holy Week) in March or April evidently entailed a more reverential form of observance. Following peninsular custom, various processions took place. On Holy Thursday, for example, local citizens formed special honor guards to accompany the consecrated host through the streets. Holy Week also furnished workers from the surrounding area with an excuse to leave their jobs for the ostensible purpose of confessing and receiving communion in fulfillment of their Easter duty, and many evidently lingered in town for a few rounds of dancing and gambling.[21]

The feast of San Felipe, the villa's other patron saint, followed a few weeks later on May 1. Again, an official religious service and a procession of local dignitaries served as prelude for fireworks and other forms of entertainment.[22] Corpus Christi, in late May or early June, rounded out the calendar of major ceremonial events in San Felipe, as it did in most other communities of the Iberian world.[23] The municipal council regularly subsidized this celebration, usually with a contribution of 100 pesos. Under penalty of stiff fines set by the corregidor and cabildo for failure to participate, local residents decorated the streets through which the Eucharist passed in solemn procession.[24]

Other religious holidays were celebrated in more modest fashion, with observances evidently limited to a single day and in some cases confined to a special liturgical function. The feast of San José (Saint Joseph), March 19, had claimed a spot on the villa's ritual calendar by the 1740s.[25] In 1758 mine operators and other principal entrepreneurs in San Felipe and Santa Eulalia enhanced the importance of this feast. At a meeting convoked by Santa Eulalia's teniente, Juan José Barrándegui, they adopted San José as the official patron of mining in the hope that the special devotions marking the occasion would breathe new life into their flagging industry. From that date forward a one-day holiday for workers and a special celebration marked this feast.[26] Other documents make passing references to religious ceremonies held in honor of Nuestra Señora de los Dolores in September and a procession on the feast of Santiago on July 25.[27]

Certain customary Mexican or Iberian festivities were evidently missing from the calendar of observance in Chihuahua, or at least they were of such minor importance that they have left few documentary traces. Although San Felipe had a cofradía dedicated to the souls in purgatory, surviving records fail to mention any special observance of the Day of the Dead (November 2), a date on which Mexicans from colonial times to the present have honored their deceased relatives.[28]

Even more striking is the absence of references to the traditional, three-day Carnival that preceded Ash Wednesday. Although at present we have little information on the early history of Carnival in Mexico, by the late seventeenth century it was celebrated with considerable gusto in Spanish cities and Indian villages alike. Residents of Mexico City danced, drank, and went about the streets in disguises that seemed to overturn the existing order of things—men dressed as women, laymen as clergy, the young as their elders. Civil and ecclesiastical authorities viewed these rituals with distaste, however. Inquisition administrators began attacking Carnival customs in 1679, forbidding laymen to wear clerical garb. In the decades following the Mexico City riots of June 1692, officials displayed even greater concern for maintaining order in the capital. The archbishop of Mexico outlawed transvestitism in 1722, the same year that Juan de Acuña, Marqués de Casa Fuerte, took over as viceroy and resolved to do his part to curb the worst excesses of the holiday. The viceroy published a decree in December 1731 threatening stringent penalties for anyone who observed traditional pre-Lenten customs during the upcoming season. Evidently the combined efforts of church and state succeeded in banishing many Carnival observances from Mexico City, relegating them to outlying settlements.[29]

The founding of Chihuahua coincided precisely with these campaigns to suppress Carnival, and the villa's leaders apparently fell into step with trends being set in the viceregal capital. Cabildo records from San Felipe el Real show no official provisions for any pre-Lenten celebration, and employers, always critical of their workers' propensity to find the slightest excuse to shirk their jobs, never complained of work stoppages during that period. On Wednesday, March 9, 1735, for example, mine owners and merchants gathered to discuss conditions that had produced the recent downturn in silver production. They grumbled that they were still recovering from the disruption of work during the Christmas holidays, and that Holy Week and Easter lay ahead, but they made no mention of Carnival.[30] Ash Wednesday that year fell on February 23; surely if any significant merriment had preceded the start of Lent, it would have been fresh in the minds of the city's major employers when they drew up their report just two weeks later.

Perhaps even more revealing is the absence of passing references to Carnival in the routine court depositions of ordinary men and women. If asked to recall when a certain event took place, people often used the ritual calendar to guide them. Phrases such as "the day before the feast of San Francisco," "during the Christmas holidays," or "shortly after Semana Santa" regularly appear in testimony. Though an occasional reference to Ash Wednesday can also be found, the colonial townspeople of San Felipe apparently did not measure time with reference to Carnival. I have found only a single mention of "the Monday of *Carnaval*," made, significantly, by an Indian from the mission pueblo of Carichic in 1770.[31]

Dynastic Observances

Even without extensive pre-Lenten festivities, people in eighteenth-century Chihuahua enjoyed numerous opportunities to escape their usual routines. In addition to observing regular religious holidays, the town council of San Felipe joined city governments throughout colonial Spanish America in organizing public spectacles to mark coronations, deaths, marriages, and births in the royal family.[32] In 1720 members of the newly formed cabildo prepared themselves for such eventualities by seeking advice on proper protocol from their counterparts in Guadalajara. Officials in the Nueva Galician capital consulted their records and extracted a detailed description of the ceremonies held there following the death of King Felipe IV in 1665.

After conducting funeral rites in honor of the dead king, the city of Guadalajara had staged an elaborate ceremony in which local dignitaries and the general populace swore fealty to his successor, Carlos II. Liveried pages and coachmen had accompanied local dignitaries to a platform erected in the main plaza especially for the occasion. Atop the platform had stood the royal coat of arms and a full-size image of the new sovereign. In a colorful procession the alférez real had carried His Majesty's banner throughout the city, stopping frequently to proclaim Guadalajara's corporate allegiance to Carlos II. At each stop the church bells had rung and the assembled crowd had shouted their "amens" and "*vivas*."[33]

Four years after receiving these guidelines from Guadalajara, cabildo officers in San Felipe found occasion to use them. On January 10, 1724, King Felipe V abdicated in favor of his sixteen-year-old son, Luis.[34] Government authorities promptly dispatched word of the dynastic change to every city in the empire. Although young Luis had already died of smallpox before news of his accession reached Chihuahua in early September, several more months passed before people on the northern frontier of New Spain learned that King Felipe had reassumed the throne.[35] In the interim the villa of San Felipe held the first of its many ceremonies in honor of the Bourbon dynasty.

Unable to match the sumptuous celebrations that Guadalajara had mounted for Carlos II, local officials in San Felipe nonetheless staged a tribute to Luis I that local residents would remember for years to come. Although he initially protested that his business affairs allowed him little spare time, Alférez Real José de Aguirre eventually played a prominent role in financing and executing the local festivities. Aguirre carried the royal banner about the city in a dignified procession, while Corregidor Bartolomé García Montero presided over the public acclamation of the new king. Following a solemn *Te Deum* in the parish church, fireworks, comedies, *bailes populares* (popular dances), the pageant of the Moors and Christians, and bullfights—involving some 200 bulls—entertained the crowd.[36]

The number of such externally mandated observances accelerated in the 1740s and beyond. In 1741 the cabildo expressed its "affection for His Majesty" King Felipe V by spending a modest 43 pesos for a mass and fireworks to celebrate the victory of Spanish forces over the British at Cartagena.[37] A few years later they received instructions to plan a public celebration honoring the marriage of Princess María Teresa to the dauphin of France.[38] The death of King Felipe in 1746 and the crowning of Fernando VI brought yet another royal decree reminding local residents of their ties to the Bourbon dynasty.[39]

A similar notice came a short thirteen years later, when Carlos III succeeded to the throne.[40] Evidently King Carlos was as energetic in promoting official celebrations throughout his empire as he was in reorganizing colonial administration. In 1771 and again in 1779 he ordered all of his subjects to observe the birth of his newest great-grandchild; at least in the latter case the governor of Nueva Vizcaya decided that a solemn mass and three nights of *luminarias* (bonfires) were sufficient.[41] Moreover, in many places the king's much-celebrated devotion to the Immaculate Conception prompted a renewed interest in staging fiestas in honor of Mary. In 1762 the cabildo spent over 1,000 pesos on observances to mark the proclamation of the Virgin of the Immaculate Conception as official patroness of Spain. The celebration featured three sermons, three comedies with music, and written invitations for members of the elite.[42] Then in 1790 and 1791 San Felipe held its customary funeral and coronation rites following the death of Carlos III and the accession of Carlos IV.[43]

Costs and Benefits of Ritual

All of these observances, religious and secular alike, gave the villa's civic leaders ample opportunities to demonstrate their own elevated social ranking and their direct links to His Majesty himself, while also instructing the local populace in the rituals of a civilized urban polity. Many also fervently believed that proper homage to San Francisco and other patron saints insured peace and prosperity in their community. In 1736 Eugenio Ramírez Calderón attributed recent epidemics, Indian attacks, and economic troubles to the villa's failure to observe the feast of San Francisco with sufficient pomp the previous year. Four years later the cabildo acted on these concerns; in the name of the town's vecinos they took a solemn oath to celebrate this occasion each year in proper style.[44] At the same time, however, elites fretted about the costs of public observances. As the local economy deteriorated after 1740, they often cut back on expenditures for these events. By the late 1770s cabildo officials even contemplated suspending the fiestas of San Felipe, Corpus Christi, and San Francisco. Although they never resorted to anything so drastic, they did halt the San Francisco bullfights for several years in the 1790s.[45]

Local authorities also worried about the effects of excessive celebration on labor discipline. As we saw in Chapter 3, employers viewed their workers as lazy and apt to abandon their tasks at the slightest provocation. The fiesta of San Francisco prompted the most frequent expressions of official concern for labor discipline. Town fathers feared that the week-long holiday would disrupt work routines, and that even the most docile employees might be corrupted by the throngs of unruly vagabonds who converged on San Felipe for the October festivities. The Christmas season also furnished occasions for lapses in social control. Employers complained that the extended period of revelry distracted workers from their promises to return to their jobs in January. Following the customary year-end adjustments of their accounts, many workers simply disappeared, often without paying their debts. Others demanded sizable advances in money or merchandise before they agreed to resume work in the new year.[46]

At the same time, civic leaders understood that a certain amount of festivity was necessary in order to maintain a stable labor supply. They frequently remarked that their employees were so given to fiestas that any curtailment of the bullfights and other expected entertainments might prompt workers to revolt or to migrate elsewhere. They may also have understood that a lively round of fiestas might attract new workers from other locations. Even Manuel San Juan y Santa Cruz, certainly no friend of the villa's working people, acknowledged the importance of fiestas in controlling the labor force. For unexplained reasons, the cabildo postponed the bullfights from the feast of San Francisco to Christmas week in 1732. San Juan y Santa Cruz, acting as diputado for the miners' guild, and Santiago Gómez de Escontría, speaking for local merchants, protested the council's decision, alleging that uncertainty surrounding the fiestas had prompted dissatisfaction among workers, harming both mining and trade.[47]

Local officials therefore faced the difficult challenge of providing sufficient pomp and ritual to fulfill their own visions of a proper urban society and enough fiestas to satisfy workers' needs for diversion, while at the same time conserving scarce municipal resources and maintaining labor discipline. The best that they could do was to juggle the schedule of events for the feast of San Francisco and other celebrations so that the festivities did not spill over into a second week. Regardless of when October 4, the actual feast day of San Francisco, fell, successive cabildos decreed that the fiestas begin on one Sunday and terminate on the next, so that workers could return to their jobs on Monday morning, presumably well refreshed and ready for the task ahead.[48]

Concern for labor discipline and the conservation of scarce resources also shaped the local celebrations of dynastic events. Whenever possible officials tried to combine these observances with regular holidays already on the calendar. When they met in October of 1724 to discuss the oath of allegiance to the new King Luis I, for example, council members explicitly voiced their apprehensions over any possible disruption in mining. Therefore they set the ceremony for December 24. The bullfights, comedies, and parades in honor of the new king simply added extra glitter to that year's Christmas festivities.[49] In 1745, the fiestas in honor of Princess María Teresa's marriage also took place during Christmas week.[50]

On later occasions the cabildo also tried to postpone the official oath of allegiance to a new king for as long as possible. When they learned of the death of King Felipe V in the spring of 1747, the council members planned an immediate funeral procession for His Majesty, complete with trumpets and kettledrums, the latter covered with black cloth. They commanded all local residents to attend, and to dress in mourning if they could afford to do so.[51] Because the swearing of loyalty to King Fernando VI involved greater pomp and thus greater expense, the council showed considerably less enthusiasm for fulfilling this part of its obligation. Initially they agreed to hold the ceremony immediately following the fiesta of San Francisco in the fall. After further discussion, however, they deferred it to June 1748, presumably to coincide with Corpus Christi. Several cabildo members expressed their opinion that the June date would cause the least possible disruption to mining.

On February 11, 1748, an official notice describing the planned festivities appeared on the door of San Felipe's municipal granary. Among the events listed was a comedy to be presented by the guilds of surgeons, barbers, and apothecaries on the afternoon of June 4. Members of these organizations lost no time in protesting the expense involved. One druggist also expressed his reluctance to cooperate with mere surgeons and bloodletters, whose trade he deemed socially inferior to his own.[52] Over the next several weeks others noted that the floundering local economy could ill afford the expense or the work stoppage that the festival would entail. At the same time a smallpox epidemic diverted people's attention from planning the celebration.

In May, long-time civic leader Alexandro García de Bustamante finally asked the council to postpone the ceremony once again. He noted that on similar occasions in the past the people of San Felipe had always shown loyalty to their sovereign. To ask them to stage the event in the face of their current difficulties would constitute tyranny and a disservice to His Majesty, García added. He suggested that the observances be delayed until the fall celebrations in honor of San Francisco, but that two full weeks be set aside to celebrate both occasions properly. Even though they undoubtedly feared the long break in mining operations, the cabildo agreed to García's proposal, setting the coronation festivities to begin on Saturday, September 21. They scheduled a full week of processions, comedies, bullfights, and mock battles of Christians and Moors following the formal acclamation of Fernando VI, so that the villa might fete the new king "with the greatest plausible ostentation." The fiesta of San Francisco would then begin on Monday, September 30.

As the fiesta approached, local guilds and militia members again complained about their projected roles in the various events. Andrés de Villalba, mayordomo of a silver refinery, heartily objected to his selection as captain of Moors, presumably because of the expense involved. He pointed out that although the cabildo had attempted to follow the example set in 1724, they had overlooked the fact that on that occasion powerful mine owners of considerably higher social status had assumed duties such as the one he had been assigned. The council overruled Villalba, however, and the festivities proceeded as planned.[53]

In 1760 cabildo members again weighed conflicting considerations of economics, social order, civic pride, and their loyalty as vassals in planning observances to mark the accession of a new king. The further deterioration of mining and the escalation of Apache hostilities had already undermined plans for that year's regular holidays even before local officials received word that Fernando VI had died. As late as September 1 no one had come forward offering to fence the plaza for the San Francisco bullfights. Local carpenters had traditionally bid for the privilege and then profited by selling space inside the fence to spectators. One Juan Ignacio Fernández Lechuga finally agreed to build the fence, but he explained that economic hard times forced him to demand stiffer terms than those exacted by previous concessionaires. The council reluctantly accepted his proposal, granting him the right to construct the fence for the next seven years without having to pay the customary annual fee to the villa's treasury.

At the same meeting the cabildo also determined that the San Francisco celebration should begin on Monday, September 29, and conclude on the following Sunday. Over the next several days, however, questions arose with regard to the actual number of bullfights the designated timetable would permit. Although the documentary evidence reveals little past clerical interference with local bullfights, Fernández Lechuga worried that church authorities might prohibit the fights on the fiesta's opening day, which happened to be the feast of San Miguel, and on the following Friday, the day of the week dedicated to commemorating the passion of Christ and one on which churchmen had sometimes objected to the holding of bullfights. Fernández Lechuga feared that he would not have sufficient opportunity to recoup the expenses he would incur in constructing the fence. Therefore he asked that the bullfights and other secular amusements begin on Monday, October 6, two days after the actual feast of San Francisco.

Perhaps Fernández Lechuga's sensitivity to clerical opinion can be traced to the presence of Bishop Pedro Tamarón y Romeral, who had recently arrived in San Felipe to conduct his general visit.[54] Cabildo members evidently agreed that their proposed schedule might prompt the bishop to limit the number of bullfights. Although some officials fretted that postponement of the fiestas would disrupt work routines even longer than projected, the cabildo agreed to Fernández Lechuga's suggestion. The members undoubtedly feared that curtailment of the bullfights might prove even more damaging to labor discipline.[55] In the meantime word of King Fernando's death finally reached Chihuahua. Now the bishop found a convenient excuse to cancel the San Francisco bullfights altogether. He persuaded the cabildo that holding them during the week of October 6 would dishonor the dead king's memory. The council therefore decided that no bullfights would be performed until Christmas of that year and that other customary San Francisco events should also be cut short. They then set funeral rites for Fernando to take place on October 13 and 14. Despite the sorry state of city finances, they allocated 557 pesos for the observances.

Again the scheduling of coronation festivities posed a problem. Some cabildo members argued that the town should express its formal allegiance to Carlos III as soon as possible, even though time, money, and respect for Fernando's memory dictated the postponement of the associated celebration. Partisans of the current alférez real felt that the ceremony should take place at least before the end of 1760, so that the incumbent could have the opportunity to perform the prestigious duties involved in swearing fealty to a new monarch. Nueva Vizcaya governor Mateo Antonio de Mendoza favored postponement of the ceremony into 1761, however, citing the cold weather that usually occurred in December. Although he recommended scheduling the celebration in April, cabildo members delayed consideration of the governor's suggestion and finally reverted to their usual strategy of combining a royal festival with the traditional San Francisco holiday. In a decree issued on July 26, 1761, they set the final agenda. The proclamation of King Carlos III would take place on Saturday morning, October 3, with the official church services planned for the following day. The customary comedies, bullfights, fireworks, and parades filled the remainder of the week.[56] Despite the usual grumbling of designated participants, the festivities went off as planned, at a cost of 695 pesos to the municipal treasury.[57]

Rituals and Elite Hegemony

The planning of public observances thus posed considerable dilemmas for local leaders as they attempted to balance the need to maintain social control and fiscal responsibility on the one hand with their desire to display patriotic fervor and local civic pride on the other. Though they frequently debated the best means to achieve these ends, they never doubted the propriety of their own roles in these events. The cabildo assumed responsibility for staging virtually all of the villa's fiestas, while they and their social peers served as directors of the cofradías that helped arrange and finance the accompanying religious observances.[58] As in other colonial towns, for example, the Archicofradía del Santo Sacramento took charge of the feast of Corpus Christi. Its officers were almost always peninsular Spaniards and, in the words of a prominent member, "the most decent people that there are in this villa."[59]

Indeed, cabildo officers and other members of the local elite shed all subtlety in their efforts to utilize local fiestas to bolster their own positions and to reinforce hierarchical values. To insure that everyone would show "due veneration" toward the cabildo on ceremonial occasions, they instructed vecinos to clean all streets and doorways through which the council would pass en route to these functions. As an additional sign of their status, cabildo officers carried the maces symbolic of their authority as they paraded through the streets. When they arrived at church they took their places in their own pew, emblazoned with His Majesty's coat of arms. Cabildo members jealously guarded their special places, on occasion forcibly ejecting royal officials who dared to sit there.[60]

Other members of the elite also struggled for positions of prominence at local celebrations. At rituals held in honor of the royal family, the alférez real and other principal participants took advantage of the opportunity to advertise their special relationship to His Majesty.[61] In 1736 members of the Archicofradía del Santo Sacramento installed their own pew at the parish church, over the objections of Alcalde José de Varaya, who apparently feared that the confraternity would thus overshadow the cabildo on ceremonial occasions. Not to be outdone, treasury officials soon constructed a pew for themselves, placing it in a position that outranked the archicofradía's.[62]

Imitating their counterparts in other colonial communities, local elites also enjoyed the accompanying public entertainment in a style befitting the social precedence they claimed. They and their families watched bullfights and other spectacles from platforms specially constructed for their convenience, while enjoying refreshments prepared for them at public expense.[63] Delicacies served to local dignitaries on the feast of San Felipe, for example, included fine wines imported from El Paso del Norte.[64] On various occasions the cabildo also appropriated municipal revenues to adorn their special viewing platforms. In 1750 fines paid by bakers who had cheated their customers helped buy carpets and candelabra, while 135 pesos from the villa's impoverished treasury were used to buy new draperies for the platform in 1773.[65]

Cabildo officials also stipulated the roles that other groups were to play in local observances. They took careful measures to bar people of color quebrado from preferred seating at major church observances and in other ways controlled the official participation of subordinate groups.[66] The lowest social ranks allowed an active role in staging festivities were the villa's loosely organized craft guilds. Groups called upon to take part, some more frequently and prominently than others, included the silversmiths, bakers, barbers, shoemakers, druggists, tailors, blacksmiths, rescatadores, candle makers, and masons. The cabildo carefully dictated the nature of their activities and accorded them a level of prestige that fell far short of that enjoyed by artisans in seventeenth-century Madrid, where major guilds watched bullfights and other ceremonial spectacles from their own special balconies on the buildings surrounding the central plaza.[67]

Guild members in San Felipe presented the comedies and built the *carros triunfales* (floats) that paraded through the streets. They may also have acted in the comedies themselves, for cabildo records contain no references to companies of specialized actors such as those that existed in Mexico City and other major urban centers.[68] A few artisans found other outlets for their creative talents. For example, a tailor named Pedro Nolasco Bañuelos not only made costumes but also composed verses for the comedies presented by his guild.[69]

The artisan guilds hardly represented the lowest strata of local society, however. The silversmiths, for example, figured prominently in many celebrations. This group included several peninsular Spaniards, and their assigned roles in most observances reflected the elevated prestige of their craft. To honor the marriage of Princess María Teresa in 1745, for example, the cabildo ordered the silversmiths to parade on horseback, dressed in all of the *lucimiento* or splendor appropriate to their calling.[70] The bakers' guild also played a major part in the villa's festive rituals, but leading businessmen, often peninsular Spaniards or foreigners, usually assumed leadership of this organization and other guilds. As we have seen, the Asturian Pedro Antonio Cadrecha used his position as head of the bakers' guild to advance to membership on the cabildo. Another leading baker was Andrés Fourzán, a Frenchman who took charge of organizing his guild's comedy for the San Francisco celebration in 1761.[71] On other occasions Félix Cuarón, a merchant originally from Genoa who had lived in Cádiz and Mexico City before making his way to Chihuahua, assisted in planning the dramatic presentations staged at local fiestas.[72]

Artisans and their social peers also played limited roles in a few of the town's cofradías. The tailors had their own organization and a specially designated pew in the parish church.[73] The confraternity of Nuestra Señora de los Dolores, which sponsored a religious observance each September, also had members from ranks below the elite. Juana Manuela Sarmiento, proprietor of a small store and wife of carpenter José Raimundo de Castro, was serving as its *mayordoma* at the time of her death in 1770. Presumably she played some role in managing the group's modest assets.[74] Few other women, however, played more than marginal roles, such as preparing food or cleaning the church, in the villa's officially sponsored fiestas.[75]

Other groups active in planning local observances included overseers of silver refineries and others of comparable social status. Such individuals were often recruited to play leading roles in the reenactment of the battles of the Moors and Christians.[76] As we saw in Chapter 2, Vicente Vargas sometimes served as Gran Turco. When he died in 1756 his burial notice listed him an español but did not accord him the honorific title of don. His family evidently lacked the means for a lavish funeral, for he was buried with a small cross.[77]

In theory, then, skilled artisans and their social peers had an opportunity to help shape the cultural messages that these observances conveyed to the assembled crowds. Not all of them welcomed the opportunity to do so, however. In 1743 José de Porras found that serving as captain of the Moors for the fiesta of San Francisco was an onerous duty, chiefly because he had difficulty persuading others to share the effort and expense of staging the ritual. Though he had invited various people to assist him, all had given their excuses. He therefore asked the cabildo to compel them to participate.[78] Such complaints became increasingly common after the mining boom collapsed in the late 1730s.[79]

Civic Ritual and Social Control

Other groups played even more marginal roles in public celebrations. The cabildo sometimes invited Indians from surrounding missions to march in processions or provide music for various festivities, and Yaquis residing in the villa accompanied the cabildo in the parade marking San Felipe's official proclamation of adherence to the dogma of the Immaculate Conception in 1762.[80] Other subordinate people seldom acted as more than passive observers in officially sponsored fiestas, however. Most rank and file workers served only as spectators or occasionally as beneficiaries of official largess when local dignitaries tossed commemorative coins to the assembled crowd to mark the coronation of a king.[81] On the other hand, workers were sometimes asked to help defray the costs of festivities. Organizers of the funeral observances for King Carlos III solicited monetary contributions from mine workers.[82] Workers might also be recruited, probably against their will, to assist if their overseer were selected to serve in some ceremonial capacity, such as captain of Moors or Christians.[83] Other formal channels of active participation remained closed to workers, however. Surviving records fail to mention cofradías or other organizations for mine workers, blacks, or any other group lower in social status than the tailors. If such organizations even existed for workers in Chihuahua, they played no significant part in civic celebrations.

Nor did these events feature any ritualized, accepted opportunities for lower classes or young people to mock the existing distribution of wealth, power, and privilege. Common in early modern Europe, such releases from customary restraints were also well known throughout the Spanish empire. Certainly the numerous fiestas conducted by cofradías in Indian villages allowed for periodic dispensation from conventional sanctions on drunkenness and other misbehavior, as well as a chance to express religious views that might run counter to Catholic orthodoxy.[84] Furthermore, as we have seen, Carnival celebrations in Spain, Mexico City, and elsewhere had traditionally offered people a chance to don disguises that blurred the boundaries between young and old, laymen and clergy, men and women. Nor was social satire absent from the festive life of colonial Mexico. In his colorful description of the "Judas-burnings" that marked the end of Lent in Porfirian times, William Beezley shows that the effigies of Judas used in these rituals in fact often resembled local dignitaries. Beezley traces this custom to medieval Europe, and he and other scholars suggest that it spread to Mexico during the colonial period.[85] Sergio Rivera Ayala also shows how plebeians in many parts of Mexico mocked their social betters in lewd songs and dances performed on various social occasions.[86]

Documents from Chihuahua contain no references to Judas-burnings or any other well-developed rituals that explicitly permitted a symbolic overturning of the social order, however. The closest that people in colonial Chihuahua may have come to such practices was in the processions featuring individuals "enmascarados ridículamente" ("ridiculously disguised"), as the ironsmiths and shoemakers appeared in the celebration honoring the marriage of Princess María Teresa in 1745. If they followed customs observed elsewhere in the viceroyalty, their disguises may have mocked local personalities. But these rituals were ordered by the cabildo, and any implied social inversion must have been very stylized at best.[87] As we have seen, by the early eighteenth century officials in Mexico City had begun to suppress the pre-Lenten rituals of role reversal. These efforts reflected the growing anxiety about social order in the wake of the Mexico City tumult of 1692, a preoccupation shared by elites in San Felipe el Real de Chihuahua.[88]

Situated atop a racially mixed society and, as they often put it, on the "frontier of enemy Indians," town council members saw little reason to encourage any parodies of social unrest. Too insecure in their own positions, they could ill afford to tolerate the kind of lower-class "countertheater" that E. P. Thompson describes for eighteenth-century England.[89] The only genuine exercise in countertheater recorded in the Chihuahua documents—marauding Apaches who desecrated churches and mocked the clergy by adorning themselves and their livestock with liturgical vestments—provided a graphic lesson of the dangers that lurked whenever "inferior" peoples found opportunities to ape and ridicule those who ranked above them.[90]

Perhaps the cabildo members' fears were groundless. Historians and anthropologists have often pointed out that the performance of countertheatrical charades can reinforce rather than undermine social stability. Elites in many parts of early modern Europe permitted and sometimes even encouraged such parodies as a kind of societal safety valve—a controlled and relatively harmless outlet for the pent-up frustrations of subordinate groups. Symbolic inversions of the social order also served important didactic functions. Youths allowed to act the parts of their elders, for example, could better understand what would be expected of them when they reached maturity. More important, even if these holiday observances allowed individuals to change places for a day or so, they still portrayed a hierarchical world in which certain people, by virtue of their office, wealth, social status, age, or gender exercised power over others. They also showed how silly it was to imagine the poor, the young, the female, or the socially inferior assuming anything other than their traditionally subordinate roles. Finally, just to make sure that no one missed the point, such rituals of inversion often ended with a symbolic return to "normal." A figure representing the license and role reversal of Carnival might be tried, executed, and buried, for example.[91] In other words, as Natalie Davis succinctly observes, symbolic inversions could carry the implied message that "a world turned upside down can only be righted, not changed."[92]

On the other hand, while not denying the importance of these festivals in reinforcing social stability, Davis and other historians have shown that such rituals might also encourage subversive thought and action. At the very least, they gave people a chance, however briefly and farcically, to envision an alternative social reality, a perspective they might carry with them when the holiday was over. Moreover, popular resentment sometimes overflowed the safe and stylized bounds of ritual. The drinking and general mayhem of festive occasions and the anonymity provided by carnival masks could spark violent confrontations with authority figures. Carnival on occasion turned to riot, as people shifted from "the language of ritual to the language of rebellion."[93]

Chihuahua's leaders evidently espoused the latter point of view. From their perspective the social order was too precarious to chance putting dangerous ideas into the impressionable heads of those whom they regarded as their inferiors. Moreover, they recognized no special status or outlets for young people. Youngsters who came from "good" families simply remained under their parents' tutelage until they married or reached the age of 25. Lower-class youths, males and females alike, went to work as soon as they were able, but authorities regarded them as particularly given to disorderly behavior. Official reports noted, for example, that young men had played prominent roles in the labor disturbances of 1735.[94]

Specific features of Chihuahua's historical development facilitated the efforts of local elites to minimize popular participation in local celebrations and ritual inversions of the existing order of things. The villa's social evolution impeded the development of the kinds of fiestas, deeply rooted in popular traditions and often linked to the seasonal rhythms of agriculture, that characterized life in early modern Europe or in the predominantly Indian villages of central and southern New Spain. Like many other mining communities in northern Mexico, San Felipe and Santa Eulalia flowered overnight on sites where no previous permanent settlement had stood. Following the discovery of silver in the opening years of the eighteenth century, people of all races and social ranks converged on the area in search of quick fortunes. Each no doubt brought memories of rituals celebrated back home and perhaps hopes of recreating this rich ceremonial life on the northern frontier.

The rhythms of production in San Felipe and Santa Eulalia offered little guidance to those interested in rekindling traditional cycles of festival life, however. Silver mining featured no regular interruptions in work routines comparable to harvest time and other seasonal pauses that had long provided obvious occasions for public celebrations in agricultural societies. Transport difficulties that held up silver shipments out of Chihuahua presented the only serious seasonal constraints on silver production. During the dry months of spring arrieros complained of insufficient pasture for their livestock on the trail, while teeming rivers and muddy roads sometimes hindered travel during the summer rainy season. On rare occasions winter snow storms might also impede work for short periods of time. For all practical purposes, though, entrepreneurs in Chihuahua saw little economic reason to keep their mines or refineries idle at any particular time of the year. The natural rhythms of economic activity more closely resembled the year-in, year-out routines of industry than the alternation between periods of intense labor and relative leisure characteristic of agricultural societies. Not until the late eighteenth century did the villa of San Felipe even have weekly market days.[95]

Lower-class people also lacked the social contacts that might have helped them in organizing their own festivals. Most workers migrated northward individually or in small groups, leaving behind the intricate web of traditional relationships that had sustained customary rituals in their home communities. Once they arrived in Chihuahua they formed part of an ethnically diverse working class whose communities of origin spanned a wide geographical and cultural spectrum. Yaqui Indians from Sonora, drifters in perpetual migration from one northern mining center to another, refugees from the embattled New Mexico frontier, and Indians from densely settled villages in central and southern Mexico joined artisans, muleteers, itinerant vendors, and emancipated Afro-Mexicans who hailed from cities and hamlets throughout the viceroyalty.

At least during the first few generations following the discovery of silver at Santa Eulalia, these people found it difficult to form elaborate social networks once they arrived in Chihuahua. There is no evidence that any kind of formal organizations existed among workers in mines, refineries, or other enterprises. Rather than turning to any kind of mutual aid society to cover a relative's funeral expenses or other financial emergencies, most workers had to depend on loans from their employers. As we have seen, elites dominated most of the villa's seven cofradías, and none of these organizations seems to have provided financial benefits for the lower classes.[96] Even the town's artisan guilds were loosely organized; they seldom enforced strict standards for membership and evidently did little more than stage civic rituals at the request of city officials.[97]

Evidence from Parral suggests that San Felipe's rapid development from haphazard mining settlement to a full-fledged municipality with a cabildo played a significant role in retarding the formation of social networks among the working classes. Like many other communities in colonial Mexico, Parral boasted a cofradía of *pardos* (dark-skinned people, probably of African ancestry), dating from the seventeenth century. The organization operated out of the Hospital de San Juan de Dios and traditionally staged celebrations in honor of Nuestra Señora de la Purísima Concepción each January. These observances featured the usual round of religious devotions and secular amusements, including bullfights and the pageant of the Moors and Christians, with pardos serving as the Gran Turco and in other ceremonial capacities. Although prominent local residents periodically tried to curb various excesses associated with the cofradía's activities and to confine its fiesta to the already "wasted" period between Christmas and Epiphany (January 6), for most of the colonial period Parral lacked a cabildo to assume official responsibility for local festivals. When a council was finally created in the late eighteenth century, it supplanted the pardos' cofradía in planning the festivities honoring Nuestra Señora de la Purísima Concepción.[98]

In San Felipe, the existence of a cabildo from its earliest days provided a vehicle for local elites to maintain tighter control over ritual celebrations, while the absence of popular organizations and traditions gave them a tabula rasa on which to set an agenda of ceremonial life. Meanwhile, their relative cultural homogeneity helped them to define the content of that agenda. As we have seen, an overwhelming majority of Chihuahua's eighteenth-century cabildo members were peninsulares, and a substantial number of them came from the geographically compact region of northern Spain. Certainly we should not underestimate the cultural and linguistic differences that separated Basques from Asturians and Galicians, but Spanish immigrants arguably faced fewer obstacles in recreating customary social networks and festive rituals than did the native Mexicans who had traveled much shorter distances to reach their new homes in Chihuahua.[99] At best the villa's elites made only minimal concessions to local or even colony-wide custom. In 1724, for example, the cabildo agreed that the mock battles of Moors and Christians to be staged in honor of the accession of Luis I be carried out "a la usanza de la tierra" ("according to local custom"), but in fact most of the key planners and participants were peninsular Spaniards.[100]

Civic leaders in eighteenth-century Chihuahua succeeded in establishing a basic calendar of observance that met the minimum requirements of "civilized" communities, while stifling popular participation and minimizing disruptions in the labor discipline that was so essential to achieving their economic goals. Their efforts to control local festivities thus dovetailed with long-term historical trends throughout Western Christendom. Beginning in the sixteenth century and gathering momentum thereafter, officials of church and state in both Catholic and Protestant countries joined forces in an attempt to suppress many genuinely popular festivals and to inject a more solemn religious observance into those that remained. Elaborate processions that displayed the pomp and power of local authorities took on added importance in all celebrations. Lower classes increasingly participated only as spectators, unless they were recruited for the necessary but menial tasks of helping decorate the streets beforehand or cleaning up afterward.[101]

Although Spain evidently lagged behind the rest of Europe in this drive to reform popular culture, such concerns had clearly found a place on the agendas of metropolitan and colonial officials by the eighteenth century. Bourbon officials on the peninsula tried to restrict popular religious dramas, pilgrimages, dances, and bullfights. On occasion they even forbade public prayers for rain out of fear of the effects on the grain market.[102] As we have already seen, the drive to suppress popular Carnival rituals began in Mexico in the late seventeenth century and accelerated after 1700, while similar gestures continued in the mother country.[103] In New Spain, late colonial viceroys and clerics, especially after about 1740, embarked on even more concerted campaigns to stifle the autonomous cultural expression evident in local celebrations, while trying to make sure that remaining rituals conveyed the proper political messages. They emphasized in particular the lapses in moral standards and the excessive expense that such festivities allegedly entailed. Many of these efforts focused on the Indian villages in central and southern Mexico and the lavish ceremonial life of the viceregal capital.[104]

Workers and Fiestas

During the first half of the eighteenth century cabildo officers in San Felipe created a cycle of civic observances that coincided with and to some extent even anticipated the modernizing impulses of the Bourbon state. They accomplished this feat for reasons of their own and with little explicit guidance from higher officials. Motivated by their own interest in maintaining social control and labor discipline, and aided by the fortuitous historical circumstances that retarded the evolution of genuinely popular forms of social organization and entertainment, they achieved substantial command over the content and form of public celebrations in San Felipe.

Yet workers still managed to assert a degree of control over their leisure activities despite their lack of formal organizations or traditionally sanctioned rituals. They also succeeded in defending and augmenting the amount of time off from work that local fiestas afforded them. The cabildo never seriously considered the possibility of limiting the San Francisco festivities to fewer than seven days, presumably because workers would never settle for it. Workers also played a role in prolonging the Christmas holidays for at least a full two weeks by refusing to return to work during the short intervals that separated Christmas, New Year's, Epiphany and other special days at year's end.[105] In other words, they had learned *hacer puente*, as their twentieth-century descendants would say—literally, "to make a bridge" between one holiday and another.

Moreover, it is evident that many mine workers enjoyed a weekly holiday of their own making. Employers never succeeded in imposing a full six-day work week. Indeed, the account books kept by administrators of mines and refineries show that many workers put in only three or four days' labor during a typical week, which in at least some cases sufficed to entitle them to the rations of maize and meat that supplemented their wages.[106] Moreover, established custom called for only a half-day's labor on Saturday. Some workers managed to prolong the weekend still further by doubling up and performing extra labor on Friday so that they could have a two-day rest. On leaving their jobs many of those who worked in the mines of Santa Eulalia set off on the three hours' walk to San Felipe, where many maintained their homes and families, and where weekend amusements proved livelier than in the mining camp. In the villa they entertained themselves on Saturday and Sunday, and, much to their employers' disgust, many extended the weekend into an unofficial holiday on Monday.[107]

Finally, workers to some degree also shaped the manner in which they would celebrate local festivals. Though they lacked formal channels of participation in these events, in due time they created their own informal traditions for festive occasions. In conjunction with officially sponsored fiestas, to honor their own weddings and saints' days, or for no particular reason at all, they organized exuberant fandangos that lasted far into the night, despite the authorities' repeated efforts to control them.[108] Indeed, recent research suggests that wherever migration and other social forces severed traditional bonds of community in colonial Mexico, fandangos assumed heightened importance for subordinate groups.[109] Cabildo records from San Felipe show increasing official concern over plebeian fandangos as the eighteenth century advanced, suggesting that over time the area's lower classes found ways to create a new form of festivity for themselves.

Surviving records also suggest that workers regularly skipped the religious observances on the feast of San Francisco and other holidays, though they rarely missed the bullfights and other merriment. Civil and ecclesiastical authorities tried various measures to induce workers to attend the religious rites. On one occasion, for example, they prohibited cockfights before one o'clock in the afternoon on fiesta days so that spectators would not be tempted to be absent from the church services.[110] But no one really assumed responsibility for seeing that workers attended mass on Sundays or other religious occasions. The villa's parish priests lacked the kind of quasi-patriarchal control over their parishioners that their counterparts in Indian missions enjoyed. Moreover, although local custom allowed employers substantial powers to police their workers' sexual conduct and other aspects of their personal lives, seldom did anyone suggest that employers should assert control over the religious habits of workers. Those who received access to Indian labor through mandamientos were expected to see to it that their assigned workers attended mass on days of obligation, and workers in rural areas were supposed to receive permission to come into town to fulfill their spiritual obligations at Easter time.[111] Few other employers even paid lip service to any concern for personal piety of workers, however. Compadrazgo might have provided ideal opportunities for them to intervene at key points in the spiritual lives of workers and their children, but, as we have seen in Chapter 3, the most prosperous employers rarely formed such ties with their workers, nor did other, less-formal bonds of paternalism develop across class lines.

Cabildo authorities also did little to foster religious devotion among the plebeians of San Felipe and Santa Eulalia. As we have seen in Chapter 4, these men framed their civic responsibilities in decidedly secular terms. They also harbored disdainful attitudes with regard to the moral and spiritual capacities of workers. Therefore when local officials referred to the need for employers and authorities to police the conduct of workers, they focused exclusively on containing such specific disruptive habits as gambling, drunkenness, idleness, sexual excess, and insolence to superiors. In other words, authorities concentrated most of their energies on rooting out conduct that directly undermined workers' productivity in the mines and refineries. They evidently saw little reason to encourage workers to participate in liturgical exercises aimed at the enlightenment of those in attendance.

Workers thus remained free to ignore the spiritual messages supposedly presented for their benefit on festive occasions. It is, of course, impossible to determine with any precision the degree to which Catholic dogma informed the worldview of ordinary men and women in Chihuahua. Certainly religion had its place in their lives. They lived surrounded by reminders of their faith; they themselves, their friends and relatives, and even the mines where they worked usually bore the names of saints. Most people reckoned the passage of time in terms of the liturgical calendar, and church bells marked the hours of the day. Throughout the eighteenth century rosaries, reliquaries, and pious images figured prominently among the possessions of many people and in the inventories of the villa's tiendas. In 1753, for example, shopkeeper Alexo de Escandón stocked more than four dozen rosaries, and a few years later a man who tended livestock by night testified that he and his companions had been about to recite the rosary when they were attacked by three Apaches.[112] Enrique de Vera was a tailor, originally from Santa Fe, New Mexico, who was apprehended for scandalous conduct in 1785. Nevertheless, among his possessions was a set of prints depicting the Stations of the Cross, two crucifixes, a statue of Saint Francis, and three other religious pictures.[113]

Men and women of all social classes also frequently reported that they had changed their behavior, especially in the area of sexual conduct, after a priest had admonished them in the confessional.[114] On occasion popular piety even assumed dimensions that troubled local authorities. In 1736 leading vecinos of the villa debated the establishment of a hospital in San Felipe, reasoning that they could probably persuade local residents to support the venture. They pointed out, with some consternation, that whenever a solicitor from further south in New Spain approached the villa with a religious image in hand, people of all social classes, including mine workers, responded with enthusiasm and lavish donations, funds that in the eyes of the town fathers might better be used to serve civic purposes closer to home.[115]

On the other hand, it is likely that the religious festivals staged for their edification did little to impart the subtleties of Catholic dogma to working-class people in Chihuahua, if the language they used in articulating their demands, complaints, and court testimony offers any indication of the level of their religious indoctrination. Of course, few workers were literate, and they therefore depended on others to draft their written petitions. Nevertheless, the absence of religious language in documents claiming to represent the concerns of Chihuahua's workers offers a sharp contrast with similar petitions, full of biblical allusions and references to Christian norms of behavior, formulated on behalf of operatives in the Mexico City tobacco factory in the late eighteenth century.[116]

Perhaps too the workers in Chihuahua rejected—or, more likely, never even understood—the lessons in cultural hegemony encoded in the ritual displays of wealth and power staged by local elites. They also found ways to celebrate official and unofficial holidays in ways not fully acceptable to those in authority. What remained closed to them, through a combination of historical accident and the deliberate strategies of local elites, were opportunities to form ongoing organizations and to stage open and officially tolerated exercises in countertheater. Except for the kinds of occasional outbursts of labor unrest that we saw in Chapter 3, they most likely found their best chances to vent their frustrations in what James Scott calls "off-stage" settings, beyond the unwelcome scrutiny of local officials—and, alas, largely hidden from the view of twentieth-century historians. The striking workers of 1730 composed songs mocking Manuel San Juan y Santa Cruz while safely encamped in their mountain stronghold outside of Santa Eulalia. No doubt their fandangos and other spontaneous social events offered other occasions to articulate their discontent.

For the most part, however, opportunities for open countertheater or deliberate, face-to-face defiance of their social superiors came sporadically, in the mundane daily transactions that took place in streets and plazas and in mines, refineries, and shops. Elites tried to control the script for these less spectacular "ritual occasions" just as they did for the town's many civic and religious observances, but with far less success. Chapter 6 examines the social dynamics of these routine encounters between elites and subordinates.

SIX

Social Etiquette in Everyday Life

THE MEN WHO exercised political and economic power in eighteenth-century Chihuahua harbored few doubts about the propriety of a hierarchical society or their own fitness to assume positions of command. As we have seen, they had little trouble identifying the villa's "decent" vecinos, who could be consulted on matters of civic concern at cabildos abiertos or be granted responsibility for helping plan local celebrations. Individuals so designated possessed sufficient economic resources to have a stake in local society and came by their fortunes through callings considered worthy of respect. They also qualified as *hombres de bien* (literally, men of good), fulfilling all of the personal and financial obligations appropriate to their status. And, not coincidentally, all of them claimed pure European descent, most because they had been born in Spain, a select few by virtue of having escaped any obvious taint of Indian or African mixture despite their Mexican origins.

Honor, Virtue, and Limpieza de Sangre

Race thus provided a convenient initial screening device in determining who qualified for local elite status and who did not. The social attitudes that underlay these assumptions of Spanish superiority long antedated the contact of Europeans, Africans, and indigenous peoples in the Americas. The protracted struggle to recapture control of the Iberian peninsula from the Moors who had overrun all but its northernmost kingdoms in the eighth century forged concepts of honor, virtue, and the right to command others that endured well past the final battle of the Reconquest in 1492. Those who proved their faith, their superior virtue, and their valor by contributing to the Christian victories on the battlefield achieved noble status. Similar notions of honor eventually extended also to those who could prove that their bloodlines had remained untainted throughout the long centuries of close association among Christians, Muslims, and Jews in medieval Spain. Though they lacked formal titles of nobility, such individuals enjoyed the coveted distinctions of *limpieza de sangre* (purity of blood) and *hidalgo* (from *hijo de algo*, or son of somebody, connoting untitled nobility), and thereby elevated status in Spanish society. Together with the titled nobility, they claimed positions of power within their communities, basing their assertions of command on medieval Spanish definitions of virtue.[1]

Spaniards who migrated to the New World brought these concepts of virtue and nobility with them. In many areas the conquest and its unsettled aftermath provided opportunities to revive medieval notions of command based on virtue as demonstrated on the battlefield. *Encomenderos* (those who could claim an encomienda) thus claimed their perquisites as a reward for having participated in the conquest or as compensation for their presumed readiness to defend the realm in case of foreign attack or native insurrection.[2] As time passed, of course, the military justification for the encomenderos' position no longer held, and new elites who had amassed fortunes in mining and commerce arose to take the places of the conquerors. Limpieza de sangre remained a highly valued credential, however, required in theory of all who immigrated legally to the Americas.[3]

Indeed, purity of blood took on compelling new dimensions in the New World, where the presence of Africans, Indians, and racially mixed "castas" presented fresh prospects for contamination. Colonial attitudes emphasizing the supposed mental inferiority and moral depravity of Indians and blacks in turn reinforced the presumed connection between nobility of birth and personal honor. Especially in new communities where an individual's personal history could not be checked, physical appearance furnished a convenient means of distinguishing those presumed to be virtuous from those who clearly were not. Quite understandably, Spanish immigrants quickly adapted their attitudes to accommodate these colonial definitions of nobility that automatically gave them preferred status, regardless of their actual antecedents. Meanwhile, by the eighteenth century Mexican elites were becoming increasingly preoccupied with lineage, and accordingly they showed greater interest in controlling the marriage choices of their offspring.[4]

The political power and social precedence of colonial elites derived substantially from their wealth and ethnicity and from the simple weight of tradition. Nevertheless, they continued to justify their positions—at least in their own minds—in terms of their superior virtue. In 1674 a leading member of Bogotá's upper class published a treatise enumerating the traits that distinguished nobles from commoners. Nobles displayed their honor and virtue in their orderly manner of living and in the sense of noblesse oblige that impelled them to lend service to their communities. In return they enjoyed the esteem of those around them. The best way to guarantee the peace and stability of a "republic" was to place such exceptional people in charge. People in the colonies and the mother country alike paid lip service to the notion that those of noble status should be able to support themselves without resort to trades or other "indecent" occupations.[5] By the late seventeenth century, however, accepted standards had changed to accommodate new economic realities. The bourgeois ethic had gained respectability, so that within certain limits nobles could work to support a lifestyle appropriate to their social status.[6]

Because few members of the titled nobility ventured to the northern frontier, Spanish immigrants arriving in Chihuahua saw few competitors in the contest for social precedence, and most of them could gloss over any possible doubts about their claim to hidalgo status. Francisco Xavier de Armenta, for example, substantiated his claim to nobility by persuading his childhood friend Pedro Soler to testify that their mutual schoolmasters and fellow students in Seville had always treated Armenta with "decency, esteem, and care," and that therefore Armenta must be a hidalgo.[7] As mining magnates and merchants, Chihuahua's immigrants also benefited from the newer, more flexible standards that permitted an individual to engage in productive enterprises without sacrificing personal honor. On the other hand, the realities of colonial society gave peninsulares and Mexican-born españoles reasons to continue valuing traditional notions of limpieza de sangre. Manuela Mauriño, illegitimate daughter of a peninsular immigrant, therefore sought proof that her teenage son was "clean of all bad races—of Moors, of Jews, and of those recently converted," before sending him off to study on a scholarship at the Colegio de San Ildefonso in Mexico City.[8] At the same time, the old idea that nobles won their honor on the battlefield evidently carried little weight by the early eighteenth century. Although many of San Felipe's founders had proven their mettle in the Indian wars of northern New Spain, they seldom pointed to their military exploits in justifying their positions of precedence in the villa. At most they referred occasionally to the notion of "Spanish valor" that soldiers should display when fighting enemy Indians.[9]

Calidad

For local elites in Chihuahua, nobility and the right to command others rightfully belonged to those of high *calidad*. Based historically and officially on race, the concept of calidad derived from legal distinctions among Spaniards, Indians, and blacks dating from the sixteenth century. But contemporaries understood, and recent scholarship has confirmed, that such characteristics as birthplace, wealth, occupation, acculturation, legitimacy, conduct, and personal honor might significantly alter one's calidad and therefore one's position in society. In sum, writes Robert McCaa, for many people in New Spain calidad might best be described as "an inclusive impression reflecting one's reputation as a whole."[10]

Local leaders in eighteenth-century Chihuahua envisioned their republic as divided into various *esferas* (spheres), each occupied by persons of a particular calidad.[11] Partisans of General José de Orio y Zubiate thus referred to him as a person "de esfera y calidad," and the wording of their statement implies that he belonged in the superior ranks of both.[12] The peninsular merchant Juan Cacho de Herrera alleged that another merchant's slanderous remarks had damaged his reputation "as an honorable man and one of those belonging to the first sphere, and esteemed in this place."[13] Privileges and responsibilities varied with one's esfera and calidad. Manuel San Juan y Santa Cruz's order against vagabondage stipulated that every man should have a job "according to his calidad."[14] In theory only those of higher spheres could carry arms.[15] Juan Antonio de Gándara, a minor functionary who accompanied judicial officers on their rounds, argued that he should not be required to work off a debt because of his status as a person of "not inferior hierarchy and calidad."[16]

It is clear that in the minds of local elites in Chihuahua the concept of calidad rested simultaneously on virtue and ethnicity. Each of the 63 men who signed the petition demanding the removal of Corregidor Juan Sánchez Camacho in 1731 possessed the requisite credentials. According to the cabildo, all of the signatories were "hombres españoles y calificados en sangre y proceder" ("Spanish men qualified by both blood and conduct") and therefore deserving of an active voice in civic affairs.[17] In point of fact, as we have seen, at least a third of these men, and perhaps many more, were peninsulares.

Spaniards and the Sociedad de Castas

Spanish immigrants in Chihuahua evidently had some difficulty in mastering the complexity of Mexico's caste system. Newly arrived in San Felipe, they faced what must have appeared to be a bewildering variety of racial designations, and they seemed hard put to classify people. In 1746 a Spanish bakery owner identified one of his workers as a mulato, while a coworker said that the peon in question was a coyote (a term that on the northern frontier usually connoted a mestizo) and the worker himself claimed to be an español.[18] On another occasion several people were asked to specify the race of an arriero involved in a legal dispute. A merchant from the kingdom of Galicia in northern Spain suggested that he was definitely an Indian because he did not speak proper Castilian, but another peninsular thought that he was probably a mestizo.[19]

On the other hand, Spanish immigrants had little trouble adapting to colonial ideology's facile equation of ethnicity with superior virtue and the right to preferential treatment. White skin was a highly valued and explicitly acknowledged defining characteristic for peninsulares, other Europeans, and favored españoles. In the early nineteenth century a man of Irish extraction born in the United States found his way to Chihuahua; local documents described him as "an español from New York."[20] References to skin color frequently appear in the villa's records. For example, a Mexican-born woman described her husband as "a white man from the kingdoms of Castilla."[21] Those identified as *cariblancos* (literally, white faces) warranted special treatment. For example, a shopkeeper questioned about the purchase of stolen merchandise explained that he had trusted the seller because he was a cariblanco.[22]

Peninsular Spaniards were also well aware that their European birthplaces gave them higher standing than those born in New Spain. Readily recognizable by speech, skin color, and general bearing, immigrants understood that theirs was the one ethnic category that would never allow "passing" by those of inferior standing. Many documents refer to individuals who claimed to be españoles, but the skepticism of those recording their statements was evident in the notation "español que dijo ser" ("español, or so he said").[23] The words "*gachupín* [or *europeo*] *que dijo ser*" are not encountered, nor are there any cases of individuals identified as Europeans in one document and Mexican-born in another. Presumably, then, peninsulares were so easy to spot that no one tried to impersonate one. At most there is a reference to a drunken individual who went about claiming at one time to be from Asturias and at another to be from the mountains of Burgos, but no one doubted that he was European.[24]

Españoles and the Sociedad de Castas

Peninsular Spaniards seldom hesitated to call attention to their European origins. When making court depositions they routinely identified themselves as "naturales de los reinos de Castilla" ("natives of the kingdoms of Castile") and often specified their hometowns as well. In contrast, those born in New Spain seldom gave their places of origin unless they were explicitly called upon to do so. Instead they simply noted the fact that they were vecinos of the villa of San Felipe if in fact they qualified as such. On the other hand, if their skin color permitted, they claimed the one attribute they shared with their peninsular neighbors, proudly proclaiming themselves to be españoles.

Indeed, throughout the Spanish empire ethnicity assumed particularly great importance for españoles of relatively humble social or occupational status and for those of mixed racial ancestry who perceived an opportunity to enter the lower ranks of the elite by passing as españoles.[25] In late colonial Buenos Aires, poor whites showed acute sensitivity over their children's choices of marriage partners, because an ill-chosen match might jeopardize their precarious social standing.[26] Españoles in Chihuahua attached similar weight to ethnicity. Miguel Francisco Jáquez de Salazar, an español and farmer from the pueblo of Santa Isabel, became involved in a dispute over a mule with José Cristóbal de Cervantes, a free mulato and arriero. Jáquez de Salazar protested that Cervantes had displayed the irritable temperament characteristic of his race and repeatedly pestered him about the animal. In his official complaint he cited royal decrees relegating mulatos to inferior status and reminded local officials to "distinguish those whom nature honored with the purity of blood of their ancestors" from people like Cervantes.[27]

Concrete advantages awaited those able to substantiate their claims to be españoles. Most people deemed the testimony of an español worthy of greater credit than that of others; it was sometimes said that the word of six Indians equaled that of one español.[28] By law españoles convicted of various offenses normally escaped the pain and indignity of public whippings.[29] For example, authorities explicitly told a mine worker apprehended for carrying on an illicit sexual affair and physically abusing his mistress that he would be exiled from the community but spared a beating because of his calidad.[30]

By the same logic officials usually lent a sympathetic ear to españoles' complaints of mistreatment at the hands of their employers. In 1720 alcalde Juan Bautista de Ibave ordered his fellow peninsular Pedro Pérez Carrasco to treat an indebted worker "como hombre español" ("like a man who is an español"), meaning without resorting to corporal punishment.[31] Anticipating such judgments, workers often phrased their petitions in terms of the preferential handling due to españoles. A worker protesting beatings ordered by mayordomos of Eugenio Ramírez Calderón noted that they had neglected to exempt from this "cruel mode of punishment those who by virtue of their calidad should be regarded with some distinction."[32] In 1736 Cayetano Jáquez complained of the severe beating that his nephew had received on the job. According to Jáquez, the young man's employer had ignored the fact that he was related to "personas limpias y honradas" ("clean and honorable people") throughout Nueva Vizcaya, especially in the city of Durango. Investigating authorities agreed that the youth was "de cuerpo blanco, al parecer español" ("white in body, and apparently español") and therefore undeserving of such abuse.[33]

In other, more subtle ways those in authority routinely reinforced the importance of race in the minds of lower-class españoles. A mine worker accused of failing to show proper respect to local officials tried to prove that he should be excused because he was español; he therefore summoned witnesses able to testify to his lineage. Prosecutors countered that even españoles were required to show deference to authority, but they tacitly acknowledged the importance of ethnicity in court proceedings by trying to discredit the man's claims to European ancestry. At one point they claimed to have secured a church document proving that he was a mulato.[34]

Social Etiquette and Interpersonal Contact

Bolstered by official endorsements of their rights to preferential treatment, peninsulares and Mexican-born españoles attempted to dictate the script for all manner of social interaction between themselves and subordinate groups. Their demands for deference went beyond anything they may have claimed in their roles as officials or employers. Regardless of their own standing in the villa's social hierarchy, persons of Spanish descent clearly expected Indians, mulatos, and those of "broken color" to show them respect on the basis of ethnicity alone. Insolence from an employee of an "inferior" race thus constituted a double offense. "Mira con quien hablas" ("Take notice of whom you are talking to," using the familiar, less respectful form of the verb), they frequently chided those who displayed any signs of disrespect.[35] They often warned lower-class people to avoid angering a gachupín.[36]

Enforcing these presumed rules posed a formidable challenge. Unlike the upper classes in eighteenth-century England, whose relatively secure position of cultural hegemony rested in part on maintaining a certain social distance between themselves and the lower classes, most members of Chihuahua's elite dealt with their subordinates on a daily basis, even if they seldom worked alongside their employees. While the English gentry "met the lower sort of people mainly on their own terms, and when these were clients for their favors; in the formalities of the bench; or on calculated occasions of popular patronage," their would-be counterparts in Chihuahua interacted with presumed social inferiors in a variety of contexts.[37] Although this social interaction might be carefully scripted during ritual observances, Spaniards, Indians, and mulatos jostled one another as they went about their daily business in the villa's streets and plazas. They also negotiated terms of employment, bargained over shop counters, and from time to time even met one another on social occasions.

As we have seen in Chapter 5, Chihuahua's elites did their best to restrain subordinate groups from playing active and officially authorized roles in civic festivals. They also clearly preferred to enjoy these occasions with their social peers while keeping the lower classes at arm's length. Accordingly, they barred those of "broken color" from preferential seating at church and from the specially constructed platforms from which elites watched the bullfights. Yet, especially during the early days of settlement in Chihuahua, substantial mixing of social classes evidently occurred at the informal gatherings held in San Felipe's streets and plazas at fiesta time and on other occasions. At the San Francisco celebration of 1724, for example, General José de Orio y Zubiate was seen drinking in the plaza with a tailor.[38]

The villa's gambling establishments often brought together people of different social classes. General Orio y Zubiate, his sons, and his servants frequently gathered with an assortment of vagabonds to indulge their passion for games.[39] *Juegos de pelotas* (ball games), evidently introduced into New Spain by Basque merchants, were popular among immigrants and native Mexicans everywhere.[40] Peninsular Spaniards and others of elite status inevitably mingled with lower classes at these events. One evening in 1723, for example, officials were summoned to investigate a homicide that had occurred at a ball game where a large crowd had gathered, "sin distinción de personas" ("without distinction between persons").[41] With the apparent exception of an establishment operated by Juan de Gálvez between 1716 and 1720, the villa of San Felipe evidently had no *pulquerías* (taverns) as such, and certainly nothing comparable to the many drinking establishments that catered to the plebeian classes in Mexico City and other communities.[42] In Chihuahua people of varying social ranks drank wine and other alcoholic beverages together at the counters of local shops.[43]

In the absence of other diversions, gachupines also participated in impromptu fandangos held by people whom they considered socially inferior. Ana María Gutiérrez Gandarilla, a woman who clearly ranked well below the villa's elite, organized one such party in January of 1750. As the hired violinist and guitarist began to play, the music attracted people from throughout the neighborhood. José Pérez Mangas, an arriero from San Juan del Río who had been staying in the house next door, decided to join the festivities. He invited another arriero and two friends, recently arrived in Chihuahua from Sonora, to accompany him. Others in attendance included José Apolinar Calderón, an unemployed mulato originally from Zacatecas, who had worked as a peon in various silver refineries during the seven years he had resided in Chihuahua. As the evening advanced others of somewhat higher social standing dropped by. At least one of these late arrivals was a peninsular Spaniard, a petty merchant who had been in town some three months. Another was a cashier for former alcalde Pedro Díaz de la Serna; he claimed that "it is customary that when such functions are held decent people come to divert themselves and enjoy the music."[44]

As we have seen, local elites in San Felipe strove to recreate the amenities of social life that they had observed in major urban centers in Old and New Spain. Therefore they attempted to copy strategies designed to limit mixing by people of different social groups then being adopted in Mexico City. By the eighteenth century, elites in the viceregal capital tried to bar the lower classes from the Alameda park on festival days and whenever possible went about the city in carriages or on horseback to avoid having to rub elbows with their social inferiors.[45] Some people in Chihuahua openly voiced similar concerns. A mayordomo of a silver refinery thus objected to his assigned role in the ceremonies surrounding the accession of King Fernando VI, in part because he believed that his duties might require him to mingle with certain people whom he regarded as beneath him socially.[46]

Local authorities also attempted to curb informal interaction across social boundaries, but several decades of effort failed to achieve the desired separation of calidades. In 1772 Alcalde Pedro Nicolás Cadrecha mentioned the need to curtail the disorders that occurred during fandangos held by the lower classes, but he also noted that people of various classes mingled at these events.[47] Some fifteen years later officials prosecuted Ramón de la Vega y Sotomayor for public drunkenness and other bad habits, not the least of which was his tendency to wander about with people of inferior status.[48] By the early nineteenth century, at last, some separation of elite and popular entertainment seems to have occurred. Festivities held to honor the coronation of King Fernando VII in 1808 featured refreshments and dancing held in arcades surrounding the plaza, apparently reserved for the elite, and a presumably separate *fandango del plebe* (fandango of the popular classes).[49]

Shopkeepers and the Etiquette of Commerce

For many Spaniards and españoles in Chihuahua, routine daily contacts with lower-class people proved far more problematic than the mixing that occurred on social occasions. Many of these encounters tested presumed rituals of deference because they involved situations for which the prescribed roles of participants remained unclear despite the efforts of elites to script all social interaction. In particular, shopkeepers and their assistants struggled over the proper etiquette that should accompany business transactions. Their customers usually included people they considered far beneath them socially—laborers, vagabonds, and even slaves who might have large amounts of money, gotten honestly or otherwise, to spend. Laborers and their families not only purchased food, fabrics, and other necessities in San Felipe's many tiendas, but also often paused for a draft of alcohol served over the counter. Lower-class people also relied on the shops as a source of credit, pawning items of value when the need arose. Shopkeepers often seemed uncertain whether to treat these customers as social inferiors or as the valued clientele on whom their livelihoods depended. In many cases, deeply ingrained racial prejudices took precedence over the etiquette of commerce. At the same time, customers seemed to sense that their economic leverage gave them certain liberties to flout the rules of deference drafted by those who claimed higher social status.

The gachupín storekeeper Martín de Echaquibel confronted this dilemma one morning in 1753, when a mulato entered his shop, asked to see some stockings, and then refused to buy any. Angered, Echaquibel reprimanded his customer, who boldly replied that he would do as he wished. The shopkeeper then pointed out the marked disparity in their respective social positions: "Mira perro que eres un mulato y yo soy muy español" ("Look, dog, you are a mulato and I am very español," using the familiar form of the second person). Although the mulato acknowledged the racial distinction, he defiantly added that he was not therefore Echaquibel's slave.[50] A similar argument took place when a mulato slave tried to reclaim a compass that he had pawned with Spanish shopkeeper Francisco Segura. During the course of their verbal exchange, the slave called Segura a "perro gachupín judío" ("gachupín Jewish dog").[51]

An incident that occurred in Parral but might just as easily have happened in Chihuahua further illustrates the social dynamics of commercial transactions between people of differing social categories. Twenty-one-year-old New Mexico native Diego Velasco and his mother operated a small shop, with a total inventory worth a paltry 119 pesos, early in the eighteenth century. One morning a mulato slave named Xavier de la Cruz entered the store and bought a handful of eggs for his owner. He soon returned, alleging that the eggs were rotten. Velasco insisted that his merchandise was good, indignantly calling de la Cruz a shameless dog and upbraiding him for daring to contradict an español. At this provocation de la Cruz broke the eggs and showered Velasco with various obscenities. The altercation then degenerated into physical conflict as Velasco grabbed the slave and wounded him. On a complaint from de la Cruz's owner, local authorities jailed Velasco, who defended himself by arguing that the slave, influenced by his "pernicious nature," had failed to display the deference demanded by the difference in their calidades. Velasco further stated that despite these indignities he had acted with "complete temperance and prudence." Although the judge ordered Velasco to pay fines and damages totaling over 50 pesos, he also admonished de la Cruz to show due respect and courtesy in future face-to-face dealings with españoles.[52]

Other daily encounters also placed Spanish immigrants and españoles in contact with lower-class individuals without clear guidelines to govern their interaction. Benito Godoy y Balcárzel was a gachupín who paid dearly for his failure to learn to deal with social subordinates in his adopted community. Late in the evening of Easter Sunday, April 5, 1733, neighbors entered Godoy's shop and found him dead of multiple stab wounds.[53] They hastily summoned Alcalde Juan de Orrantia, who immediately began an investigation of the apparent murder. Recent experience and cultural assumptions suggested robbery as the most obvious motive. Theft was commonplace in Chihuahua, and other merchants had been killed for the valuables they kept in their well-stocked tiendas.[54] A quick examination of Godoy's inventory revealed that nothing had been taken, however, and authorities had to explore other possible reasons for his killing. The results of their investigation offer telling insights into the dynamics of Chihuahua's multiethnic society.

Known to his neighbors as "el Gallego [the Galician] Don Benito" or simply "el gachupín," Godoy was born about 1691 and must have been in his early twenties when he left his native province of Galicia in northern Spain. After a sojourn in Mexico City, he established himself in San Felipe at least as early as 1719. From then until his death he devoted most of his energies to commerce, often accepting goods on consignment from other merchants, although he also dabbled occasionally in silver mining.[55] Tall and thin, Godoy wore his hair in the customary braid. He was a bachelor and something of a loner. He lived the frugal lifestyle often attributed to gachupín shopkeepers in the New World, sleeping and eating in a simple room behind his store.[56]

Godoy's claims to elite status rested exclusively on his ethnicity, birthplace, and modest economic success. He never held office on the cabildo, and indeed his name rarely appears on lists of merchants or leading vecinos convoked to discuss matters of local interest. He was not, for example, among those who signed the petition requesting the ouster of Corregidor Juan Sánchez Camacho in 1731, although four years earlier he had joined his fellow vecinos in signing a petition complaining about an incompetent physician.[57] He evidently formed few of the ties that his countrymen found so useful in advancing their own interests. Just once did anyone even ask him to serve as godfather for a child, and only on a single occasion did he testify in favor of another merchant in a legal dispute.[58] Evidently a hard-nosed businessman, he showed little sympathy for the many people who owed him money, never hesitating to have them thrown into jail. His contentious temperament drew him into frequent conflict with neighbors and fellow merchants.[59]

Like other bachelors in San Felipe, Benito Godoy admitted no knowledge of cooking and therefore needed to pay someone to prepare his meals. During a two-month period shortly before his death he employed three different women who came to his house to cook every day. Each of them quit after just a few weeks rather than endure the excessive demands of this "hombre temerario y mal sufrido" ("rash and unbearable man"). He repeatedly complained about the quality of the food, insulted the women verbally, and threatened to beat them. Finally he contracted with a male caterer named Juan Ricardo, who provided similar services to a number of other unmarried merchants in the villa. Ricardo agreed to have a noon meal, supper, and bedtime chocolate brought to Godoy's residence each day.

Godoy immediately angered the messengers hired by Ricardo to carry the food to his customers. One of them, an Indian from New Mexico, simply refused to make further deliveries to Godoy or any other gachupín. A more recent employee, a young mulato named José Lorenzo Graciano, alias Chico, found Godoy no more agreeable.[60] The Spaniard liked none of the food and voiced his objections in highly offensive terms, ranging from a simple chiding—"Don't you know how to cook?"—to insults about Chico's mother. The messenger's tactful suggestion that Godoy might more properly address his complaints to the cook elicited only further taunts from the cranky gachupín. On Saturday, April 4, Godoy lunged at the young man after claiming to have found a hair in his soup. The next day, Easter Sunday, found Godoy in no better humor. At noontime he reprimanded Chico and slapped him on the face for arriving late and bringing him pork that was already cold. That evening's supper featured beef that Godoy likened to the flesh of a dead dog, adding that the meat was burned and not enough oil had been used in its preparation. Again he showered the young messenger with physical and verbal abuse. Later that same evening Chico returned to Godoy's house to collect the supper dishes. This time he came with his friend and compadre, Juan de Dios de los Reyes, and the gachupín could not resist asking Chico an insulting question about his companion. Exact details of what happened next are unclear, but after the ensuing scuffle the two young men fled the shop, leaving the ornery shopkeeper to bleed to death.

Benito Godoy lost his life in part because of his exceptionally cantankerous nature, but also because there were few well-fixed rules to guide him in his relationship with people like Chico and the women who cooked for him. Accepted norms of interpersonal behavior certainly stipulated that servants should display deference toward their masters, but none of the individuals who fed Benito Godoy worked in his exclusive employ or remained under his direct control in the manner of live-in domestic servants. The women all lived in their own homes, and under prevailing patriarchal attitudes they answered to their husbands rather than to Godoy. Indeed, one of the women quit her job at her husband's behest after the Spaniard insulted her in his presence. Chico was neither Godoy's servant nor even his employee; he worked for Juan Ricardo, and the angry gachupín was a customer. According to established colonial precedent, Chico owed Godoy respect by virtue of the vast difference in their calidades, but these rules derived not only from blatant assertions of racial hierarchy but also the tacit assumption that those of inferior category would always find themselves in an unequivocal position of servitude vis-à-vis their social superiors.

Benito Godoy, Martín de Echaquibel, and other Spaniards experienced difficulties in coping with their adopted social environment because 200 years of colonial rule had simply not sufficed to allow the evolution of new standards of conduct to govern a wide variety of relationships involving the exchange of money for goods and services, especially when so many of those who claimed precedence were Spanish immigrants only recently initiated in the complexities of Mexico's caste society. A new, more impersonal form of commercial etiquette had yet to emerge. Strangers arriving on the northern frontier carried in their racial appearance a rough index of their social status and of the degree of formal courtesy to which they were entitled. When a Spanish vendor faced a mulato customer across a shop counter in Chihuahua, the obvious disparities in their racial categories precluded any formulaic greetings connoting mutual respect, even though the gachupín's livelihood might heavily depend on precisely this kind of trade.

Elites and Privileged Space

Even higher-ranking members of the local elite who were spared the indignity of waiting on lower-class customers or depending on the services of people like Chico still had frequent contact with those whom they regarded as their social inferiors. Claims to social precedence in eighteenth-century Chihuahua rested not so much on hereditary status or symbolic power as on highly visible economic success, which in turn hinged on one's prowess in marshaling actual control over resources and people. Few of the area's economically powerful people were absentee owners. Even though Spaniards and others aspiring to social prominence avoided manual labor whenever possible and proprietors of most enterprises had overseers to assist in management, successful operation of a mine or refinery demanded the periodic intervention of its owner. In communities as small as San Felipe and Santa Eulalia, workers usually knew their employers by sight and often observed them going about their daily routines.

These same employers, along with the town's more prominent merchants, exercised political power as alcaldes and regidores on the cabildo, while even some of the more humble shopkeepers ranked among those invited to play a role in civic affairs. While performing their official duties, alcaldes and other authorities may have carried their varas and other symbols of rank, but their subordinates could simultaneously picture them in other roles and contexts—as employers not immune to the insolent retorts of workers, as merchants whose profits depended on the trade of lower-class people, and as fallible humans who all too often fell victim to the temptations of drinking and gambling. When leading vecinos gathered for a cabildo abierto, workers and vagabonds could undoubtedly recall these same individuals displaying far less dignity over their shop counters.

Unlike the eighteenth-century English gentry, who might retreat to their enclosed deer parks or behind the high walls of their estates, even the most prestigious of Chihuahua's local elites enjoyed relatively little privileged space away from the inquisitive gaze of their social subordinates.[61] The wealthy people of San Felipe lived in somewhat more substantial houses than others, and they enjoyed the seclusion of their private patios, but at most a few blocks might separate their residences from those of lower-class workers and drifters. The moment they stepped into the street, they entered public space—and often encountered people who might question their claims to deference and respect.

Precisely because their facade of social privilege revealed so many cracks, mine owners, merchants, and other members of the villa's elite agonized over any public breach in the rules of social etiquette that they had formulated. Any kind of open quarrel furnished cause for alarm if the contenders differed markedly in their calidad, and especially if a lower-class audience was watching.[62] In 1727 a gachupín named Juan de Bonilla, who served as scribe to the cabildo, became involved in a public dispute with a local butcher over the quality of meat that one of Bonilla's servants had bought for him. The butcher's angry response prompted Bonilla's immediate concern because a crowd of impressionable vecinos, most of them mulatos, had witnessed the altercation.[63] When Mateo de Herrera wounded a mayordomo of José Antonio Villar in 1722, Villar complained that the assault was particularly harmful because Herrera not only had injured "a white man of recognized obligations," but also had acted in full view of "so many servants of [Herrera's] same calidad and nature."[64]

Martín de Echaquibel, the same shopkeeper who had so much difficulty dealing with his lower-class clientele, also experienced considerable consternation when his mulato servant, Plácido de Rivas, publicly insulted him. Some twenty years after his tussle with the uppity customer described above, Echaquibel had expanded his business ventures from commerce to include mining and refining, but had evidently become no more adept in dealing with people he regarded as his social inferiors. Rivas called his master a drunkard and even dared to suggest that Echaquibel's social peers held him in poor repute. Charging that Rivas had verbally and physically challenged his "public and well-known nobility," Echaquibel observed that the offenses were doubly injurious coming from a mulato. He also admitted his chagrin when friends approached him in the street with questions about his inability to command his servant's respect.[65]

Even a socially marginal peninsular could set a bad example for the lower classes. In 1772 the corregidor heard complaints that a Spanish cook named Felipe Castillo not only refused to attend mass on days of obligation but also went about the streets of town threatening to bludgeon all the statues of the saints and proclaiming that a certain local lady was more beautiful than the Virgin Mary. Those bringing charges against Castillo cited the need to curtail such scandalous behavior, "especially in this villa, which is home to different classes of people who might become infected by bad example."[66] Moreover, even insults from their social peers alarmed local elites, because they felt compelled to maintain appearances of group solidarity in front of the lower classes. In 1734 Alcalde José Antonio de Uranga chided his fellow merchant Lorenzo Mendívil for insulting him in the town's plaza. Uranga reminded his adversary that all the witnesses were people of color quebrado.[67]

Those who claimed social precedence in Chihuahua displayed as much, and perhaps even more, concern over asserting their rights to deference in the arena of interpersonal encounters than over proving their nobility of lineage on paper. They remained keenly sensitive to the possibility of disrespect or even ridicule from those who ranked beneath them. They responded with particular alarm, for example, whenever a literate subordinate dared to mock them in verse, which evidently happened from time to time.[68] In other words, they conformed to James Scott's general description of uneasy elites who "frequently sense that they perform before an extremely critical audience which waits in eager anticipation for any sign that the actors are losing their touch."[69] Undoubtedly they shared the anxiety of their counterparts in late colonial Buenos Aires, who were reluctant to join the militia because people of the lower classes might gather to watch them drill and delight in their mistakes.[70]

Local elites in Chihuahua fretted so much over maintaining the formal and informal rituals of deference because they saw what appeared to be compelling proof that they had failed to achieve sufficient hegemony over the lower classes around them. As they went about their business in the bustling streets and plazas of San Felipe, they faced constant evidence of insubordination on the part of the villa's more affluent mestizos and mulatos, who paraded about in fancy finery supposedly reserved for those of higher standing. Like their social superiors, many people of Chihuahua's lower classes had seen the luxuries to be had in Mexico City and other major urban centers, and they saw no reason to deny themselves whatever share of elegance they could manage, honestly or otherwise. As we saw in Chapter 3, even a mule-tender's wife could indulge a passion for Flanders lace. When bakery owner Juan García dismissed a peon who owed him 52 pesos, the worker left behind two pairs of pants made of English flannel, decorated with silver braiding and buttonholes, in lieu of payment.[71] The Chihuahua archives are replete with complaints lodged against slaves and others of low social standing who persisted in dressing above their rank.[72]

Honor, Obligations and Cultural Hegemony

From another perspective, however, we might conclude that the troubles of Chihuahua's elites stemmed in part from the fact that they had succeeded only too well in convincing at least some of their subordinates to share the racially based ideology they had fashioned in order to justify their own positions in society. As we have seen, those able to mount even the slightest claims to Spanish ancestry eagerly embraced the argument that white skin equaled superior virtue, which in turn conferred preferential status. Even more remarkable, however, were the ways in which those with absolutely no title to superior ethnicity still managed to carry elite values to their logical conclusions and demand a certain amount of dignity for themselves.

Local elites widely and self-righteously touted the degree to which their authority derived from virtue rather than from naked assertions of precedence based exclusively on race. They maintained therefore that their superior deportment and bearing entitled them to exercise command and to receive respect from those who ranked beneath them. Those in subordinate positions quickly grasped the logic of this argument and turned it on its head, contending that if dignity and honor rested fundamentally on strength of character and adherence to prescribed behavioral norms, anyone displaying such attributes of virtue deserved to be treated accordingly. Many men and women clearly relished the opportunity to call the bluff embedded in the self-justifying rhetoric of local elites. Those in positions of authority were therefore caught in a trap of their own making. Because civil and ecclesiastical officials had endeavored so strenuously to encourage lower-class people to work hard, to avoid drinking, gambling, and other vices, and in general to emulate the conduct that supposedly distinguished their social betters, they could hardly protest when mestizos, mulatos, and others presented evidence that they had in fact tried to conform to these dictates of church and state.

Moreover, all of those who exercised formal or informal power routinely reiterated the notion that for everyone, regardless of social rank, honor resided in fulfilling the obligations appropriate to one's station in life. These duties varied in number and prestige according to social status; they included scrupulous attention to the requirements of one's job, respect for law and order in the community, the faithful discharge of family commitments, and the payment of one's debts. For those in the higher ranks of local society the notion of obligations embraced older views of status based on virtue as well as newer ideas of status derived from wealth. Members of the elite were expected to be responsible stewards of their wealth and to assume the burdens of community office, and they seldom hesitated to point out their own ponderous responsibilities when listing the many reasons they deserved respect.

Anyone who lived up to his or her prescribed obligations merited some measure of preferential treatment, however. Lower-ranking peninsular Spaniards often cited the many burdens they shouldered and the deference they accordingly deserved. Jailed for assaulting a mulato, a young Spanish immigrant named Francisco Sotomayor Flores pointed out that he was a "man of well-known obligations in this kingdom as in those of Castile and Andalusía."[73] In 1731

Diego de Robles, a native of Jérez de la Frontera in Spain, became involved in an argument with a mulato from Querétaro named Salvador Villareal. Alcalde Manuel de Uranga ordered both participants jailed while he investigated the incident. Meanwhile, the two men patched up their differences. Robles then asked Uranga to release them both, citing the many obligations incumbent upon each of them.[74] Similarly the merchant Francisco Gómez was excused from jail confinement—also following a dispute with a mulato—after he pointed out his "calidad, honor, and pressing obligations." Officers of the court explained that Gómez could not settle his accounts if he remained in prison.[75]

In a variety of contexts people of different social ranks cited their obligations and the personal honor conferred through the faithful discharge of these responsibilities. A mulato accused of assault was released on bond after his employer argued that the accused had the "obligations of a married man with children."[76] The concept also furnished a convenient excuse to challenge an employer's impertinence. In 1724 Joaquín Lechuga, a mayordomo at Juan Antonio Tarín's charcoal-producing estate, challenged his boss for having insulted his personal honor and that of other workers. In his verbal retort, and again in a written complaint filing criminal charges against Tarín, Lechuga alluded to his own obligations as a married man.[77] Francisco Pallares similarly complained that his son had suffered mistreatment at the hands of overseers at the refinery where he worked. Such abuses constituted a "grave excess," noted Pallares, because his son was an "español of well-known obligations."[78]

People accused of crimes also utilized the notion of obligations when pleading for lenient treatment in court. Cristóbal de Avila was a self-proclaimed español (and a nephew of Mateo de Olague, whom we met in Chapter 2). He had worked as a barretero and agricultural laborer in Zacatecas and other mining centers before migrating to Chihuahua in 1746. Jailed for alleged complicity in a homicide, he protested his innocence and appealed to the corregidor for help. He explained that he had left his wife and children in the town of Jérez, near Zacatecas, and had come north in order to fulfill his family obligations. He stated further that unless his good name were restored, he could not return home without besmirching the honor that he and all of his relatives had struggled to maintain.[79]

Those with only tenuous claims to español status used these notions to boost themselves into the ranks of honorable men and women. In 1724 Miguel Verdugo lodged a criminal complaint against Juana de Vargas, his brother's mother-in-law, after she allegedly asserted that Verdugo's mother had been a slave. When questioned about the incident, Vargas denied the accusation, pointing out that if she had indeed insinuated that her daughter had married the offspring of a slave, she would have sullied the entire family's reputation. How could she have done that, she asked, when they were all "españoles, well-born and with obligations"?[80]

In the examples given above, people joined the notion of honorable obligations with Spanish ethnicity, but even those with no hope of passing themselves off as españoles could still claim personal honor based on the fulfillment of their responsibilities. Manual laborers routinely couched their demands for greater compensation on their need to live up to their obligations to support their families properly.[81] For people in the lower ranks of society, these duties obviously involved physical labor, and for these people hard work in and of itself conferred a certain measure of honor. In the first decade of the nineteenth century, a self-admitted mulato in Parral asserted his right to marry a woman of higher racial standing by pointing out that he was "a man who attends to his work."[82] Similarly, a court-appointed defender for a young stonecutter accused of robbery recommended leniency because in this "land so prone to idleness" the alleged offender and the older brother with whom he lived had an honorable calling, one by which they could support themselves in a respectable fashion "by their sweat and their labor." Prosecuting authorities, who struggled to force the villa's many thieves and vagabonds to seek acceptable jobs, could hardly counter this argument. The alcalde hearing the case accordingly dismissed the charges against the youth and released him to his brother's custody.[83]

Some measure of dignity quite clearly lay within the reach of many people. Thus a peon could easily claim to be an "hombre de bien en la esfera que le toca" ("a man of good within his appropriate sphere").[84] Testimony given in 1737 by the mulata slave Cecilia Dorotea de Lugo and petitions drafted on her behalf show that notions of personal honor extended far down the social scale. Her master was a rather ornery Spanish baker named Lorenzo Gutiérrez, who continually accused Lugo and her husband José de la Cruz Enríquez of theft and therefore refused to accept the money she offered in exchange for her freedom. She filed a complaint against Gutiérrez, alleging that he had dishonored her and cast aspersions on her spouse, ignoring his status as a free man and a recognized hombre de bien—even though he was an Apache Indian. At one point Enríquez had responded to the Spaniard's verbal taunts with blows and had landed in jail as a result. Court-appointed defenders for the Indian argued that he had acted justifiably and quite understandably because Gutiérrez had repeatedly called him a dog—a "very injurious and provocative word." Although Enríquez spent several months in jail while the case was pending, he was ultimately exonerated, evidently due in part to his "honrados procederes aunque indio apache" ("honorable conduct though [he is] an Apache Indian"). Meanwhile, Cecilia Dorotea de Lugo also won her freedom.[85]

We cannot know, of course, how readily or fluently lower-class people themselves utilized the language of personal honor or how skillfully they proclaimed the dignity of honest work. The eloquent petitions presented to authorities on their behalf may reflect no more than the rhetorical devices used by trained advocates who usually received payment for their services. Even documents purporting to present the sworn testimony of humble men and women may in fact reveal nothing more than a scribe's idealized version of how one should speak in court. Regardless of how faithfully the surviving record summarizes the worldview of lower-class people or reproduces their actual words, however, we cannot underestimate the importance of the very fact that literate men wrote these documents.

The ability to read and write, let alone the capacity to manipulate complex legal formulas and to produce the well-crafted petitions that abound in the colonial municipal archives, placed these obscure scriveners well within elite ranks in San Felipe, where so few people had access to formal education. That such men thought it proper to invoke concepts of personal honor for the villa's lower-class residents cannot have failed to make a strong impression on their clients and on others in attendance. Slaves routinely heard references to their legitimate aspirations to liberty and humane treatment.[86] Even the killers of the merchant Benito Godoy, though presumed guilty from the outset of their trial and eventually executed for their deed, had court-appointed defenders who argued that Godoy had provoked them without cause by failing to show them proper respect.[87]

Although the finer points of legal language may have lain beyond their comprehension, many petitioners must have grasped some of the sentiments voiced in their behalf. Moreover, after a witness testified in court the scribe customarily read the statement back to him or her for verification. Even if scribes put words into witnesses' mouths on occasion, perhaps later those witnesses might recall the language on their own. Such formal encounters with authorities gave them opportunities to rehearse the rhetorical equation of obligations, personal honor, and the right to dignity that lay at the heart of the more high-minded self-justifications that their social superiors used to explain their own positions of precedence. Consider, for example, the recorded testimony of Jacinto Roque Romero, who may have been a carpenter but in any case was not a member of the villa's elite. Answering an insult to his personal honor, he reportedly insisted, "I have maintained myself in good opinion and repute, jealously guarding my house, indoctrinating my family members with good life and customs and trying in my work to maintain my obligations by the sweat of my brow."[88] Whether or not the surviving documents recapture Romero's exact words, the court proceedings gave him a succinct recapitulation of the duties incumbent on him as a respectable vecino, and the privileges he might expect if he fulfilled those expectations. Perhaps it is true, as Ramón Gutiérrez asserts in his study of Spanish values of honor in colonial New Mexico, that "the most vice-ridden aristocrat always enjoyed more honor-status than the most virtuous peasant," but at the same time people of lower-class standing in Chihuahua had many opportunities to refine their understanding of the moral justification on which honor supposedly depended. They also had chances to convince themselves that they in some measure deserved the respect that accompanied virtue.[89]

Just because lower-class people internalized some of the moral arguments articulated by local elites does not mean that they accepted the racial assumptions on which those arguments ultimately rested. R. Douglas Cope has recently suggested that the racial components of elite ideology carried relatively little weight for most plebeians living in Mexico City in the late seventeenth and early eighteenth centuries. Mestizos, mulatos, and other castas failed—or refused—to appreciate the Spaniards' near obsession with the importance of bloodlines and racial boundaries. While dominant groups in the viceregal capital proudly lavished great attention on the surnames that betokened their distinguished pedigrees, their social subordinates often knew little of their own lineage or anyone else's, and often bore no surname at all until they married.[90]

People of lower rank in Chihuahua evidently showed similar disregard for the intricacies of lineage.[91] Moreover, as we have seen, they bristled whenever local elites, especially the arrogant gachupines, blatantly asserted their racial superiority and claimed social precedence on that basis alone. On many occasions lower-class disdain spilled over into open disrespect for Spaniards and others who claimed social precedence over them. They further voiced their rejection of Spanish racial ideology in their persistent assertion that honorable behavior provided an acceptable and theoretically accessible avenue to decent treatment, even for Apaches and others whose pedigrees fell far short of the limpieza de sangre so prized by Spaniards.

Men and women of color quebrado absorbed Spanish notions of honor, virtue, and obligation or at least mastered the associated rhetoric, because they heard these ideas constantly repeated at church and in court. Moreover, they could grasp the concept of obligation and apply it to their own situation because officials of church and state, even alcaldes without a smattering of formal legal training, continually invoked it when referring to the most commonplace and intimate aspects of people's lives—home and family. Firmly convinced that patriarchal authority was the key to peace and stability in their community, local elites allowed even the humblest man to exercise substantial power within his own household. In effect all men became the deputies of the elite in the struggle to maintain control over unruly women, servants, and youth. Any man, regardless of social rank, who successfully controlled the behavior of his family fulfilled the most important of the obligations imposed on him, and could therefore claim the respect due an honorable member of the community. Chapter 7 explores the implications of this patriarchal ethos in greater detail.

SEVEN

The Ethos and Practice of Patriarchy

BY THE TIME Spain extended its dominion to the far reaches of the New World, philosophers in Western Europe had long acknowledged the social and political importance of the family governed by a patriarch. Theologians and political theorists alike saw the well-ordered family as the foundation and the model of the well-ordered state. The paterfamilias who exercised firm, benevolent, and divinely granted authority over his wife, children, and servants helped guarantee peace and stability in the realm and symbolized the ideal relationship between a sovereign and his subjects. Kings in turn were expected to rule in paternalistic fashion, while setting a good example by maintaining discipline and order within their own households. Patriarchs and monarchs alike understood that the behavior of females demanded special vigilance, because prevailing views of human nature stressed women's innate moral inferiority and their propensity to disrupt the peace of households and of kingdoms.[1] As Louis XIV of France reportedly reminded his grandson, the young King Felipe V of Spain, "The queen is the first of your subjects."[2]

Spanish tradition further underscored the importance of the patriarchal family and the subordination of women. A family's claims to limpieza de sangre obviously depended on restraining the sexual activity of its female members.[3] Moreover, during the centuries-long struggle to overthrow the Muslim kingdoms of the Iberian peninsula, properly ordered families, and duly subservient females in particular, played crucial roles in reestablishing Christian hegemony in newly resettled territory. Fighting men were essential to the Catholic victories on the battlefield, and municipal governments in reconquered areas had little choice but to tolerate their periodic binges of sexual excess. Women's contribution to the Reconquest, on the other hand, hinged on their observance of prevailing norms of feminine seclusion and domesticity. By fulfilling their traditional duties as wives and mothers, they helped recreate Christian civil society at the grassroots level. Because women's sexual misconduct might easily disrupt the fragile social order being established on the frontier, their transgressions were punished more severely than men's. Heath Dillard concludes that "the sharp contrast between worthy and wicked women was less a judgment of the female sex than recognition of their ability to threaten colonization at its primary level, the established and prolific household."[4]

Iberian notions of patriarchy continued to evolve in the centuries that followed the Reconquest. Spanish moral philosophers responded to the rapid social changes of the sixteenth century by continuing to expound on the importance of promoting family life and controlling the behavior of women as a means of safeguarding public order.[5] Meanwhile, these attitudes easily crossed the Atlantic and acquired new urgency as Spaniards confronted the challenge of settling a new world. Wherever possible colonial policy aimed to convert swashbuckling conquistadores, who might otherwise threaten royal authority, into solid citizens and padres de familia. From the earliest days of colonization married men took precedence over bachelors in the distribution of land grants and other favors. Single men who received Indians in encomienda were legally required to marry within stipulated periods of time, and married men risked loss of their encomiendas if they failed to bring their wives to live with them.[6] Although male domesticity thus assumed greater formal importance in the colonies than it did in Spain during the Reconquest, no one in authority questioned the subordination of women within the colonial social order. Meanwhile, Spanish missionaries saw the imposition of the patriarchal, monogamous nuclear family as essential to the process of converting indigenous peoples to Christianity.[7]

The nuclear family and patriarchal values assumed particularly compelling dimensions in northern New Spain. Frontier Indian conflicts rekindled medieval attitudes emphasizing the valor of fighting men. Franciscan and Jesuit priests touted the importance of family life among the neophytes gathered in their missions. Civil and ecclesiastical authorities also cited submission within the family context as a model for the subordination expected of pacified Indians. They spoke readily of "reducing" Indians to civilized living in their pueblos, using the same verb to describe the domestication of women, children, and servants under the authority of husbands, fathers, and masters.[8] In addition, the respectable Spanish household provided a major vehicle of acculturation for captive Apaches and other Indians "ransomed" into Spanish society as domestic servants. Finally, in the absence of convents, orphanages, correctional institutions, and other shelters, local authorities also depended on substantial vecinos to take in children abandoned by their parents and women who supposedly needed proper patriarchal supervision to control their propensity toward unruly behavior.

Patriarchy in Chihuahua

Patriarchal values and the family as a metaphor for civil society occupied central positions in the governing ideology of Chihuahua's colonial elites. As we saw in Chapter 4, the villa's political leaders readily cast themselves as paternal figures as they went about their official duties. They regarded marriage as a sign of stability and respectability in a man and used it as a criterion in determining whom to summon to cabildos abiertos. They also pressured men who had left wives behind in Spain or elsewhere in Mexico to return to their familial obligations. Moreover, they openly shared prevailing negative assessments of women's character and, while documents make frequent reference to the moral fragility of both sexes, local officials embraced the assumption that loose women were responsible for men's transgressions. A woman who went about from one fandango to another, for example, was criticized for "placing men on the precipice of perdition."[9] Men routinely questioned women's veracity and tried to impugn their sworn testimony.[10] Women's use of indecent sexual insults raised official eyebrows no more than when men employed such language.[11] When women became drunk and disorderly local authorities never registered any surprise, and references to women smoking or gambling similarly fail to suggest that such conduct was anything other than expected.[12] Authorities often tried to prevent men and women from mixing at gambling establishments, cockfights, and other public diversions, not because they felt that women might be corrupted by such entertainment but because their presence might lead to disorder.[13]

Male authorities also emphasized women's alleged greater propensity toward sins of the flesh. Rape victims therefore bore the burden of proof if they hoped to see their assailants brought to justice. They had to prove that their prior reputations were unsullied and that they had done nothing to provoke the attack. The author of a document dated 1780 lamented that prisoners seized by marauding Apaches sometimes adopted "barbarous customs" from their captors. He added that women especially yielded to the sensuous liberties afforded them in Indian society.[14]

These attitudes regularly surfaced when local officials reminded people to fulfill the commitments appropriate to their station in life. Their injunctions to married men showed that, whatever the deficiencies in their formal education, Chihuahua's leaders had grasped the essential vocabulary of European political thought. They believed that the foremost obligation of any married man, regardless of his class or ethnicity, was to attend to "the government of his house and family."[15] Officials employed other political terms to describe how the ideal domestic unit should function. Women, children, and servants were to live in "subjection" to male heads of households, as vassals were subordinate to their sovereigns. Women who refused to be "reduced" to the "dominion" of appropriate male relatives were guilty of "treason" or "rebellion," and a marital dispute might be termed a "revolution."[16]

Padres de familia, whatever their social status, were expected first of all to support their families, providing them with food and shelter, as well as clothing sufficient to allow their wives and children to dress with "decency."[17] In some cases this responsibility even took precedence over that of sexual fidelity to wives; on occasion a man jailed for adultery might be released so that his family would not be left destitute. Above all, however, authorities expected honorable men to monitor the sexual behavior of their female relatives and servants. Men of all social ranks took very seriously any implication that they had failed to contain properly the excesses of their wives and other female relatives. One man remarked that his wife's infidelity had caused him "notable scandal and public dishonor."[18] Pedro Pérez Carrasco, a prominent mining entrepreneur, said that the mere fact that his wife refused to live with him reflected poorly on his "credit."[19] A pregnant, unwed daughter cast a very negative shadow on her father's honor.[20]

Even the slightest suggestion of female sexual misconduct drew alarmed responses from padres de familia. Late one evening in 1774 the physician José Orellana returned home from his rounds to find his wife in a bedroom with Fernando de Mendoza, a widower and the proprietor of a local gambling establishment. Although the two were fully clothed and protested that they had been merely conversing, Orellana explained that he had retreated to his study "shamed by the loss of my honor." He nonetheless hesitated to press formal charges against Mendoza, hoping instead that his wife would "maintain the good reputation and fame that she had had until that time." He was therefore horrified when a third party, perhaps fearing for the woman's physical safety, persuaded her to abandon her home, whereupon the vicar placed her in yet another household. To Orellana's utter chagrin, soon everyone in town knew of the incident. Although Corregidor Pedro Antonio Queipo del Llano's investigation revealed no evidence of adultery, he nevertheless ordered Mendoza permanently banished from San Felipe, and a legal advisor from Durango upheld his verdict.[21] In most cases, furthermore, authorities did their utmost to keep rumors of such scandals from circulating in the community, primarily in order to protect the honor of aggrieved husbands. They routinely omitted from the record the names of individuals involved in such incidents, for example.

Husbands were so sensitive to the possibility of a wife's infidelity that "*cornudo*" and "*cabrón*," both terms denoting cuckolds, ranked among the most serious insults that could be leveled at a man.[22] Even more injurious were the insinuations that a man consented to his wife's infidelity or acted as her *alcahuete* (pimp), bartering her sexual favors to other men.[23] Though often uttered in obvious jest or blind rage, any of these epithets usually elicited a swift and vigorous denial, regardless of the social class of the victim or his antagonist. For example, a sirviente employed by the teniente of Babanoyaba noted that his boss had insulted him in this manner when in fact he had "maintained his wife in good opinion and fame."[24]

The importance of safeguarding the sexual conduct of female household members reinforced the quasi-political authority of padres de familia. Men received frequent admonitions to control the behavior of their wives, daughters, sisters, and female servants even in matters seemingly unrelated to sexuality. When a middle-aged woman named María Josefa de Ornelas quarreled with another woman, Corregidor Fernando de Torija y Leri briefly jailed her husband, ranchero Ignacio Portillo, in connection with the incident. He later released Portillo, advising him to "counsel, correct, and, if necessary, contain" his wife in the future, and threatened him with further punishment if he failed to do so.[25]

Patriarchy and Domestic Violence

Throughout colonial Latin America, padres de familia were allowed and even expected to administer a certain amount of physical "correction" to their wives, children, and servants, and a man neglected his obligations if he failed to discipline his household sufficiently.[26] A woman suspected of adultery could certainly anticipate a beating, and the law typically exonerated a husband who killed his wife and her lover after catching them in the act.[27] Bernardo Antonio Sánchez provided the exception that proves the rule when he admitted that he had refrained from mistreating his wife who had returned to him after an extramarital affair.[28] Men routinely beat their wives for alleged inattention to domestic duties and for other trivial reasons as well.

When women left their husbands they most often cited excessive corporal punishment as the reason, probably because they knew that authorities would certainly believe them, whether or not the charges were actually true.[29] Petitions written on behalf of women who had been brutally beaten by their husbands usually claimed that the men had acted without justification, implying that under some circumstances a beating might be warranted.[30] Though wives were the most frequent targets of domestic violence, children and particularly stepchildren also suffered at the hands of abusive padres de familia.[31] José de Ochoa explained that he had beaten his twelve-year-old stepdaughter because she had failed to make tortillas, run errands, and care for her younger siblings.[32]

Battered wives and children sometimes enlisted the help of priests, corregidores, and alcaldes, who might arrange temporary protective custody for them in some other household. More commonly, though, authorities persuaded couples to reconcile after warning the husbands not to be so abusive in the future.[33] In 1718 Catalina Cos Madrid went to the parish priest's house and showed him the bruises she had received from her husband, Pedro Pérez Carrasco. Joining forces with General José de Orio y Zubiate, the priest convinced her to return home. Two years later, however, Alcalde Juan Bautista de Ibave supported Cos Madrid's petition to be allowed to separate from Pérez Carrasco.[34]

Most women, however, bowed to the official pressure that supported maintenance of the conjugal unit at all costs. Vicente de Irigoyen reportedly struck his wife Juana López so often that on four separate occasions she took refuge at the home of Juan Antonio Mariño and his wife Antonia Téllez Xirón. Each time Mariño and Téllez had persuaded the couple to reconcile after Irigoyen had promised not to harm his wife in the future, but he repeatedly went back on his word. Finally, one day in 1751 he beat her so severely that he dislocated her shoulder. Covered with bruises and vomiting from the effects of a head injury, López again appealed to her friends for help. This time Mariño decided to enlist the support of local authorities. The alcalde ordered Irigoyen jailed and then allowed him to present his side of the story. After Irigoyen persuaded the alcalde that such altercations were common between spouses, his wife agreed to drop the charges against him and return home.[35]

Authorities of church and state regularly cited a man's obligation to support his family to explain why abusive husbands should be released from custody after their wives had filed complaints. In 1778 José Hernández, a mule-tender at the hacienda Tabalaopa, answered charges that he had beaten his wife, Juana Juliana Quesada. One evening he arrived home from a hard day at work, tired and frustrated after a dispute with his mayordomo. His wife had gone out, leaving many of her domestic chores undone. When she returned a short time later, he had reprimanded her with what he thought were *razones suaves* (gentle arguments), but she had failed to show him the respect he expected. Finally, "to contain her and to frighten her into acknowledging the error of her ways," he had whipped her with a *reata* (rope). Jailed and brought before Corregidor Pedro Antonio Queipo del Llano, Hernández pleaded to be released so that he could attend to his familial responsibilities. The corregidor then convinced Quesada to accept her husband's promise to mend his ways, whereupon he released Hernández with a stern warning that he would face more severe punishments if similar incidents occurred in the future.[36]

Even when civil officials took women's complaints seriously, they often responded in the same manner as they did when presented complaints from workers punished by employers. In other words, they displayed as much concern for any possible infringement on their own jurisdiction as for the plight of the petitioner. In 1718 Juana de Berdugo threatened to report her husband to the authorities for beating her and her five children. The husband responded by asserting that he alone had jurisdiction over his family, boldly proclaiming, "As far as I am concerned there is no such thing as a judge. . . . I am enough for one or many alcaldes." When local officials heard about his boast, they ordered him jailed, not because he had abused his family but because he had failed to show proper respect to representatives of the king.[37]

Patriarchy and Social Status

As long as husbands refrained from gross misuse of their power, the sanctity of patriarchal authority and the respect due any man who judiciously exercised that authority extended, at least in theory, to the lowest of the villa's social ranks. Local officials acknowledged that even slaves bore responsibility for supporting their families and were therefore entitled to adequate compensation for their labor. In 1766 the governor of Nueva Vizcaya ordered a master to give a male slave his customary ration, so that he could feed his wife, a free woman.[38] Authorities also conceded the importance of maintaining tranquility between husbands and wives even in the villa's most humble households and on occasion admonished a peninsular Spaniard for disturbing the peace of a lower-class family.[39]

Men of all social ranks had compelling reasons to internalize the ethos of patriarchy and to join authorities of church and state in articulating and reinforcing its behavioral imperatives. As we have seen, one's rank in society, and one's claim to attendant perquisites and deference, rested on calidad, a subtle and socially constructed mix of ethnicity, wealth, occupation, and personal conduct. In theory, many people could make incremental improvements in their calidad—for example, by covering mestizo or mulato roots in order to "pass" as españoles or by improving their economic fortunes. In most cases, however, they could expect their social superiors to block their upward mobility. Those with surer claims to español status seldom welcomed the ascent of obvious mestizos or mulatos into their caste, and employers hardly relished the prospect of workers who enriched themselves with higher wages or graduated into the ranks of petty entrepreneurs. When lower-class men attempted to advance themselves by governing their households as hombres de bien, however, they could often anticipate the endorsement of local authorities. By subscribing to the patriarchal ethos, men stood to gain honor and esteem in local society and a certain amount of control over what happened in their own households. Moreover, because virtually all men shared that ethos, women had little choice but to phrase their own claims to respectability in terms of their adherence to accepted norms of feminine submission and domesticity.

For most men and women, then, the standards of patriarchy underwrote their claims to respectability, and they reacted with alarm whenever anyone questioned their observance of those standards, even in jest.[40] Therefore popular insults continued to focus on misplaced sexuality, regardless of the target's gender, throughout the eighteenth century. Epithets aimed at women accused them of sexual misconduct, while those directed at men questioned their ability to control the behavior of women subordinate to them. In some other societies, by contrast, a gendered differentiation of insult accompanied the growth of commercial activity: women's honor remained centered on their sexual conduct, while men proved increasingly sensitive to accusations of financial irresponsibility. In Chihuahua, and evidently elsewhere in Mexico, sexually based insults remained the norm for men and women even as society became ever more commercialized in the eighteenth century. Indeed, it appears that the aggressively masculine tone of popular insult intensified in the late colonial and early national periods.[41] Such insults continued to evoke strong emotional responses in Chihuahua because personal honor—defined in gender-specific terms—provided a crucial vehicle for ordinary men and women to enhance or at least preserve their social standing.

In other words, the ethos of patriarchy was no laughing matter. The accepted code of social etiquette failed to provide opportunities for anyone to suggest that its essential norms of conduct might on occasion be breached. Even the most off-handed insult to an individual's personal honor elicited a swift and intensely angry response, and there is no evidence that the villa's residents ever publicly ridiculed cuckolds or hen-pecked husbands with the kind of ritual charivaris common in early modern Europe. Moreover, as we have seen, public observances rarely furnished opportunities for any kind of symbolic inversions of the social order. Therefore it should come as no surprise that rituals mocking the subordination of women to men, evidently common in early modern Europe, found no place on the ceremonial calendar of San Felipe.[42] In fact, just to be on the safe side, men evidently denied women all but the most marginal roles in staging the villa's public celebrations.

The men who governed colonial Chihuahua looked to patriarchy as the one set of interpersonal rules that seemed familiar in an exotic, sometimes frightening environment where all other social relations appeared subject to constant renegotiation. Though we know little about their lives in Spain, it is safe to say that before emigrating to the New World few of these men had had much experience commanding a large labor force in a quasi-industrial setting comparable to that of colonial silver mining. As children they had no doubt heard stirring tales of their forebears' valiant campaigns to banish Muslim infidels from the Iberian peninsula, but nothing could have prepared them to deal with recalcitrant Apaches who rejected sedentary lifestyles and threatened the very existence of communities like San Felipe el Real. The multiethnic society of northern New Spain and the absence of any well-defined rules governing the mundane transactions of daily life baffled many immigrants and brought tragic consequences for men like Benito Godoy. On the other hand, the well-established rules regarding the separate duties and responsibilities of men and women seemed to require no adjustments in their new environment. Even if immigrants could not easily distinguish between Indians and coyotes, mulatos and mestizos, at least their society still remained divided into the biologically determined and presumably constant categories of male and female.

Of all the Spanish cultural baggage that crossed the Atlantic between the sixteenth and the eighteenth centuries, patriarchy arguably changed least in transit. Once transplanted, it found enthusiastic adherence among males who had every other rational reason to question Spanish cultural and political hegemony. Accepted notions of masculinity and femininity also provided a readily comprehensible model for all other contexts of subordination and domination. Thus, as we saw in Chapter 3, the workers who submitted too quickly to their employers' demands found their manhood ridiculed by their own wives and children.

Patriarchy therefore furnished what appeared to be a coherent and widely supported underpinning for social relations in the new community of San Felipe el Real de Chihuahua. The extent to which reality actually conformed to the envisioned ideal is another issue, however. Surviving colonial documentation amply demonstrates that men and women routinely flouted the norms that were supposed to confine sexual activity within the matrimonial unit. Moreover, the practical necessities of living in a society riven by deep divisions of class and ethnicity sometimes undermined the patriarchal authority of lower-class men, even españoles. For example, such men were more likely than their affluent neighbors to be accused of profiting from their wives' infidelities. In 1723 the mestiza María Rosa Gómez carried on an adulterous affair with one of the villa's "principal men"—none other than the regidor Francisco de Salcido. The pair evidently violated all locally accepted standards of propriety and discretion. Salcido bought expensive finery for his mistress and publicly escorted her and her sisters to the plaza on the feast of San Francisco. When his fellow cabildo members finally investigated the affair, however, they preferred to focus on the alleged complicity of Gómez's husband, a vecino of Santa Eulalia who had declared himself an español when the couple married in 1712.[43]

Men of "inferior" ethnic groups sometimes found their patriarchal authority mocked in even more striking ways. The mulato slave Antonio de Anduaga and his wife Brígida de Ramos lived in Parral early in the eighteenth century, but their story could as easily have occurred in San Felipe. One evening a pesky and arrogant gachupín named Francisco de la Iseca followed Ramos as she went to draw water from the river. After teasing her and tossing stones at her, he hurled her to the ground with the apparent intent of raping her. At that moment Anduaga arrived and pounced on Iseca, calling him a "pícaro" ("rascal") and a "gachupín dog" and wounding him with a rock. Although under most circumstances colonial law recognized a husband's right to defend his wife from sexual attack, local authorities reprimanded Anduaga for daring to assault someone far superior to him in ethnicity and social rank. He spent over three months in jail, paid the costs incurred in his prosecution, and received a stern warning to avoid future demonstrations of disrespect toward Spaniards.[44]

The day-to-day routines of working-class families also limited the effective authority of husbands and fathers. Wives who worked as domestic servants in upper-class households, especially those who did so on a live-in basis, fell under the patriarchal sway of their employers rather than that of their own male relatives.[45] Migration patterns and housing shortages during the early stages of the mining boom also caused many households to deviate from the nuclear family model. Working-class families often supplemented their earnings by taking in boarders from among the hundreds of unattached males looking for lodging. In the eyes of local authorities, the presence of these paying guests often disrupted the peace of the conjugal unit.[46] The quasi-industrial mode of labor organization also undermined male workers' dominion within their households. Men who worked in mining, refining, and many other jobs were gone from home all day. Others stayed away all night, working as watchmen or in the many mines, refineries, bakeries, and other enterprises that operated after dark.[47] Moreover, as we have seen, many workers left their families in the villa of San Felipe all week while they ascended to the mines in Santa Eulalia.

Many married women—and men—thus enjoyed considerable freedom to deviate from prescribed norms of sexual conduct. Juana Mariana de Mena, for example, carried on a protracted affair with a young unmarried cajero while her husband worked in a local refinery.[48] In 1725 Salvador Núñez, a barretero who worked in Santa Eulalia while his family remained in San Felipe, also suspected that his wife was unfaithful in his absence. One evening after work he left Santa Eulalia, arriving home three hours later. He climbed over the wall of a corral to gain access to his house, where he found his wife in bed with a man who boarded with them.[49]

Even if they remained sexually faithful to their husbands, working-class women often exerted substantial control over the day-to-day operations of their households. Responsibility for the routine care and discipline of children obviously fell to them. In many cases too women went directly to the overseers of mines and refineries to collect their husbands' rations, to obtain cash and other items that were then debited to their husbands' accounts, and to negotiate wages and other terms of employment for their grown sons.[50] Married women also approached the authorities to protest mistreatment that their husbands or sons had suffered at the hands of employers or supervisors.[51]

Women's Employment Outside the Home

Significant numbers of married women supplemented their husbands' earnings by pursuing occupations that took them out of the prescribed seclusion of their homes. Some, of course, became cooks or domestic servants in more affluent households. Others worked as midwives or *curanderas* (healers), learning their crafts by word of mouth from their mothers and grandmothers. A few earned small amounts of money wrapping and preparing corpses for burial. Others took in laundry or did sewing for the many bachelors in town.[52] It was especially common for women to prepare meals for the area's many unattached males. Ignacia Gertrudis Benítez was an española, age 22, who supplemented her husband's income in this manner. One of her clients was the irritable Spaniard Benito Godoy, who paid her a single real, plus small amounts of saffron and pepper, for two meals daily.[53] Master saddlemaker Felipe de Escobedo y Robledo explained that with his permission his wife Ana María Sepúlveda had established a *bodegón* (restaurant or inn) in Santa Eulalia, where he evidently assisted her in feeding bachelor merchants.[54] The mulata María Rita García also catered meals; she and her husband, also a free mulato, were servants of assayer José de la Borbolla.[55] Other women, married and single, sold fruit and other foods in the plaza.[56] In rural areas wives often helped with plowing, the tending of livestock, and other chores, and managed ranchos and other properties in their husbands' absences.[57]

Wives of shopkeepers and other petty entrepreneurs routinely assisted in the family business. In the 1720s and 1730s the gachupín Lorenzo Gutiérrez and his wife Juana de Dios Fernández de Lugo owned a bakery, which she reportedly "governed and administered."[58] Other married women operated shops and bakeries more or less on their own, though technically they needed their husbands' consent to do so.[59] Juana Manuela Sarmiento, an illiterate native of Guadalajara and the wife of the carpenter José Raimundo de Castro, was one such merchant. She and her husband had no children, so she was able to devote substantial energy to her business.[60] Rosa María de Salas operated a bakery in Santa Eulalia in the 1720s; she explained that her profits derived exclusively from "my sweat and labor."[61]

Women such as Salas often found it in their interest to make such claims in order to prevent their husbands' creditors from seizing the assets of their businesses. There is no doubt, nevertheless, that many entrepreneurial wives acted on their own in managing their shops and bakeries. These women stood at the center of the elaborate networks of petty credit that facilitated local commerce in eighteenth-century Chihuahua. Rosa María de Salas and other bakers obtained flour and other supplies on credit, while female shopkeepers joined their male counterparts in making loans to the villa's humble residents who pawned items of value. Juana Manuela Sarmiento extended credit to a long list of local vecinos, many of them women. She in turn borrowed from the town's more substantial citizens, including José María Cantelmi, a peninsular merchant who later served as corregidor of Chihuahua. In 1768 Sarmiento even spent a brief time in jail for failure to pay her debts.[62]

Despite the lip service paid to patriarchal ideals, only a handful of elite wives could afford to spend most of their time secluded within the presumably chaste and secure confines of their homes.[63] For women who lacked domestic servants, routine housekeeping duties entailed frequent trips to markets and shops for food and other necessities, and many obtained short-term loans, often from female merchants, to tide them over difficult times. Many women also trudged down to the river at least once a day to haul water to their homes or to do their laundry. Wives of workers managed their households during their husbands' absences and dealt routinely with owners or mayordomos of mines and refineries, while married women who managed shops or bakeries came into daily contact with a wide range of local citizenry. In eighteenth-century Chihuahua and throughout colonial Latin America, female *recogimiento* or seclusion existed more in the rhetoric of clerics and officials than in the everyday routines of most women.

Unmarried Women

If the lives of most married women failed to conform to the prescriptions of the patriarchal ethos, the large numbers of unattached women further undermined its assumptions. Women outnumbered men and played important economic roles in cities and towns in many parts of colonial Spanish America.[64] San Felipe el Real de Chihuahua was no exception. The earliest complete census that we have for the villa dates from 1785, when adult females outnumbered adult males by almost two to one (1,612 women, 826 men). These totals include 436 women designated as widows but only 47 widowers, 345 bachelors and 747 *solteras* (women who had never married). The figures may slightly overstate the adult female majority, because young women may have been counted as adults at an earlier age than young men; the census lists 700 boys and only 590 girls. Still, women outnumbered men by a substantial majority and headed 250 of the villa's 700 households, or just over 35 percent. Although female-headed households tended to be slightly smaller than those headed by men (see Table 6 in the Appendix), approximately 31 percent of San Felipe's residents lived in households headed by women. In Santa Eulalia and in the area's rural settlements, on the other hand, the numbers of men and women tended to be about equal.[65] The preponderance of women in San Felipe continued into the nineteenth century. Among adults over the age of seventeen in 1821, females again outnumbered males, 1,564 to 1,106; these figures included 338 widows and only 61 widowers.[66]

Silvia Arrom points out that colonial and nineteenth-century Mexican censuses often listed a widow as head of her household as a courtesy, when in fact a grown son or other male relative might live with her and exercise de facto authority within the family.[67] Those who counted Chihuahua's population in 1785 seem to have made some kind of determination about power relations in each household they visited. In some cases they listed a woman as head of the household even if an adult male relative resided with her, but in other cases they listed widows as members of households headed by their sons or sons-in-law. In any event, widows who lived with adult male relatives frequently represented the household to the outside world. Even more often than married women, widows negotiated with their sons' employers over wages and credits.[68] Others evidently exercised considerable authority over their sons and sons-in-law. In the 1760s an Apache widow named María Rosa Serrano, known to local residents as "*la frutera*," ("the fruit vendor") maintained a small orchard and sold her produce in the streets of San Felipe. On many occasions she ordered her young son-in-law to run errands for her, sometimes sending him as far as Parral.[69] Meanwhile, many other widows and solteras headed households peopled entirely by minor children or other single women.

Unfortunately, in the absence of earlier censuses, we cannot determine precise sex ratios for the decades prior to 1785. We do know that large numbers of unattached men flocked to Chihuahua to seek their fortunes in the early days of the mining boom, but the evidence suggests that the villa's population included many women who were on their own as well. The municipal archives contain numerous references to women who registered titles to *solares* (parcels of land on which to build houses) in the 1720s and 1730s. Many of these women were evidently of relatively low social status; a few, including one María de la Encarnación, even lacked Spanish surnames.[70] Married women were sometimes abandoned by husbands who left Chihuahua fleeing debts or searching for better opportunities elsewhere. After 1740 the intensification of Indian attacks undoubtedly left many women widowed, while others faced life alone after their husbands went off to serve long terms in frontier presidios. An inventory of a silver refinery in 1753 lists the humble shacks occupied by workers and others resident on the property, together with the name of the head of household occupying each dwelling; several of those enumerated were women.[71]

With the notable exception of María Rosa Ortiz de Campos, widow of Juan Antonio Trasviña y Retes, few unmarried women figured among Chihuahua's economic elite.[72] The most prosperous widows usually remarried within a matter of months. For example, the alférez real and wealthy miner José de Aguirre died in September of 1728; in February of the following year his widow Nicolasa de Orio y Zubiate, daughter of the late General José de Orio y Zubiate, wed Juan de Urrutia.[73] In a similar case, María Josefa Dosal became a widow in January of 1748 upon the death of her husband, former alcalde José Velarde Cosío. Within eighteen months she married Antonio Gutiérrez del Castillo, another prominent peninsular immigrant.[74]

Very few unmarried women owned mines or refineries in Chihuahua. In his inspection tour of 1716 Governor Manuel San Juan y Santa Cruz listed one Diega Núñez as proprietor of a refinery and a shop, and other sources suggest that she may have also owned a mine. Existing documents fail to reveal her marital status.[75] A few other women dabbled in mining. In 1727 the widow Andrea de Govea, a vecina of Santa Eulalia, registered a modest claim that she intended her three sons to work.[76] In 1766 Manuela Mouriño, daughter of the scribe Isidro Mouriño and one of a handful of women in eighteenth-century Chihuahua able to sign her name, owned a share in a silver mine as well. She had been a widow for at least 25 years.[77]

For the most part, however, widows and solteras supported themselves and their families by pursuing occupations similar to those of their married counterparts. Ana María Suárez was a widow whose husband had been a slave. In 1763 she opened a bodegón that catered to mine workers.[78] Numerous single women also established bakeries in San Felipe and in Santa Eulalia. The española María Teresa de Rivera was married at least twice, once to a soldier and later to a man who worked variously as a tailor and a rescatador, but she supported herself during her widowhood by running a bakery in San Felipe.[79] The widow María Josefa Alvidres supported herself and her "dilatada familia" ("large family") with the proceeds of her bakery in the 1730s.[80] An enterprising slave named Isabel María set aside money to purchase her freedom from the profits of her bakery. She bought flour, sugar, and other supplies on credit from local merchants, and even entered into a kind of limited partnership with another female slave who supplied her with 100 pesos, presumably in return for a promised share of the bakery's earnings.[81]

Several women known collectively to townspeople as "Las Rosareñas" (a nickname that presumably denoted their geographical origins in the town of Nuestra Señora del Rosario in Nueva Galicia) also operated bakeries over the course of several decades, beginning in the 1720s.[82] María de Alcaraz y Rentería, an illiterate soltera originally from Nuestra Señora del Rosario, probably belonged to this group. The first documentary reference to her bakery dates from 1736. From then until her death in 1769, she continued in business, selling bread and other supplies at her modest tienda. Unlike many other female bakers, she evidently had some access to the villa's elite; her sister was married to the baker, merchant, and cabildo member Pedro Antonio Cadrecha. As a token of respect, her fellow vecinos addressed her with the honorific title Doña, and from time to time authorities confined errant women in her bakery for discipline and correction.[83]

Single women, and to a lesser extent some of their married counterparts, often escaped the scrutiny of husbands, fathers, or other male authority figures as they went about their daily routines. In another sense, however, they could not ignore the fact that they lived in a society whose governing principles rested solidly on assumptions of patriarchal supremacy and female fragility. Local clerics and civil officials therefore enjoined widows and solteras to adhere to all of the prescribed norms governing women's behavior, especially with regard to their sexual conduct. Indeed, sometimes officials held widows to even stricter standards than other women. For example, a widow who allowed a couple to use her home for an adulterous rendezvous received a more severe penalty than the woman involved in the affair.[84] At the same time female heads of households were supposed to exert authority similar to that of male patriarchs over their children and servants, policing their morals and administering corporal punishment when warranted.[85] Unattached women who ran afoul of any of these societal expectations faced numerous difficulties in conducting their businesses and managing their households.

Juana de Cobos

The remarkable biography of Juana de Cobos provides telling insights on the status of female heads of households in colonial Chihuahua. She belonged to a family of relatively poor españoles whom we first met in Chapter 2. Her life spanned virtually the entire eighteenth century; she was born in El Valle de San Bartolomé in 1706 and died in San Felipe in 1797.[86] She married Juan Muñoz de Olvera in San Bartolomé in 1722, and in the 1730s they settled in Chihuahua along with several of their children. Sometime over the next several years the couple began living apart, although they evidently failed to obtain a church-sanctioned separation. Existing documents reveal no trace of Juan's doings thereafter, except to imply that he remained in San Felipe.[87] By the early 1740s Cobos had established a bakery, using the proceeds to support six children and a number of grandchildren for several decades to come. Although she evidently never learned to read or write, she became a familiar figure in local commerce. Her name appears in scores of documents dealing with the bread trade in colonial Chihuahua.[88]

Like many other women, Juana found managing a bakery to be hard work. She invested what to her was a substantial amount of capital in her ovens and other equipment and relied on elaborate credit arrangements to obtain necessary supplies. Much of the labor was performed at night, so that she could deliver fresh bread to local shopkeepers early each morning. Cobos and other women who operated bakeries then faced the task of collecting sums owed them by their customers. Meanwhile, she supervised a staff of three or more servants, including Indians "ransomed" from New Mexico. She disciplined her workers when they did not perform as expected yet extended credit to them in an effort to hold them to their jobs. She also endured constant scrutiny from cabildo officers who regularly reprimanded bakers for failure to adhere to established schedules for the price of bread.[89]

Competing with male bakers probably posed the greatest challenge for Cobos and other women, however. Female bakers' retail outlets were seldom as imposing as those of the peninsular immigrants who dominated the local bread trade. These men enjoyed substantial economic advantages because they could afford to buy supplies in bulk and benefit from other economies of scale.[90] The most successful of them participated in merchants' juntas and a few, like Pedro Antonio Cadrecha, even gained positions on the cabildo. Meanwhile, they accorded women only the most marginal of places within the town's loosely organized bakers' guild. While they expected female bakers to help defray the expenses of comedies and other activities staged by the organization on ritual occasions, they never allowed women any voice in planning these events, and they were quick to criticize any woman who proved too assertive for their taste.

Over the years Juana de Cobos earned a reputation among the town's prosperous male bakers for being outspoken and often uncooperative and for encouraging other women to follow her example. In 1748 she resisted paying her assessment to help underwrite the comedy planned by the bakers to commemorate the coronation of King Fernando VI. Pedro Antonio Cadrecha thereupon complained to the cabildo that she and other females, also delinquent in their dues, had employed impolite language and frivolous pretexts in explaining why they had not paid.[91] Cobos also evidently led the way in breaking bread prices in 1760, underselling her competitors and eventually forcing them to lower their prices.[92] She was also the only woman among dozens of vecinos asked to contribute funds to help attract a trained physician to the villa. She demurred, citing her own lack of funds as well as the fact that previous efforts to secure a doctor had been unsuccessful.[93]

Juana de Cobos not only violated accepted norms of female submissiveness in her business activities, her personal life came under the critical scrutiny of her neighbors as well. Her decision to live apart from her husband automatically made her suspect in the eyes of local authorities. Women who refused to live with their spouses could expect some kind of official inquiry about their situation.[94] Cobos paid lip service to the notion that married women required their husbands' permission to operate businesses or to engage in other financial or legal transactions. In 1753, for example, she presented a petition to the alcalde demanding payment for 25 pesos' worth of bread that she had supplied on credit to a local shopkeeper. She explained in her complaint that she conducted her business with her husband's blessing but without any assistance from him.[95]

In most other respects, however, she acted as if Juan Muñoz de Olvera played no part in her life at all. It is possible also that in her early to mid-forties she had an illegitimate daughter. A little girl died in San Felipe in June of 1755; parish registers list her parents as Juana de Cobos and the español Crisóstomo Domínguez.[96] Meanwhile, Juana's grown daughter Mariana Muñoz emulated her mother's lifestyle. Born in 1725 in El Valle de San Bartolomé, Mariana was the second child of Cobos and Juan Muñoz de Olvera. In 1746 she married Juan José de Arroyo in Chihuahua.[97] Six years later they had separated, however, and Mariana and her two children had taken up residence with her mother.[98]

A seemingly trivial dispute that occurred in 1752 reveals not only the marginal position of two assertive women who flouted prevailing patriarchal norms but also the ways in which concepts of honor and ethnicity came into play in the daily contacts of different groups in local society.[99] On the evening of September 3, Mariana happened to walk past the home of Josefa García de Noriega. A recent widow, García de Noriega was about to marry Miguel Mayor Rico de Cuesta, a peninsular merchant in his mid-thirties who had arrived in Chihuahua from his native Burgos several years earlier.[100] Although he never held office on the cabildo, he definitely belonged in the ranks of the villa's respected vecinos. In 1759, for example, he was summoned to a cabildo abierto.[101]

Sitting in the window of his fiancee's home that September evening, Mayor Rico noticed Mariana as she passed by. He called out to her, laughing and asking her where she had gotten the new chintz garments she was wearing—and openly suggesting that she had traded her sexual favors for new clothes. Mariana retorted with an insult of her own, calling Mayor Rico a *cochino* (pig) and his mother a whore.

Evidently she returned a few hours later and continued the quarrel. Meanwhile her brother learned of the incident and reported it to their mother. Juana de Cobos immediately hurried over to García de Noriega's house, forcing her way into the principal parlor and joining her daughter in insulting the personal honor of García de Noriega and her female servants, suggesting pointedly that the widow failed to observe proper feminine seclusion or recogimiento. Only with the help of several neighbors did García de Noriega finally succeed in ejecting the pair from her home.

The next morning García de Noriega filed a criminal complaint against the two "alborotadoras y escandalosas" ("troublesome and scandalous") women. She presented witnesses who routinely referred to Cobos as a mulata, even though parish registers and most other documents regularly listed her and her children as españoles. Others stressed Juana's quarrelsome nature, pointing out that she had had a similar argument in recent weeks with a woman named María Josefa de Armendáriz. Several witnesses also asserted that Cobos had left El Valle de San Bartolomé in disgrace, expelled for her scandalous behavior.

Summoned to answer the charges against her, Juana de Cobos boldly proclaimed that the insults of Mayor Rico and García de Noriega had brought unwarranted discredit to her own reputation as a married woman. She also pointed out that Mayor Rico's vicious taunts had provoked the incident. She explained that she had had previous arguments with Mayor Rico; on one occasion he had refused to sell her a particular item when she had entered his shop. Still, Cobos knew that she faced a losing battle. She understood that as a peninsular Spaniard Mayor Rico was well connected to other powerful figures in the villa. When he and García de Noriega eventually married in December of 1752, their *padrinos* or sponsors were Micaela Gerónima Trasviña, daughter of Juan Antonio Trasviña y Retes, and her husband José Antonio de Uranga—who was none other than the alcalde handling the case![102]

Uranga's ruling, issued just a few weeks before the wedding of García de Noriega and Mayor Rico, therefore came as no surprise to Juana de Cobos. Hoping to prevent further friction between the quarreling parties, the alcalde ordered her to move to a more distant part of town and avoid passing García de Noriega's house in the future. Cobos vigorously protested that compliance would entail serious financial hardships for herself and her family. She anticipated considerable difficulty in finding another house close enough to her established clientele and equipped with a sufficiently large oven. Constructing a new one would cost a prohibitive 40 pesos or more. Even if she did find acceptable facilities, she expected her rent to rise considerably. Meanwhile, Mariana's husband appeared in Chihuahua just long enough to scoff at Uranga's dictum and urge the women to defy it before he left town again.

Arguments and counterarguments continued into 1753, but Uranga's successor proved no more sympathetic to Cobos. In fact, the new alcalde became so convinced of her "perverse nature" that he decided to order her exiled from San Felipe. He stressed the importance of using Cobos and Muñoz as examples to other women who might commit similar excesses while claiming the deference due to married women. Again Juana protested, arguing that she would lose all of the amounts owed her by customers and workers if she had to leave town. She also implicitly cited her own social standing in explaining the origins of her quarrel with María Josefa de Armendáriz. Cobos's son had become involved with a woman of low calidad, she claimed, and Armendáriz had evidently interfered with her efforts to put an end to the affair. Although Cobos was eventually allowed to remain in San Felipe, she did relocate her residence to the outskirts of town. She subsequently reported that her volume of business had deteriorated substantially since the move. Whereas formerly she had used between five and seven *quintales* (hundred-weights) of flour per day, by February of 1753 she was using about half that amount.

Defeat in this particular case did not daunt as determined a woman as Juana de Cobos. She remained one of the villa's most prominent bakers for many years to come, and enjoyed a certain degree of respect from her fellow townspeople. At least some documents—even a few dating from the year of her fight with García de Noriega and Mayor Rico—accord her the honorific title of Doña.[103] In 1769 Alcade Francisco Duro, a peninsular well connected to other members of the villa's elite, even considered Cobos's bakery a worthy place in which to confine and discipline other women accused of sexual misconduct.[104] Although her name is missing from a list of bakers cited in an official investigation of the bread trade conducted in 1772, she still employed a number of workers in 1780.[105] In contrast to most other official records, which listed her as an española, the census of 1785 enumerated Juana de Cobos as the 80-year-old mestiza widow of Juan Muñoz. At that time she headed a household that included six adult males, most of whom were probably servants of some sort.[106] Perhaps in her last years Juana de Cobos took consolation in the fact that she had outlived both of her adversaries of 1752. García de Noriega died sometime before 1779, while Mayor Rico lived until 1790.[107] Even in death she claimed a measure of deference; she was buried "with a large cross" in December of 1797, and the parish register lists her as Doña one last time. Her burial listing notes, in parentheses, that she was the widow of Don Juan Muñoz.[108]

Juana's children also earned spots, if not among the local elite, at least among those who enjoyed the esteem of some of the town's more respectable citizens. In 1766 her son Gregorio Antonio, who often assisted her in managing the bakery, formed a business partnership with the scribe Juan Antonio Mariño de Cadaval, who was probably a peninsular.[109] One Dolores Muñoz, who shared with Cobos the nickname of "La Vallera" (connoting origins in El Valle de San Bartolomé), was probably her daughter. Dolores married Domingo Antonio Noriega (presumably no relation of Josefa García de Noriega), a Spaniard from Burgos; Juana's children Gregorio Antonio and Mariana served as godparents for a child born to them in 1758.[110] If Dolores was indeed Juana's daughter, she also shared her mother's reputation for a feisty temperament. In 1766 local authorities investigated a quarrel between her and another woman who resided in the villa.[111] Documents from the early nineteenth century also refer to a baker named Victoria Muñoz de Rivera—perhaps the scribe meant to write "Muñoz de Olvera"—who might have been Juana's granddaughter but in any event followed her example. In 1816 her male competitors, one of them a peninsular Spaniard, accused her of violating municipal ordinances governing the price of bread. They asked the cabildo to order her bakery closed and commented on her "depravado ánimo" ("depraved spirit") when she resisted.[112]

Although she ultimately prevailed in some measure, throughout her lifetime Juana de Cobos faced considerable obstacles in operating her business and earning the esteem of her fellow vecinos. Any objective reading of the documents from the 1752 dispute suggests that Miguel Mayor Rico and his fiancee were at least as much to blame for the altercation as Cobos or her daughter, but she alone suffered adverse consequences. Though usually regarded as española, she ranked lower in social status than García de Noriega or Mayor Rico and lacked their connections to powerful figures in the villa.

Patriarchy and Women's Autonomy

Juana de Cobos's deviation from customary patriarchal norms further damaged her case and provided a readily comprehensible basis for any and all attacks upon her. While local officials could scarcely overlook the large numbers of unattached women who lived in the villa, they expected such women not only to display proper sexual decorum but also to assume the posture of helpless females, dependent on the paternal benevolence of the cabildo and the charity of their fellow vecinos. Scribes who wrote petitions on behalf of women invariably stressed their clients' vulnerability, presumably because they understood that such requests were more likely to find favor from men in power. A widow might ask for pity by calling herself a "pobre viuda desamparada" ("poor destitute widow"), for example.[113] Even married women found it advantageous to stress their weakness if they suddenly became responsible for the welfare of their families. When María de la Encarnación Romero brought charges against another man who had assaulted and temporarily disabled her husband, her petition mentioned that she was burdened with children and without assistance—"mujer al fin" ("a woman, after all"), and as such ignorant of the intricacies of the judicial system and at the mercy of those in power.[114]

Women who rejected this image of feminine weakness in favor of the sturdy, self-reliant model offered by Juana de Cobos found their personal conduct subject to minute scrutiny and risked punitive action for any and all infractions. Juana Anaclita Carrillo, who catered food to a group of soldiers during her husband's absence, was accused of having an affair with one of them. One afternoon in 1772 Alcalde Pedro Nicolás Cadrecha came to her house in San Felipe, tied her up, and led her off to jail. When she succeeded in escaping, Cadrecha issued warrants for her arrest and warned authorities in Santa Eulalia to be on the lookout for her. A short time later he apprehended Carrillo again, temporarily jailing her mother as well, and reportedly dealing them a generous dose of verbal abuse as he took them into custody. Carrillo then received a beating for her behavior. Afterward Cadrecha explained that it was necessary to restrain her because she hosted all-night fandangos in violation of municipal ordinances and otherwise scandalized the villa's citizenry.[115]

Authorities clearly preferred to return troublesome women to their husbands or fathers for "correction," but they entertained few qualms about forcibly confining females who lacked male relatives capable of "reducing" them to acceptable behavior. Most commonly they resorted to the familiar tactic of "depositing" women in respectable households, usually but not always headed by men. Throughout colonial Mexico, civil and ecclesiastical officials used the practice of *depósito* to remove women from all manner of undesirable situations. Women of unblemished reputation might be placed in the protective custody of households other than their own if they needed shelter from abusive husbands or relief from family members attempting to exert undue influence on their choice of marriage partners. But everywhere authorities also considered the properly ordered household as a suitable vehicle for monitoring and controlling the behavior of recalcitrant females.[116]

The household as refuge and reformatory for women assumed particular importance in areas such as Chihuahua, which lacked the institutional alternatives of convents and *recogimientos de mujeres* (protective and corrective shelters for women) available in Mexico City and other large urban centers.[117] Authorities in San Felipe certainly utilized the coercive infrastructure available to them, however. As we have seen, women sometimes faced incarceration, and indeed the villa's jail had special quarters reserved for women being held for questioning in criminal cases. In 1750 María Manuela Corral spent more than seven months in solitary confinement while authorities investigated her husband's death, allegedly at the hands of a peninsular Spaniard with whom she had been having an affair. She was allowed to leave her cell only on Sundays, when bailiffs escorted her downstairs to hear mass.[118]

Women as well as men who threatened the stability of local society also faced terms of involuntary servitude, during which they would supposedly learn to contain their unruly behavior. Men alone risked being posted to frontier presidios or ordered to work in silver refineries as punishment for their misconduct, but working-class people of both sexes were often confined and forced to work in bakeries. On occasion, too, women were sent to the obraje at Encinillas or that of San Felipe, though all of those interned at the the latter factory in

1810 were men.[119] Whether sent to a bakery, an obraje, or a private household, most women detained for disciplinary reasons were expected to work. Only women of high standing, who were placed in households of local officials and other social peers, escaped domestic chores during their confinement. Those of lower rank routinely served as maids and cooks in the houses that accepted them.[120] Even female prisoners held in the town jail were ordered to grind maize and prepare meals for male prisoners.[121]

The case of María Antonia de la Cruz was typical. In 1768 she was convicted of attempting to kill her husband, reportedly because he had continually mistreated her and bartered her sexual favors to other men. Interim Corregidor Antonio Gutiérrez del Castillo found her guilty and ordered her to undergo public humiliation and a beating in the town plaza, with a placard detailing her crime to be placed around her neck. When it became obvious that she was pregnant, Gutiérrez del Castillo lifted these penalties but nonetheless prescribed her placement in a bakery or other "house of service." Eventually she ended up in the household of the villa's jailer, who was to supervise her "Christian education" so that "her eyes might be opened to her blind passion."[122]

Local officials clearly viewed the deposit of females in bakeries and households as a form of incarceration. In 1712 María de Marmolejo, a mulata whose husband was absent, was having an affair with Manuel Molina. After Molina wounded her in a fit of jealousy and then fled Santa Eulalia, the teniente placed her in a household where she was to work, with her wages going to pay the surgeon who had treated her injuries. The teniente ordered her not to leave this *carcelería* (confinement) on pain of 200 lashes.[123] María Terrazas, whose husband had been missing for a decade, allegedly scandalized the community with her immoral behavior. In 1725 ecclesiastical and civil authorities joined forces to deposit Terrazas and her daughters in the "cárcel" ("prison") of Antonio Escobedo's home.[124]

Men in authority were likely to question the sexual conduct of, and find excuses to punish, any self-supporting woman who challenged prescribed norms of female submission. During the height of the mining boom the mulata Josefa de San Diego and her three daughters operated a catering business, but detractors claimed that it provided a front for prostitution and that the four women served as madams for españolas who sold their sexual favors. Their scandalous behavior reportedly aroused considerable murmuring among townswomen whose husbands patronized these services. Cabildo officials repeatedly cautioned the four to live honestly, but were unable to persuade them to change their ways. Finally in 1730 they conducted a thorough investigation, proceeding discreetly in order to protect the identities of "respectable" vecinos who might have been involved. They then ordered Josefa de San Diego and her daughters banished from Chihuahua, justifying their action on the grounds that the mulatas were not in fact vecinas of San Felipe. Although the women initially complied, within a short time they returned to the villa. Cabildo officials promptly ordered them jailed, beaten, and personally escorted to El Paso del Norte, more than 200 miles to the north.[125]

In fact, charges of sexual impropriety and even prostitution lurked just beneath the surface in virtually any prosecution of a woman, whether or not the case had anything to do with sexuality. A woman questioned about her possible complicity in the theft of ore was turned over to the custody of her aunt, who received strict admonitions to keep her *recogida* (literally, secluded, but usually implying separation from temptations of the flesh).[126] Juana Efigenia Gutiérrez was an española and a middle-aged widow who lived with her teenage daughter. The two women evidently supported themselves by sewing for bachelors in town. One evening one of their customers, a peninsular named Diego Godoy, stopped by their home to chat. While he was there another man sought him out. A quarrel ensued between the two men, and Godoy ended up killing his adversary. Local officials ruled the killing accidental but banished Godoy from town to avoid future disturbances. Although Gutiérrez and her daughter were detained briefly for questioning, records of the investigation contain no evidence that they were accused of any wrongdoing, sexual or otherwise. Nevertheless, cabildo authorities concluded the case with a warning to the two women to live "honestly and secluded." If they were involved in any such incident in the future, they would face "prosecution without mercy."[127]

Although authorities were quick to accuse recalcitrant females of organized prostitution, in fact most women who bartered their sexuality appear to have done so on an ad hoc, one-to-one basis. To be sure, male relatives might coerce women into sexual relations with other men and pocket the proceeds themselves. But women on their own were largely free to negotiate the terms of the bargain for themselves. For whatever reason, local officials in Chihuahua declined to set up legalized brothels like those that existed in early modern Spain and in some of the colonies' larger cities. Whether or not this decision reduced the traffic in sexual favors, it deprived the authorities of a chance to control and contain prostitution within limits defined by men, except, of course, in those cases where they succeeded in apprehending and prosecuting a woman for her freelance trade.[128] Women who emulated the self-reliant example of Juana de Cobos remained substantially in control of their own sexuality and its "market" value, and it is little wonder that men in authority focused so often on the possibility that such women might exploit that situation to their own advantage.

Patriarchy and Single Men

For local authorities, women who rejected patriarchal authority seriously threatened the already fragile order of a multiracial frontier society. At the same time, these officials had to ponder the potentially disruptive effects of the large numbers of males whose living arrangements and personal behavior also failed to conform to prescribed notions of proper domesticity. Lower-class men often lived as boarders in other workers' homes or in the makeshift huts that surrounded the mines in Santa Eulalia. Some petty merchants, like the disagreeable Benito Godoy, lived alone, while others resided with other males, sometimes related to them but in any case similar to them in social status. José Fernández de Hinojosa and Salvador de Lemus, both peninsular merchants who later married and served as alcaldes, lived together in the early 1730s, as did Juan and Fernando de Pruneda, merchants from Asturias. All of these men had meals delivered to their homes by the infamous José Lorenzo Graciano, alias Chico.[129]

The villa's more prosperous bachelors added servants to their households. The merchant Francisco Calderón lived with four male servants, three of them españoles and the fourth a "ransomed" Indian. Calderón once stated that he and his sirvientes customarily gathered in the evening to recite the rosary together.[130] The Spaniard Juan Gordillo de Toro, a miner and owner of a refinery, headed a similar household that included two male mulato slaves, an Apache *indizuelo* (youngster), and an elderly Apache woman.[131]

Local officials certainly prosecuted single men whose sexual exploits proved disruptive to peace in the community, and they issued decrees that supposedly banished the most troublesome offenders from San Felipe and its environs. As we have seen, from time to time authorities also ordered men to return home if they had abandoned their wives in Spain or elsewhere in Mexico. Men found it fairly easy to sidestep most of these measures. Employers who hesitated to dismiss workers who ran up enormous debts or habitually skipped work on Mondays could hardly be expected to support official efforts to remove workers from the area as punishment for sexual improprieties. Thus a sentence of exile imposed on the barretero Manuel Morales for an illicit affair carried a proviso that suspended the penalty if he owed anything to his employer, who was none other than Manuel San Juan y Santa Cruz.[132]

Men also evaded orders to leave the jurisdiction by arguing that their military roles in fighting hostile Indians required their continued presence in Chihuahua.[133] Indeed, military service evidently furnished a pretext to excuse all manner of unacceptable conduct. Tomás Luis de Vera y Maraber was an itinerant merchant in his late forties who had left behind a wife in Seville to seek his fortune in northern New Spain. He had an affair with a married woman that lasted over a year, until he finally killed her husband in May of 1750. He fled to Sonora, where he fought against the Pima and Seri Indian uprisings. He eventually returned to Chihuahua and cited his military service as evidence that he had rendered proper retribution for his crimes.[134]

Men of any substance could use their business affairs or other obligations as an excuse to delay compliance with official orders to return to their wives. Domingo Cuarón Leyva y Santa Bárbara, a former captain in the Manila galleons who opened a shop in San Felipe in the early 1720s, had left his wife in Pavia, Italy, more than six years earlier to seek his fortune in the New World. Ordered to depart for Veracruz within eight days to return to her, he explained that he needed more time to liquidate his inventory at fair prices and to pay off debts to suppliers in Chihuahua, Parral, and Mexico City. Surviving documents do not indicate whether or not he eventually returned to Europe, but he managed to remain in Chihuahua for several years after being told to leave.[135] In 1735 Blas de Seda, a peninsular merchant whose wife resided in the diocese of Puebla in central Mexico, used similar arguments to avoid returning to her.

Governor Juan José Vertiz y Ontañón tried to facilitate matters by ordering Seda's many creditors to come forward and legally acknowledge their debts, but he evidently remained in Chihuahua for years to come without ever complying with the governor's decree. His name appears in parish registers and other documents as late as 1742, but nowhere is the presence of a wife mentioned.[136]

Single men of any social standing also apparently received the benefit of the doubt with regard to their sexual transgressions, especially if they involved women of inferior status. As we have seen, Regidor Francisco de Salcido flouted accepted norms with impunity. In the late 1720s and early 1730s the peninsular cashier Miguel Jiménez de Leorín had a long-standing affair with a light-skinned mulata named María de Guadalupe, whom he employed as his cook. He reportedly paid her rent and subsidized the numerous fandangos that she hosted. He also instructed local merchants to debit his account for any clothing she wanted; watchful vecinos reported that as a result she went about town adorned in finery far too elegant for her humble station in life. Local authorities evidently failed to pressure the couple to marry, and they chose to discipline María de Guadalupe rather than Jiménez de Leorín. They ordered her exiled from the villa, while he remained.[137] Although he never held public office, his fellow citizens held him in sufficient esteem that they invited him to sign the petition demanding the ouster of Corregidor Sánchez Camacho in 1731. He remained in San Felipe until his death in 1751, and there is no evidence that he ever married.[138]

As we have seen, men who failed to marry were less likely to be elected to local office or be counted among the socially responsible citizens summoned to cabildos abiertos and other civic gatherings, and relatively few bachelors ranked among the most prosperous mining entrepreneurs and merchants of San Felipe.[139] Nevertheless, the presence of servants or subordinate relatives within their households enabled some single men to exercise patriarchal authority comparable to that wielded by those who were married. Mindful of what he called "the zeal with which an hombre de bien should see to the government of his home and family," bachelor merchant Martín de Echaquibel carefully supervised the conduct of the two female servants he employed.[140]

Single men, especially those who possessed any property or skilled trade, bore many of the "obligations" that conferred respectability in local society. They could point to their faithful execution of the duties inherent in their occupations, and those with any financial resources could mention their prompt and responsible payment of debts. Men who headed households of any size could also cite their duty to govern those who lived with them. In other words, a man did not need a wife to claim status as an hombre de bien.

The "Obligations" of Women

Behavioral expectations for women, on the other hand, revolved around their relationship to men—obedience for those who lived in patriarchal households, an unrealistic seclusion for those who did not. Eighteenth-century documents suggest that the concept of "obligations" and its associated validation of personal honor pertained much more often to men than to women. As we have seen, working-class men could at least cite the duties inherent in their occupations and earn respect literally by the sweat of their brows. The more affluent could point also to their punctual payment of debts and their civic responsibilities, and men of any status could in theory claim a certain degree of community respect by fulfilling their commitments as husbands and fathers. Although businesswomen were certainly expected to pay their debts, the rhetorical concept of female obligations dealt exclusively with the conduct prescribed for wives, who were to remain sexually faithful to their husbands, uphold the honor of their households, and perform normal domestic tasks.[141] At most a wife might be her husband's "companion in honorable occupations."[142]

Only in very exceptional circumstances did the notion of obligations extend to unattached women, and even in these cases the documents suggest that women's obligations centered on observance of proper sexual conduct. In 1730, for example, Francisco Lecumberri faced prosecution for having an affair with a widow described as "a young woman with obligations," although the documents do not indicate the nature of those commitments.[143] Similarly, in 1735 local authorities chastised a middle-aged shopkeeper named Juan de Mendoza for impregnating a young girl who was "of calidad and obligations."[144]

The only officially acknowledged duties for women not directly related to their sexual conduct and subordination to men centered on their roles as mothers. Maternal responsibilities sometimes gained women a reprieve from the consequences of their misconduct. Pregnant women escaped beatings and public humiliations, and mothers were sometimes released from jail to attend to their families. In 1772, for example, several men and women were jailed on charges of theft. The women were released after they testified so that they could care for their children, while the men remained in custody throughout the investigation.[145] In other cases, however, authorities might disregard a woman's maternal duties and focus on her sexual conduct as the only "obligation" that really mattered. Petra de Sosa was a widow living in rural San José de Julimes in 1732. On reports that she was carrying on an illicit affair, the local teniente ordered her jailed, separating her from her three children for more than six months.[146]

Obligations incumbent on women, whether married or single, generally excluded any relationship with the world outside their own households. Men, in contrast, had public responsibilities regardless of their social class. Local authorities expected men to work and focused considerable attention on ways to compel them to do so, because men's labor produced profits for their employers. Female idleness as such never provoked the same kind of official concern. As we have seen, most women held in "deposit" were required to work, but this was primarily because useful labor would teach them proper submission and subdue their unruly impulses, not because their labor held much economic value. However much men depended on women to prepare their meals, care for their children, and manage petty retail establishments, prevailing ideology in Chihuahua largely ignored the worth of women's labor in household and marketplace alike. Although the Bourbon monarchs of the late eighteenth century and their deputies in New Spain had begun to recognize the potential contributions of women in the labor force, these attitudes found few adherents on the northern frontier of New Spain. In 1810 local leaders briefly entertained the idea of establishing a cigar factory in San Felipe and opening its doors to male and female workers alike, but, as we shall see in the Conclusion, their major concern was social control, not economic utility.[147] By the time these new ideas gained currency in Madrid and Mexico City, Chihuahua had already entered its cycle of economic decline. In the troubled times of the late colonial period, the leaders of San Felipe found it increasingly difficult to find profitable uses for the men in their community. They therefore had few incentives to experiment with putting women's energies to productive economic purposes.

As a result, the productive contributions of women like Juana de Cobos went largely unrecognized. Cobos played a variety of public roles, arguably more than any other female in eighteenth-century Chihuahua. She operated a business for several decades, stood at the center of an intricate network of credit, contributed to the villa's food supply, employed several people, supported a large household, and helped underwrite community festivities. Yet her petitions for fair treatment in the dispute with Miguel Mayor Rico never invoked these roles in the way that men's petitions routinely cited their work, business, and civic obligations along with their familial responsibilities. Instead, Cobos based her claim to greater respect on her age (46) and her status as a married woman. Behavioral expectations for women thus remained firmly rooted in centuries-old attitudes that linked personal honor with family honor. Norms applied to men also stressed the fulfillment of their duties as husbands, fathers, and heads of households, but new obligations of the marketplace offered them supplementary avenues to deference and esteem, even if popular insults remained firmly grounded in references to sexual conduct.[148]

Like most other people in most other times and places, the men and women of eighteenth-century Chihuahua sought at least a modicum of material comfort and personal dignity for themselves and those for whom they cared. An individual's prospects for success in reaching these objectives depended heavily on calidad, an amalgam of class, ethnicity, and personal honor, the latter based largely on one's reputed adherence to gender-specific norms of behavior. Assembling an optimal combination of these components was no easy task for anyone, male or female, who ranked below the town's acknowledged elite. Women who by choice or by force of circumstance lived outside the confines of patriarchal households faced especially difficult challenges in this regard. In effect, they attempted to put together the complicated jigsaw puzzle known as calidad while missing one of its most crucial pieces. Unlike unmarried men, they could not claim economic or civic responsibilities in place of fulfillment of their obligations as wives.

Social Negotiation and the Rules of Patriarchy

As we have seen, eighteenth-century Chihuahua was a society in which certain social boundaries were flexible and many norms governing interpersonal relations remained subject to varying interpretations. Even the well-articulated rules that supposedly confined sexuality to marriage and placed all women under the direct supervision of male heads of households in fact found little consistent adherence in San Felipe and Santa Eulalia. Still, clear and seemingly immutable biological boundaries separated males from females, and the ethos of patriarchy allowed less room for negotiation than those standards that purportedly upheld the status quo in matters of class and ethnicity.

For example, prevailing political philosophy provided workers with a rhetorical tool with which to challenge the existing distribution of wealth. When striking mine workers of the early 1730s repeated the familiar refrain, "Viva el rey y muera el mal gobierno" ("Long live the king and death to bad government"), they in effect implied that if the King of Spain were to climb the twisted paths leading to the mines of Santa Eulalia he would sympathize with them rather than with the likes of Manuel San Juan y Santa Cruz or his allies in local government. One might argue that His Majesty had even greater reason to support the ambitious entrepreneurs who filled the royal coffers with tax revenues—provided, of course, that they could be compelled to pay their rightful share—and that he took as given the notion that some people should toil for others. But Spanish ideology still cast the king as a pious and benevolent ruler interested in the welfare of all his subjects, even down to those of humble station. Meanwhile, the rules that supposedly dictated appropriate conduct and privileges for each of the colony's ethnic groups provided an equivalent opening for those of lower status to question the pretenses of their putative social betters. As we have seen, elites grounded their assertions of precedence in the presumption of their own moral superiority. In so doing they gave others an opportunity to claim better treatment if they adhered to the behavioral norms stipulated for them by officials of church and state.

Although we might debate the practical utility of these loopholes for most people, the rules of gender allowed even less flexibility of interpretation. Women who chafed under the restrictive code of patriarchy could hardly argue that King Felipe V might ratify their bids for greater autonomy if he could only step into their kitchens, their bedrooms, or even their bakeries—not when His Majesty received precise indoctrination on the propriety of feminine submission from the Sun King himself. Nor could women win reprieve from the constraints of patriarchal restrictions by citing their superior virtue. For women, correct behavior won them a certain amount of deference and respect, and more benign treatment within the existing set of rules that allocated privilege and responsibility according to gender, but not the freedom to alter the rules in any meaningful way. The lifestyle of Juana de Cobos clearly flouted those standards, and perhaps she and women like her passed many a day free from obvious intrusions of patriarchal authority. But whenever they faced a challenge to their reputations and their livelihoods, they could invoke no alternative ideology in their defense. At most they could point to whatever elements of the patriarchal prescription they in fact observed—in Juana's case, the fact that she was, after all, a married woman. In other words, patriarchy furnished a relatively stable, non-negotiable set of governing principles even when all other rules came into question.

Conclusion: Chihuahua and Colonial Mexico

THE FOREGOING chapters have described how the men and women of eighteenth-century Chihuahua made crucial decisions as they set up a new community on the Nueva Vizcaya frontier. As we have seen, a handful of peninsulares who figured among the first settlers of San Felipe and Santa Eulalia exerted paramount influence over the collective decisions being reached. Their connections to the colonial bureaucracy and to financial networks in Mexico City and Guadalajara enabled them to make their fortunes and capture control of local government. These economic and political resources strengthened their hand in labor negotiations and afforded them strong and sturdy vehicles in which to ferry their favorite cultural "baggage" to the northern frontier. The most pretentious among them brought elegant lace and taffeta, their coaches and coachmen, and wigs that might have graced an elegant court in Europe, but the European immigrants also effectively transported their conception of how a society should be organized. Peninsulares laid out a town that matched their vision of a properly ordered community, then built a church worthy of a much larger Spanish municipality and claimed their positions on its most prestigiously situated pews. Meanwhile, they determined the calendar and content of ritual observance in the emerging villa of San Felipe el Real.

The immigrants also succeeded in forming new social and familial networks to replace the ones they had left behind in Spain. Facing the unfamiliar and unsettling social landscape of Nueva Vizcaya—the hostile Indians and the multihued representatives of Mexico's sociedad de castas—peninsulares evidently gravitated toward one another, setting aside at least some of the political, cultural, and linguistic barriers that might have separated them back home. Whether Basque or Asturian, Galician or Castilian, one could at least count on a fellow European to understand the ethos of living in a civilized republic. The most fortunate of Spanish newcomers also found a ready welcome as compadres or even sons-in-law of countrymen who had already secured places within the town's elite. With relative ease, then, the European immigrants of Chihuahua formed a cohesive group with shared values and mutual interests, and they quickly devised institutions and rituals that promoted their political and cultural agendas.

Most of Chihuahua's Mexican-born settlers found it much harder to advance their interests in collective fashion. All of its first-generation residents were certainly special people, self-selected men and women who had demonstrated considerable courage and resourcefulness in attempting to better their fortunes by migrating hundreds of miles to Nueva Vizcaya. But it is significant that all of these españoles, Indians, and castas had opted for individual solutions to their problems, choosing to walk away rather than to pursue their goals through concerted action back home. Such decisions may have represented realistic assessments of the possibilities open to them, but the fact that migrants traveled alone or in the company of a few trusted associates seriously limited their capacity for cooperative initiative once they arrived in Chihuahua. No emerging network of economic and political privilege embraced them as it did the more fortunate of their peninsular counterparts, nor did they receive any help in transporting their own "cultural baggage" to northern New Spain. Each person brought only what he or she could carry in the form of individual memories of how things were back home. Even if ethnic distinctions meant relatively little to plebeians in colonial Mexico, it still took time to forge new bonds of community among men and women of such diverse geographic provenances. Moreover, those who left central Mexico, however much personal fortitude and initiative they may have possessed, probably counted among those least integrated into the rituals, power networks, and support systems of their native communities. After all, those who were so connected presumably had far fewer incentives to take off for the remote frontiers of Nueva Vizcaya. Certainly workers arriving in Chihuahua quickly made new acquaintances, social peers who became their friends, compadres, lovers, and spouses, but these ties hardly compared with the interpersonal networks and institutions that were at least theoretically available in their communities of origin.

Neither indigenous peoples native to Nueva Vizcaya nor lower-class newcomers could call upon the long-established rituals and traditions, based in part on prehispanic custom, that underwrote community solidarity in the Indian villages of central and southern Mexico. They had no acknowledged leaders as skilled in the manipulation of colonial law, and in deflecting intracommunity discontent toward external enemies and away from themselves, as the more politically astute Indian caciques to the south. Chihuahua's laboring classes also lacked the cofradías and mutual aid societies that gave people of lower social standing in Indian villages and larger cities—and even in older mining centers such as Parral—an opportunity to help one another, a corporate identity, and a place in the civic ritual of their community. At least for the first generation or two after the founding of Chihuahua, working-class solidarity was ephemeral at best. As we have seen, mine workers in Chihuahua briefly came together to challenge existing economic arrangements in the 1730s, but their coalition quickly dissolved when confronted by the powerful Manuel San Juan y Santa Cruz and his well-connected allies.

The men who assumed command during San Felipe's formative decades further strengthened their positions because they achieved a limited form of cultural hegemony over at least some of their social subordinates. To continue with the transport metaphor, local elites were able to transfer so much of their cultural baggage to northern New Spain because they persuaded people of lower social rank to carry some of the load. They may not have convinced very many castas that superior virtue inhered exclusively in those able to document an unsullied Spanish lineage in a distinguished surname, but they did nevertheless succeed in teaching many people to draw the connection, often explicitly articulated in their own self-justifications, between proper behavior and a certain measure of social deference.

Meanwhile, the patriarchal ethos, transported virtually intact from Europe to the northern frontier of New Spain, insured an enthusiastic audience for this lesson. Regardless of their ethnicity or social standing, most men could earn at least some degree of membership in the community of hombres de bien by attending to their obligations as padres de familia. To be sure, lower-class men might exploit this logic to demand various concessions from the elite. In return, however, local rulers exacted a certain amount of good behavior from men eager to claim the rewards of superior virtue. Moreover, their willingness to delegate to virtually any adult male the power to "govern" his own family and household gained them valuable allies in the struggle to contain troublesome women, youth, and servants. Patriarchal attitudes, then, assisted elites in achieving a kind of cultural hegemony and a measure of social control.

The social configurations established in Chihuahua during the first six decades of the eighteenth century owed much to the conscious designs of local elites, the tactical advantages that their personal, political, and financial alliances afforded them, and the durability and portability of traditional concepts of honor and patriarchy. Taken together, these factors produced a community that in many ways resembled others to the south. Labor relations, though often the focus of bitter struggle, in the end featured no significant innovations not also present in other mining centers and in many other types of enterprises throughout the viceroyalty. Political life also replicated that of other municipalities in New and Old Spain. Cabildo officers in San Felipe el Real consciously aped their counterparts in larger towns, imitating whenever possible the actions, rhetoric, and symbolic display they had witnessed in Mexico City or Guadalajara. At the same time, they fell into step with the Bourbon monarchy's efforts to contain popular celebrations that might prove disruptive to social order. Those who claimed special privilege in Chihuahua mouthed the same self-serving equations of nobility, virtue, and ethnicity that resounded in every corner of the Iberian world, while in Nueva Vizcaya, as in Buenos Aires, those who hovered near the outer fringes of privilege agonized most visibly over the social boundaries separating españoles from less desirable castes. Finally, assumptions governing the respective duties and liberties of males and females displayed virtual uniformity from California to Cape Horn.

Despite historians' efforts to consign Chihuahua to the "fringes" of the Spanish empire, social relations in San Felipe and Santa Eulalia bore strong resemblance to those observed throughout New Spain. The preponderant influence of Spanish immigrants accounts for a substantial portion of this similarity. Moreover, as we have seen, the men who commanded local government harbored fears and concerns that echoed throughout the viceroyalty, from Santa Fe to Mexico City, in the decades following the Pueblo Rebellion and the great tumult of 1692. But we must also look to the habits and attitudes of ordinary men and women to explain Chihuahua's likeness to other parts of colonial Mexico. Lower-class migrants left much behind as they traveled north. Still, they managed to carry with them the practices of social negotiation they had learned back home. They had no doubt met arrogant gachupines like Benito Godoy or Martín de Echaquibel before and witnessed many arguments over land or wages, racial classifications or courteous treatment, weekend liberties or the right to wear Belgian lace. And they certainly had no reason not to expect the debates to continue once they relocated in Chihuahua.

It is likely, though, that Chihuahua differed from many other parts of New Spain in the degree of certainty with which participants in these negotiations faced one another. Although Chihuahua's emergent elites ultimately won many rounds in the competition, they had little reason for confidence when they first set up their mines and shops in Santa Eulalia and San Felipe, while they could well imagine what might happen if social control broke down. Most had passed through Mexico City, where they no doubt observed evidence or heard impassioned accounts of the tumult of 1692. Once they arrived in Nueva Vizcaya, the future leaders of San Felipe found additional proof that a "civilized" polity, as they knew it, rested on the most precarious of bases. Tales of the Pueblo Rebellion still lingered, while the menacing presence of Apaches and other indigenous peoples who rejected the constraints of Spanish law and religion provided a near-constant reminder of the challenge facing those who attempted to govern at San Felipe. Especially before the reorganization of imperial defense, which occurred after 1763, the leaders of San Felipe could expect little effective help from the motley contingent of poorly equipped and ill-trained soldiers assigned to the handful of presidios scattered along the frontier.[1]

Elites in Chihuahua thus entered the process of social negotiation fully cognizant of the grave consequences that might result if they faltered. To be sure, their counterparts in Mexico City had seen the breakdown of social order at first hand as flames swept the viceregal palace and the city council chambers that fateful evening of June 8,

1692. But the capital soon marshaled its impressive arsenal of political and economic resources to repair the buildings on an even grander scale.[2] The magnificent edifices surrounding Mexico City's central plaza, and the scores of imposing churches, convents, and private residences lining its downtown streets, provided everyone, regardless of rank, with powerful visual suggestions of social stability. As R. Douglas Cope has recently observed, these monumental structures also "shaped the plebeians' concept of urban space" in the capital, as people testifying in court often used monasteries and other ecclesiastical structures as handy geographical reference points, much as they used the church's ritual calendar to reckon the passage of time. Thus a mulato slave called before the Inquisition noted that he lived "next to the great monastery of San Francisco."[3] Residents of Chihuahua found far less architectural evidence of the power wielded by local elites. San Felipe's imposing parish church, when finally completed at midcentury, certainly served as a focus of town life, but the blocks surrounding the central plaza boasted few other landmarks to shore up the elite's self-confidence and hegemony.

Dominant groups in Chihuahua also lacked other benefits enjoyed by elites in the major cities of New Spain. No titles of nobility bolstered their assertions of social precedence, and none could claim descent from the original Spanish conquerors of Mexico. The ties of kinship, compadrazgo, economic partnership, and ideological consensus that formed among successive generations of San Felipe's dominant group only faintly resembled the powerful alliances that bound together elites in larger and longer-established communities. Though sizable by local standards, the assets accumulated by mining and commercial magnates in Chihuahua were paltry sums alongside the great fortunes of those who commanded local affairs in Mexico City and Guadalajara. Familiar as they were with the order of things in these larger urban centers, Chihuahua's political and economic elites must have tacitly acknowledged the relative paucity of resources available to them in their struggle to fashion a form of social organization favorable to their interests. Perhaps as a result they pursued their goals with sharpened vigilance and intensity, unable to harbor any smug illusion that the social bargains underwriting their precedence had been fixed for all time.

Elites in Chihuahua, and those aspiring to join their ranks, also faced more frequent and more direct pressure to renegotiate their position than their counterparts in larger cities and towns across the viceroyalty, where the sheer weight of numbers and the evolution of a more complicated social hierarchy limited encounters among representatives of sharply different social categories. On ritual occasions and in the conduct of their daily business, ruling groups in major municipalities managed to sequester greater physical and institutional space for themselves. More of them were able to afford coaches that enabled them to travel through streets and plazas without rubbing elbows with the lower classes, and the practice of separating elite celebrations from popular festivities had developed more fully in big cities than in the frontier communities of Nueva Vizcaya. Significant numbers of Mexico City's upper classes also escaped the occupational demands which placed some of Chihuahua's elites in daily touch with their social inferiors. The powerful wholesalers who dominated commerce in the viceregal capital were spared the indignity of waiting on customers in person, while many highly placed bureaucrats could count on a cadre of compliant subalterns to shield them from contact with the rabble.

Those who commanded the capital's highest levels of power and prestige, and who therefore possessed the greatest capacity to maintain or alter existing local allocations of responsibility and privilege, experienced fewer occasions requiring them to reiterate or renegotiate the manner in which those bargains applied directly to themselves. In San Felipe el Real, by contrast, a narrower social distance separated the villa's most powerful officials and entrepreneurs from the lower classes, and those wishing special deference had to reassert their claims on a more regular basis. Those aspiring to social precedence in San Felipe therefore appreciated what was at stake in the nearly constant jockeying for position that marked interpersonal relations in their community, and they also had ample reason to question their own ability to swing the end result their way.

Those relegated to subordinate positions may not have recognized fully the tactical advantages that elite vulnerability afforded them. Moreover, the absence of strong associational networks among the area's lower classes tipped the balance in favor of customary allocations of power and privilege. In other regions of colonial Mexico, social struggle often took the form of litigation in which a collective entity—an Indian village or an organized guild or cofradía—spoke for those who might otherwise lose the battle and invoked protective legislation or customary notions of moral economy on their behalf.

Such contests were fewer in Chihuahua, and social negotiation more often played itself out in one-to-one confrontations over routine transactions—the purchase of a few eggs or a pair of stockings, the delivery of a lonely bachelor's supper. As we have seen, few "rules" explicitly governed such encounters, and while they generated considerable anxiety for local elites, in the end they did little to disturb existing allocations of resources, power, or privilege. An angry mulato might gain momentary vindication by stalking out of a gachupín's shop without making a purchase and muttering insults as he went. But someone of his calidad could only push his own claim to respectful treatment so far, and then only by observing the much more clearly defined rules that stipulated precise obligations for one of his station in local society. He could gain recognition as an hombre de bien within his "sphere" by the sweat of his brow, his ability to discipline his own family, and his willingness to show proper deference to figures in authority, who might well be the kinfolk or compadres of the shopkeeper who had offended him in the first place. If any such confrontation resulted in his criminal prosecution, he could probably expect that a court-appointed defender would plead his case, sincerely or otherwise, but he could count on no institutional infrastructure to engage in an ongoing battle to advance the collective interests of mulatos. Chihuahua's elites, then, may have lacked some of the advantages available to their counterparts in other communities, but those who might challenge their position had even fewer resources at their command.

Late Colonial Changes

Peninsular Spaniards and their close associates thus wielded considerable influence over the political and cultural bargains struck in Chihuahua during the first generation or two after the discovery of silver at Santa Eulalia. After 1740, and even more decisively after 1760, local elites faced potential threats to their hegemony. By then it was clear that the best days of silver mining had ended, despite years of earnest prayers to San Francisco and other celestial advocates. The region's economic decline and its heightened vulnerability to Indian attack posed obvious challenges for those who commanded local government. Their own ranks thinned, in fact, as fewer individuals came forward to seek positions on the cabildo, and those who remained in power had fewer resources to co-opt dissidents or coerce them into submission. Meanwhile, a more sizable proportion of Chihuahua's working men and women were now native to the area. The greater attention paid by late colonial authorities to plebeian fandangos suggests that the lower classes had finally lived in one place long enough to develop more durable social networks among themselves and to "sequester" a larger piece of ritual space they could call their own.

Other circumstances facilitated the efforts of local elites to consolidate and maintain their control during the final four decades of the eighteenth century, however. Here we must consider first the simple weight of social inertia. In our search for grand explanations of human behavior, historians sometimes overlook the obvious—that men and women fall into familiar routines without leaving detailed, self-reflective explanations for their children and grandchildren, much less for meddlesome scholars who come along two or three centuries later. Over time, then, people may lose sight of the reasons, profound or prosaic, why their ancestors adopted a particular type of conduct in the first place. Even if Chihuahua's working classes had formed tighter networks of neighborhood and family by the last third of the eighteenth century, they could not suddenly recreate the community rituals and institutions that their grandparents had left behind in central Mexico several decades before. As far as most of them could see, people of their social rank had "always" been relegated to the margins of official celebrations. Late colonial elites may have known otherwise but obviously had little reason to share that privileged information.

In other ways, too, the historical reality of the late colonial period discouraged the renegotiation of bargains previously reached. Although fewer peninsulares now entered the region than had earlier, more of those who did arrived with bureaucratic or military appointments in hand, and therefore with more clearly defined "tools" and "scripts" to use in dealing with social subordinates. Even more important in maintaining elite hegemony was the ability of local elites to adapt to changing times. As we saw in Chapter 4, the cabildo of San Felipe el Real remained viable, even as municipal institutions atrophied elsewhere in the Spanish empire, because the town's governing minority proved willing to open its ranks to ambitious bakers like Pedro Antonio Cadrecha and other small-scale entrenpreneurs. Thoroughly respectable and well-versed in the logic of elite hegemony even if they lacked the more substantial fortunes and political connections of the miners and merchants who had previously dominated the cabildo, Cadrecha and his fellow newcomers to local government ensured that the villa always had a critical mass of politically active townsmen with a stake in maintaining social order.

Local elites also proved themselves capable of altering the assumptions that underlay labor relations in the light of changed economic circumstances in the late colonial period. As mining deteriorated and as refugees from outlying settlements entered the villa of San Felipe seeking protection from hostile Indian attacks, employers and civic leaders now for the first time confronted a potential surplus of workers, and fresh challenges for social control as well. As one alcalde reported to his colleagues on the cabildo, these people escaped not only the discipline of productive labor but also the supervision of the clergy. Lacking amos, they had no one to advance the sums they needed to pay for burials and other services of the church.[4]

To be sure, Chihuahua had always attracted a steady stream of drifters more interested in gambling and other forms of mischief than in useful work, and, as we have seen, local authorities from the very first days of the mining boom had attempted to formulate strategies to compel them to work. Late colonial leaders adopted comparable measures. In 1775, for example, Corregidor Pedro Antonio Queipo del Llano y Galarza noted the preponderance of idle *forasteros* (outsiders), whose unauthorized fandangos frequently disturbed the peace. The corregidor therefore ordered that every newcomer register with the authorities upon arrival in San Felipe and that those who failed to find a job within three days be placed in some mine or hacienda.[5] But the depressed economy of the late colonial period could not generate enough jobs to accommodate every potentially disruptive individual. In the 1760s and 1770s local authorities continued the practice of sending male prisoners to forced labor in area silver refineries, but they did so with rapidly declining frequency thereafter.[6] They therefore turned more and more to institutions that ostensibly were productive enterprises but in fact served more as instruments of social control.

For decades the obraje at the hacienda of Encinillas had offered a convenient place to confine troublemakers, and it continued to play a similar role even into the beginning of the nineteenth century.[7] Meanwhile, a new obraje within the villa of San Felipe itself offered an alternative during the final decades of the colonial period. The peninsular merchants Martín de Mariñelarena and Manuel de Urquidi established the factory in 1780 and sold it to the cabildo six years later. Thereafter the town government paid an administrator to oversee its operations, and the regidores took monthly turns assuring that he did his job properly. The cabildo leaders harbored few illusions about the obraje's profitability, however. They spoke often of its utility as a means of social control and by 1812 had taken to calling it a "correctional hospice," but rarely did they cite its economic productivity. In fact, they had difficulty selling its output, and its balance sheets usually showed a loss. Its labor force consisted almost exclusively of individuals confined there against their will. Indians being held for alleged subversion, youngsters committed by parents unable to discipline them any other way, and even an occasional person suffering from dementia all found themselves detained in the obraje at San Felipe el Real. Few of these "workers" knew anything of textile production when they entered, and fewer still became sufficiently expert to turn the factory into a profitable venture for the town government.[8]

Of course, Spanish colonial authorities had long emphasized the importance of labor as a way of uplifting degenerate and potentially disruptive Indians, Africans, and castas and of teaching them their proper place in "civilized" society. During the heyday of the mining boom, employers in Chihuahua energetically touted the morally and politically beneficial effects of labor when explaining why the town's vagabonds should be subjected to the rigorous discipline of silver mines and refineries. But whenever they succeeded in subjecting such individuals to a work routine, they not only reaped an increased measure of social peace but also added to their personal fortunes. Only as a last resort did they "waste" potentially productive muscle power in such relatively unprofitable enterprises as textile production.

By the late colonial period, however, their successors had come to appreciate more fully the value of labor as a means of social control over and above any economic advantage it might confer. Ideally, these later leaders sought solutions that would subdue the disorderly elements in their community and render some useful commodities as well. The scores of rebel Indians confined to the villa's jail in the 1770s and 1780s therefore supposedly learned how to work hides into reins, boots, and other utilitarian items.[9] By 1810 local residents even talked of establishing a cigar factory at San Felipe, comparable to those of Mexico City and other major urban centers, to provide employment for men and women in the town.[10] But cigars and saddles were not silver, and late colonial authorities increasingly viewed social control as the major, and at times the only, reason to put otherwise idle hands to work. The increased importance of the workplace as an instrument of social control may help explain why Juana de Cobos's stature in the community increased ever so slightly during the final decades of her life. However much the assertive conduct of her middle years may have flouted accepted standards of feminine submission, at least her bakery provided one more alternative site in which to confine potentially disruptive elements of the local population.

In other respects, too, the civic leaders of Chihuahua in the late eighteenth century demonstrated heightened concern for maintaining order in their community. To the extent that their limited resources permitted, they emulated their counterparts in Mexico City, Guadalajara, and other cities in paying closer attention to policing the population under their command. In 1793, for example, they subdivided the town into four formal barrios and assigned a regidor to preside over each one. In their roles as *comisarios* (commissaries) of their designated barrios, the regidores were to monitor gambling, fandangos, and all other mischief.[11] However serious the challenges to social order, then, local elites proved sufficiently flexible and inventive to meet and contain them, while plebeians still had comparatively few resources to alter the bargains reached in previous generations. The final decades of colonial rule thus presented continued opportunities for social negotiation in San Felipe and Santa Eulalia, but not with the frequency and intensity of the period before about 1760.

Social Change in Mexico, 1750–1850

In this respect Chihuahua may seem to part company with the rest of New Spain. Virtually every study that has concentrated on the late colonial period has emphasized the profound political, economic, and social changes that swept the viceroyalty after 1760. In many areas the expansion of commercial agriculture drastically altered patterns of land tenure and utilization and intensified the level of conflict over land and water. Silver output expanded, and mine workers fell subject to increasingly harsh regimens of labor discipline. Population growth, recurrent epidemics, ecological crises, and the unsettling effects of commercial and administrative innovation—the so-called

Bourbon Reforms—all further accelerated the pace of social transformation in late colonial New Spain. The already fragile boundaries separating "Indian," "casta," and "Spanish" society crumbled even further, while authorities in Madrid and Mexico City even reconsidered traditional concepts of gender and began to emphasize the importance of educating females and the economically productive value of women's labor.[12]

Chihuahua failed to partake fully in these changes of the late colonial period, but we cannot attribute the area's relative inertia solely or even chiefly to its peripheral relationship to the so-called core regions of the viceroyalty. After all, even the far more geographically remote province of New Mexico evidently experienced significant social change in the closing decades of the eighteenth century, thanks in part to the Bourbon dynasty's efforts to promote economic development there. Demographic growth and the expansion of a cash economy placed increasing pressure on available resources, and more people worked for wages, often bound by debts to their employers, on lands they did not own.[13] In Chihuahua, by contrast, the growing trade with New Mexico and the provision of supplies for the expanding military establishment failed to restore local economic activity to the levels achieved during the mining boom of the 1720s and 1730s.

We might also argue that many of the social changes so evident in other parts of late colonial New Spain failed to take place in Chihuahua because they were largely irrelevant there. In fact, the social arrangments forged in San Felipe and Santa Eulalia early in the eighteenth century in certain crucial respects anticipated changes throughout the rest of the colony that are usually associated with the years after 1760. The erosion of barriers separating the Indian and Spanish republics meant little in the villa of San Felipe, which had never had separate quarters reserved exclusively for Indians, other than the tiny neighborhood of well-acculturated Yaquis. Meanwhile, in the outlying Tarahumara mission pueblos, the transformation from Indian villages to mestizo farming communities proceeded at a pace commensurate with or well ahead of that observed in central Mexico. In a similar manner, employers and local authorities in many mining centers moved to eliminate customary partidos for workers in the 1760s, but their counterparts in Chihuahua had taken similar measures some 30 years before.[14] Furthermore, as we have seen in Chapter 5, by 1760 Chihuahua's leaders had succeeded in streamlining the calendar of ritual observance in their community, and their lack of resources further curtailed local festivities in subsequent decades. As a result they had little reason to replicate Viceroy Revillagigedo's efforts in the 1790s to reduce the number of frivolous holidays and fiestas in central Mexico. Guild restrictions tended to deteriorate, often with official encouragement, in late colonial New Spain, but again such changes could have little meaning in Chihuahua, where a formal structure of craft guilds had never developed in the first place.

The men and women who settled in Chihuahua during the first six decades of the eighteenth century also had numerous chances to rehearse the kinds of social dynamics that most certainly intensified in other parts of New Spain after 1760. Late colonial administrative reforms, economic changes, and ecological crises generated massive migration throughout the viceroyalty. Greater numbers of Spanish immigrants arrived to take up posts in the expanding bureaucracy and army or to seek their fortunes in new commercial ventures made possible by the easing of old mercantile restrictions. Meanwhile, thousands of lower-class men and women moved about as economic opportunities expanded in some places and contracted in others. Peasants denied access to land or water in their villages might seek greater security as permanent employees of nearby haciendas, while elsewhere the intensification of commercial agriculture displaced many who who had previously lived on the haciendas as sharecroppers. Countless numbers abandoned the countryside altogether, adding to the population of Mexico City, Guadalajara, and other towns. In many parts of New Spain, then, the years after 1760 brought more new faces in touch with one another than ever before.

As we have seen in Chihuahua, however, men and women settling in new surroundings may simply reprise old debates without altering the underlying premises of society, and those with the greatest reason to change the existing order of things are precisely those who possess the fewest tools with which to do so. Further research is therefore necessary in order to determine whether or not the myriad social, political, and economic innovations that occurred in Mexico during the late colonial period in fact modified social relations of the everyday, face-to-face variety that we have studied in the preceding chapters. Several years ago Eric Van Young wrote that "modes and social relations of production, family and gender relationships, certain characteristics of state structure and action, appear to have been substantially in place by the middle of the eighteenth century, and to have altered more between 1700 and 1750, or between 1850 and 1900, than between 1750 and 1850."[15]

Other scholars have identified specific points of continuity, and their findings suggest that the kinds of social bargains reached in Chihuahua during the first six decades of the eighteenth century endured in many parts of Mexico well past the achievement of political independence from Spain. The ethos of governance articulated by cabildo members in San Felipe el Real echoed in the words of the nineteenth-century statesman Lucas Alamán, who saw the hombre de bien as "a man of faith, honor, property, education and virtue," and best suited to assume positions of command in the new nation. It went without saying, too, that such qualities inhered most consistently in those of European ancestry, even if the doors of civic participation did in fact open for a handful of respectable mestizos and others. Hombres de bien who were active politically also voiced frequent worries about maintaining the stability of the social order over which they presided. They shared these values despite their disagreements on other questions of political import, and on a national scale they formed a closely interwoven ruling class, linked by ties of kinship and commerce, at least somewhat reminiscent of the interlocking coterie that governed at San Felipe el Real. If Basques and Galicians could set aside their regional differences in colonial Chihuahua, the hombres de bien who came to the forefront of national politics in post-independence Mexico displayed "loyalty to their class, a social solidarity which allowed bitter rivals to maintain respect for one another, and . . . to switch their allegiance whenever it suited them."[16]

If the ideas of governance voiced in Chihuahua during the early eighteenth century emerged substantially intact from the turmoil of late colonial and independence periods, there is also evidence to suggest that in other ways the social relations that we have observed in San Felipe endured in many parts of Mexico after 1810. The rage directed at arrogant gachupines during and after the wars for independence suggests that latter-day counterparts of Benito Godoy were no more adept than he in dealing with representatives of Mexico's sociedad de castas.[17] In 1828 the lower classes of Mexico City sacked the Parián market, where many of the capital's remaining Spanish merchants sold their wares. Even if their actions stemmed from a new kind of popular political mobilization that emerged after independence, as Silvia Arrom convincingly argues, it is likely that a long run of insulting exchanges, of the sort we witnessed over the shop counters of San Felipe el Real, focused the crowd's angry attention on the Parián. Arrom goes on to say that many of the people who participated in the riot were recent arrivals in the capital, and as such "they lacked the communal structure and leadership that facilitated organization in Indian villages," while "they had not yet developed strong associational organizations that would foster collective independent action." As a result, the hombres de bien who controlled the city's political life moved quickly and effectively to ward off similar outbursts in the future.[18] In Mexico City in 1828, as in San Felipe a century earlier, the appearance of new faces in the crowd strengthened the hold of social bargains previously reached.

The reforms introduced by the Bourbon monarchy in the late colonial period also failed to modify prevailing assumptions on the proper roles of men and women in any meaningful way. The late eighteenth and early nineteenth centuries may have witnessed expanded educational and occupational possibilities for at least some women in Mexico City, but those changes counted most for women of the middle and upper classes, who had access to schooling and to careers in teaching and other "respectable" professions. Similarly, advances in the legal rights of widows and single adult women meant most to women of the propertied classes. These changes did little to alter traditional suspicions against lower-class women whose work removed them from the confines of patriarchal households, and Mexico's economic troubles in the early nineteenth century closed off previously opened opportunities in manufacturing and artisan trades. Meanwhile, even though new attitudes known collectively as *marianismo* raised the possibility that women might emulate the Virgin Mary rather than the temptress Eve, those who looked for sources of social equilibrium in times of rapid change took comfort in stressing traditional gender roles. As Arrom observes, "Sex roles and family patterns must have seemed reassuringly stable to people confronting the problems of self-rule, foreign invasions, the loss of half the national territory, Caste uprisings, governmental instability, and recession."[19] The men who governed Chihuahua a century before had reached similar conclusions in the face of Indian hostilities, economic troubles, and the perpetual insouciance of mestizos and mulatos all about them.

In the foregoing discussion I do not wish to minimize the importance of the changes that swept Mexico in the late colonial and early national periods, but merely to suggest that it is not yet clear whether or not these changes produced fundamental transformations in the way that men and women understood, articulated, and manipulated the power relations they confronted on a daily basis. Figures in authority could, after all, claim to speak for the nation rather than the king, yet still stress traditional habits of deference and couch them in familiar terms. For the time being, then, it is safe to assume that in many parts of Mexico the years after 1760 brought increasingly numerous occasions for the type of social negotiation that characterized the history of Chihuahua during the early eighteenth century. The outcome of those debates in San Felipe suggests that the fundamental principles of honor, social hierarchy, and patriarchy had enormous staying power, enabling them to survive the trek to northern Nueva Vizcaya in the early eighteenth century and the monumental political, economic, and social transformations that occurred throughout Mexico after 1750.

Appendix

Selected Demographic and Political Data for San Felipe el Real and Its Jurisdiction

TABLE I

Alcaldes Ordinarios of Chihuahua, 1718–1821

Year	Name	Birthplace
1718–1719	José de Orio y Zubiate	Guipúzcoa
	Diego de Vilchis Tovar y Cordera	Granada
1720–1721	Alonso Montaño Vidal	?
	Juan Bautista de Ibave	Spain
1722	Domingo Pérez de Bustillos	?
	Alexandro García de Bustamante	Spain
1723	Juan Felipe de Orozco y Molina	Seville
	José Antonio Villar	?
1724	Juan Antonio Trasviña y Retes (died Sept. 12, 1724)	Asturias
	Ignacio Alfonso de Riaza	Guadalajara, Spain
1725	Pedro Ruiz de Azua	Guipúzcoa
	Santiago Gómez de Escontría	Spain
1726	Antonio José de Paniagua	?
	Juan Ignacio de Perea	Spain
1727	Antonio José de Paniagua	?
	Juan Ignacio de Perea	Spain
1728	Pedro González de Almoina	Spain
	José Velarde Cosío	Spain
1729	Juan Sánchez Palacios	?
	Santiago Sánchez de la Güera	Spain
1730	Domingo Vélez del Ribero	Burgos
	José de Varaya	Durango, Vizcaya

TABLE I
(continued)

Year	Name	Birthplace
1731	Juan Bautista de Ibave	Spain
	Manuel de Uranga	Spain
1732	Domingo Basoco	Vizcaya
	Juan Cacho de Herrera	Asturias
1733	Pablo Benito Rodríguez Rey	Vizcaya
	Juan de Orrantia	Spain
1734	José Antonio de Uranga	?
	Esteban de Arenívar	Spain
1735	Ignacio Alfonso de Riaza	Guadalajara, Spain
	Pedro Soler Pardo	Seville
1736	José de Varaya	Durango, Vizcaya
	Domingo del Valle	Asturias
1737	Matías del Solar	Spain
	Antonio de Orrantia y Santa Coloma	?
1738	Pedro González de Almoina	Spain
	Miguel de la Sierra	?
1739	José Velarde Cosío	?
	Baltasar de Arechavala	?
1740	Juan José de Aramburu	Navarre
	Pedro Gómez del Campo	Burgos
1741	Domingo Antonio García	?
	José Gómez de Barreda	Spain
1742	Pedro Díaz de la Serna	?
	Juan Manuel Castro y Bravo	Spain
1743	Manuel de Güemes	?
	Pedro de la Bárcena	Spain
1744	José Gómez de Barreda	Spain
	Francisco del Castillo	?
1745	José Gómez de Barreda	Spain
	Santiago Gómez de Escontría	probably Spain
1746	Pedro Díaz de la Serna	?
	Francisco del Castillo	?
1747	Baltasar de Arechavala	?
	José Fernández de Hinojosa	Seville
1748	José Gómez de Barreda	Spain
	Domingo de Escandón	Burgos
1749	Francisco Antonio Martínez	?
	Domingo Antonio González de Novoa	?
1750	Francisco Antonio Martínez	?
	Domingo Antonio González de Novoa	?
1751	Baltasar de Arechavala	?
	Antonio de Echaquibel	probably Spain
1752	José Antonio de Uranga	?
	Domingo del Valle	Asturias
1753	Domingo del Valle	Asturias
	Antonio Gutiérrez del Castillo	Asturias

TABLE I
(continued)

Year	Name	Birthplace
1754	Antonio Gutiérrez del Castillo	Asturias
	Manuel Gómez del Pinar	Burgos
1755	Fernando Velarde	Burgos
	Salvador de Lemus	Spain
1756	Domingo Antonio González de Novoa	?
	Manuel García	presumably Spain
1757	Francisco Antonio Martínez	?
	José de la Borbolla	probably Asturias
1758	José de la Borbolla	probably Asturias
	Pedro José de la Fuente y Rivero	Spain
1759	José Antonio de Uranga	?
	Pedro Antonio Cadrecha	Asturias
1760	Manuel García	presumably Spain
	Francisco Duro	Galicia
1761	Ramón Martínez	Galicia
	Agustín de Urquidi	Guipúzcoa
1762	Fernando Velarde	Burgos
	Juan José Barrándegui	?
1763	Alexandro Manuel de Quijano	?
	Alonso de la Cadena	Spain
1764	Juan José Caballero	?
	Antonio Gutiérrez del Castillo	Asturias
1765	Francisco Antonio Martínez	?
	Antonio Gutiérrez del Castillo	Asturias
1766	Pedro Antonio Cadrecha	Asturias
	Manuel Antonio de Escorza	Santander
1767	Juan José Barrándegui	?
	Manuel Gómez de Salazar	?
1768	Pedro José de la Fuente y Rivero	possibly Spain
	Martín de Mariñelarena	Navarre
1769	Francisco Duro	Galicia
	Francisco Xavier del Campo	Madrid
1770	Juan José Barrándegui	?
	Juan Antonio de Orduño	?
1771	Martín de Mariñelarena	Navarre
	Manuel de Urquidi	Guipúzcoa
1772	Pedro Nicolás Cadrecha	probably Chihuahua
	Miguel Ruiz Galdeano	Navarre
1773	Francisco Lozada	Galicia
	Andrés de Calles	Cádiz
1774	Martín de Mariñelarena	Navarre
	Francisco Ormáegui	?
1775	Francisco Duro	Galicia
	Andrés de Calles	Cádiz
1776	Francisco Lozada	Galicia
	Francisco Antonio Trespalacios	Oviedo

TABLE I
(continued)

Year	Name	Birthplace
1777	Leonardo María de Calo	Spain
	Pedro Antonio Velarde	Spain
1778	Francisco Xavier del Campo	Madrid
	José Antonio de Irigoyen	?
1779	Manuel de Urquidi	Guipúzcoa
	Francisco Antonio de la Torre	?
1780	Francisco Guizarnótegui	Guipúzcoa
	Manuel Ruiz	?
1781	Ventura do Porto	Coruña, Galicia
	Francisco Lozada	Galicia
1782	Pedro Antonio Velarde	Spain
	Francisco Antonio Trespalacios	Oviedo
1783	Pedro Sandoval y Moscoso	Nochistán, Guadalajara, Nueva Galicia
	Ignacio Antonio González	?
1784	José Antonio de Iribarren	?
	Juan José Ruíz de Bustamante	Santander
1785	Manuel Ruíz	?
	Diego Ventura Márquez	Galicia
1786	Francisco Gerónimo del Valle	?
	Ventura do Porto	Coruña, Galicia
1787	Francisco Antonio Trespalacios	Oviedo
	Andrés Manuel Martínez de Alballe	Galicia
1788	Francisco Antonio Trespalacios	Oviedo
	Manuel Ruiz	?
1789	Manuel Ruiz	?
	Francisco Gerónimo del Valle	?
1790	Francisco Gerónimo del Valle	?
	José María Cantelmi	Andalusia
1791	José María Cantelmi	Andalusia
	Pablo Mestre	Cádiz
1792	Ignacio Antonio González	?
	Pablo de Ochoa	Spain
1793	Pablo de Ochoa	Spain
	Juan José Colsa de la Borbolla	Spain
1794	Francisco Gerónimo del Valle	?
	Juan José Ruiz de Bustamante	Santander
1795	Juan José Ruiz de Bustamante	Santander
	José Manuel de Elguea	?
1796	José Manuel de Elguea	?
	Justo Pastor de Madariaga	Guipúzcoa
1797	Justo Pastor de Madariaga	Guipúzcoa
	Pedro Ignacio Irigoyen	?
1798	Pedro Ignacio Irigoyen	?
	Francisco Gerónimo del Valle	?

TABLE I
(continued)

Year	Name	Birthplace
1799	Francisco Gerónimo del Valle	?
	José Alvarez	probably Spain
1800	Bernabé Martínez	possibly Galicia
	José Alvarez	probably Spain
1801	Pedro Ignacio Irigoyen	?
	Andrés Manuel Martínez de Alballe	Galicia
1802	José Maria Ruiz de Bustamante	?
	Rafael Zubia	?
1803	Bernabé Martínez	?
	Juan de Elguezábal	probably Vizcaya
1804	Juan José Ruiz de Bustamante	Santander
	Andrés Manuel Martínez de Alballe	Galicia
1805	Simón de Ochoa	Burgos
	Pedro de Valois	Vizcaya
1806	Justo Pastor de Madariaga	Guipúzcoa
	Sabino de la Pedrueza	Viscaya
1807	Rafael Zubia	?
	Juan José de Arenas	?
1808	Bernabé Martínez	?
	Pedro de Valois	Vizcaya
1809	Justo Pastor de Madariaga	Guipúzcoa
	Lope de la Vega	Santander
1810	Simón de Ochoa	Burgos
	Juan José de Arenas	?
1811	Pedro de Valois	Vizcaya
	Rafael Zubia	?
1812	Miguel de la Huerta	Vizcaya
	Eugenio Vizoso	Galicia
1813	Juan José Ruiz de Bustamante	Burgos
	Juan José de Arenas	?
1814[a]	Francisco José de Jáuregui	Spain
	José Félix Trespalacios	Chihuahua
	Pedro de Valois	Vizcaya
	Rafael Zubia	?
1815	Francisco José de Jáuregui	Spain
	Manuel Zubia	?
1816	Justo Pastor de Madariaga	Guipúzcoa
	Mariano Orcasitas	Chihuahua
1817	Eugenio Vizoso	Galicia
	Miguel de la Huerta	Vizcaya
1818	José Antonio Ruiz de Bustamante	?
	Pedro de Valois	Vizcaya
1819	Mariano Orcasitas	Chihuahua
	Francisco Orvañanos	?
1820	Eugenio Vizoso	Galicia
	Joaquín José de Marichalar	Vizcaya

TABLE 1
(continued)

Year	Name	Birthplace
1821	Mariano Orcasitas	Chihuahua
	Pablo Guerra	?

SOURCES: Almada, "Lista de los alcaldes," gives the names of all alcaldes and the years in which they served. Birthplaces have been determined through a variety of sources, including parish registers and documents in the Archivo del Ayuntamiento de Chihuahua microfilm. For specific citations, consult Martin, "Name Index."

[a] In 1814 Jáuregui and Trespalacios were elected under the terms of the Constitution of Cádiz. New elections were held after the restoration of King Fernando VII, and Valois and Zubia were chosen.

TABLE 2
Numbers of Known Peninsulares Living in Chihuahua Jurisdiction, by Decade, 1700–1819

Decade	Number	Decade	Number
1700–1709	12	1760–1769	65
1710–1719	56	1770–1779	105
1720–1729	118	1780–1789	76
1730–1739	159	1790–1799	72
1740–1749	133	1800–1809	29
1750–1759	104	1810–1819	24

SOURCE: Figures compiled from Martin, "Name Index."

TABLE 3
Numbers of Peninsular Spaniards Living in Chihuahua Jurisdiction in Selected Years

Year	Number	Year	Number
1720	42	1760	44
1730	80	1770	41
1740	93	1780	49
1742	88	1790	44
1750	68	1800	23
1753	59		

SOURCE: Figures compiled from Martin, "Name Index."

TABLE 4
Origins of Peninsular Immigrants to Chihuahua

Region	Number	Percent[a]
Andalusia (provinces of Huelva, Seville, Cádiz, Córdoba, Jaén, Granada, Almería)	48	16.5%
Aragón (provinces of Huesca, Saragossa, Teruel)	2	0.7
Asturias	29	10.0
Baleares	2	0.7
Cantabria	8	2.8
Castile-La Mancha (provinces of Madrid, Guadalajara, Cuenca, Albacete, Ciudad Real, Toledo)	10	3.4
Castile y León[b] (provinces of León, Palencia, Burgos, La Rioja, Soria, Zamora, Valladolid, Segovia, Avila, Salamanca)	65	22.4
Catalonia (provinces of Lleida, Girona, Barcelona, Tarragona)	14	4.8
Extremadura (provinces of Cáceres, Badajoz)	2	0.7
Galicia (provinces of La Coruña, Lugo, Pontevedra, Orense)	41	14.1
Navarre	17	5.9
País Vasco[c] (provinces of Vizcaya, Guipúzcoa, Alava)	48	16.6
Valencia	4	1.4
Total of those with known birthplaces	290	100.0%

SOURCE: Figures compiled from Martin, "Name Index."

[a] This column indicates the percentage of immigrants known to have been born in each region listed relative to the total number of peninsular immigrants whose birthplaces are known.

[b] Of those from Castile y León, 51 were from Burgos. They constituted 17.6 percent of those whose birthplaces have been determined.

[c] Of those from the País Vasco, two were from Alava.

TABLE 5

Numbers of Baptisms, El Sagrario Parish, San Felipe el Real de Chihuahua, Selected Years

1715	
Españoles	39
Indios	44
Mestizos	17
Mulatos	8
Others	4
Adults[a]	1
Total	113
1720	
Españoles	78
Indios	70
Mestizos	28
Mulatos	23
Others	18
Adults[a]	2
Total	219
1725	
Españoles	84
Indios	97
Mestizos	33
Mulatos	25
Others	59
Adults[a]	31
Total	329
1730	
Españoles	45
Indios	74
Mestizos	56
Mulatos	32
Others	74
Adults[a]	26
Total	307
1735	
Españoles	145
Indios	93
Mestizos	57
Mulatos	65
Others	102
Adults[a]	20
Total	482
1740	
Españoles	108
Indios	56
Mestizos	109
Mulatos	18
Others	93
Adults[a]	7
Total	391
1750[b]	
Españoles	110
Indios	53
Mestizos	27
Mulatos	38
Others	70
Adults[a]	18
Total	316
1755	
Españoles	77
Indios	77
Mestizos	51
Mulatos	53
Others	70
Adults[a]	11
Total	339
1760	
Españoles	94
Indios	76
Mestizos	39
Mulatos	65
Others	99
Adults[a]	2
Total	375
1775[b]	
Españoles	66
Indios	32
Mestizos	124
Mulatos	13
Others	93
Adults[a]	0
Total	328
1780	
Españoles	58
Indios	32
Mestizos	99
Mulatos	66
Others	40
Adults[a]	0
Total	295
1785	
Españoles	78
Indios	13
Mestizos	93
Mulatos	6
Others	65
Adults[a]	0
Total	255

TABLE 5
(continued)

1790		1805	
Españoles	49	Españoles	58
Indios	11	Indios	6
Mestizos	116	Mestizos	154
Mulatos	0	Mulatos	0
Others	42	Others	21
Adults[a]	0	Adults[a]	0
Total	218	Total	239
1795		1810	
Españoles	56	Españoles	73
Indios	18	Indios	1
Mestizos	183	Mestizos	188
Mulatos	1	Mulatos	0
Others	24	Others	50
Adults[a]	0	Adults[a]	0
Total	282	Total	312
1800		1815	
Españoles	50	Españoles	112
Indios	10	Indios	0
Mestizos	180	Mestizos	102
Mulatos	2	Mulatos	0
Others	13	Others	48
Adults[a]	0	Adults[a]	0
Total	255	Total	262

SOURCES: Chihuahua (El Sagrario) Parish Registers, Baptisms, GSU microfilm, reels 0162660, 0162661, 0162662, 0162663, 0162664, 0162665.

[a] In most cases the documents list no race for adults baptized, but presumably most were Apaches or other Indians captured in New Mexico and brought to Chihuahua.

[b] The data for 1745, 1765, and 1770 are incomplete.

TABLE 6

Household Structure, Villa de San Felipe el Real de Chihuahua, 1785

Ethnic classification	No. of households	Avg. no. of persons
Households headed by men		
Español "Don"[a]	113	6.51
Español[a]	87	5.46
Mestizo	165	5.38
Mulato	44	5.57
Indio	24	4.75
Other or unknown	6	6.0
Households headed by women		
Española "Doña"[a]	66	5.39
Española[a]	56	3.68
Mestiza	73	4.44
Mulata	29	4.55
India	13	3.92
Other or unknown	13	3.92

SOURCE: Archivo del Ayuntamiento de Chihuahua, second supplement, microfilm copy at the University of Texas at El Paso Library, film no. 502, reel 3, exp. 23.

[a] Includes "españoles europeos" and "españoles" born in Mexico. "Don" and "Doña" were titles of respect and generally connoted a class standing somewhat higher than that of people who lacked these titles.

TABLE 7

Ethnic Composition of Population, Villa de San Felipe el Real de Chihuahua, 1785

Ethnic classification	Number	Percentage of total
Españoles[a]	1,307	34.8%
Mestizos	1,715	45.7
Indios	227	6.0
Mulatos	484	12.9
Slaves	21	0.6
Total	3,754	100.0%

SOURCE: Archivo del Ayuntamiento de Chihuahua, second supplement, microfilm copy at the University of Texas at El Paso Library, film no. 502, reel 3, exp. 23.

[a] Includes "españoles europeos" and "españoles" born in Mexico.

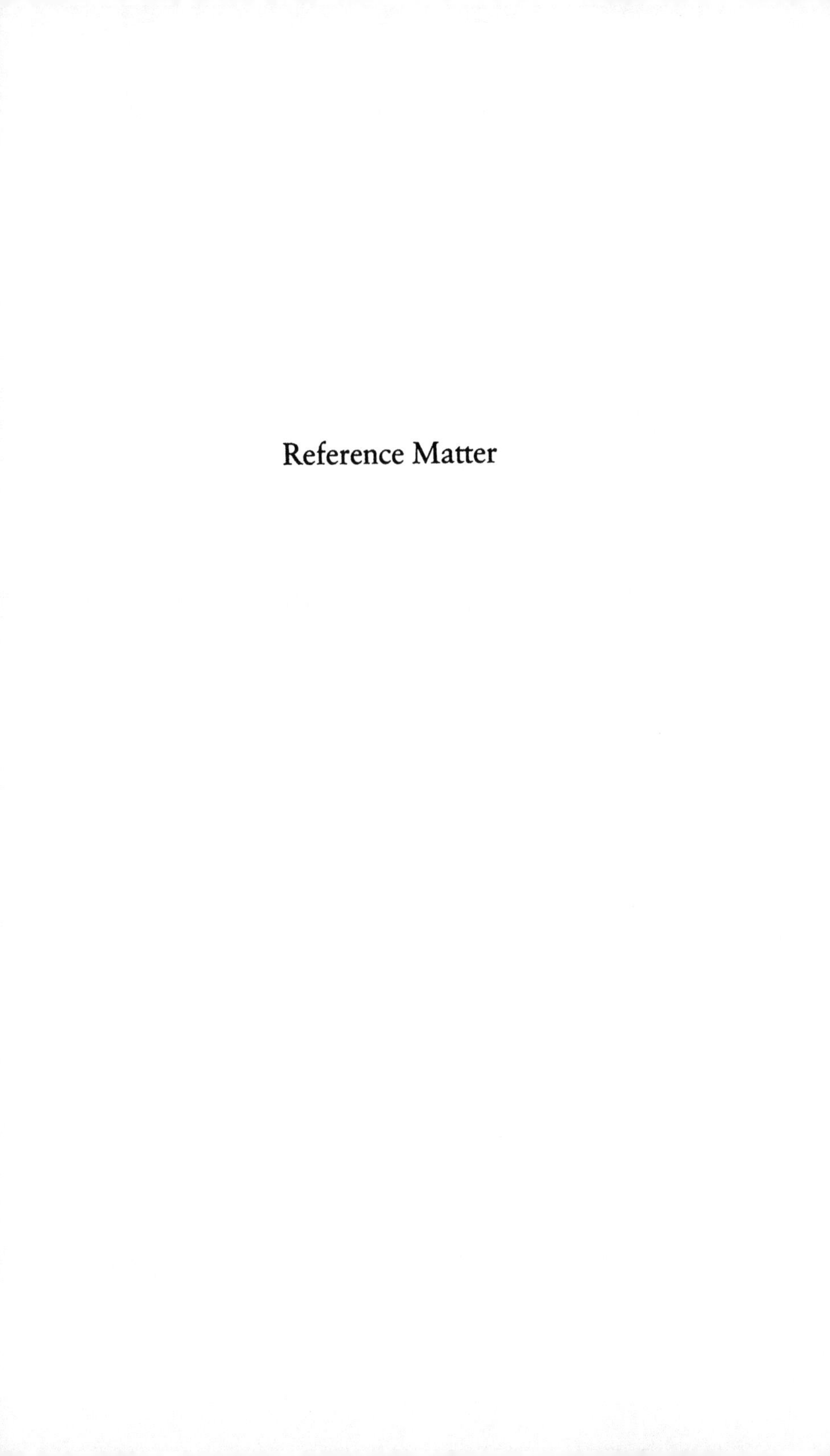

Reference Matter

Glossary

alcalde judicial officer and member of town council, elected for one-year term by permanent members of council; also referred to as *alcalde ordinario*

alcalde mayor district magistrate, representative of Spanish crown; equivalent in function to *corregidor*

alférez real royal standard bearer

alguacil mayor chief constable

amo master, employer

arriero muleteer

audiencia court of appeals; Chihuahua fell under the jurisdiction of the audiencia of Guadalajara

barretero pickman

bodegón restaurant or inn

cabildo municipal council

cabildo abierto ad hoc meeting of leading townsmen, convoked by *corregidor* to discuss matters of civic importance

cacique leader of Indian community

cajero cashier

calidad measure of positive social standing in community; affected by factors such as race, ethnicity, birthplace, wealth, occupation, legitimacy, conduct, personal honor, and level of acculturation (plural, *calidades*)

casta person of mixed racial ancestry

cendradillero owner of small-scale silver refinery

cofradía confraternity of laymen, organized for pious or charitable purposes

colegio college or school

color quebrado literally, broken color; used to describe persons of mixed racial ancestry

compadre godparent of one's child, or parent of one's godchild (feminine, *comadre*)
compadrazgo ritual kinship of compadres
corregidor district magistrate, representative of Spanish crown; equivalent in function to *alcalde mayor*
coyote person of mixed racial ancestry; in northern Mexico, usually someone of mixed Spanish and Indian background
diputado elected spokesman for local miners or merchants
Don title of respect given to men
Doña title of respect given to women
encomendero holder of an *encomienda*
encomienda grant of Indians as laborers and/or tribute payers
español person claiming Spanish descent; used in this study to describe people claiming Spanish descent who were born in the New World (plural, *españoles*; feminine singular, *española*)
fandango dance
fiel ejecutor inspector of weights and measures
gachupín somewhat derogatory term used by natives of Mexico to describe Spanish immigrants (plural, *gachupines*)
Gran Turco literally, captain of the Turks; ceremonial role in recreations of medieval battles between Christians and Moors
hombre de bien literally, man of good; used to describe man of honorable reputation
limpieza de sangre literally, purity of blood; denotes absence of Moorish, Jewish, or racially "inferior" lineage
mandamiento grant of Indian draft laborers; local variant of *repartimiento*
mayordomo majordomo or supervisor
mestizo person of mixed racial ancestry, appearing to be of Spanish and Indian extraction (feminine, *mestiza*)
mulato person of mixed racial ancestry exhibiting African physical characteristics (feminine, *mulata*)
obraje textile factory
padre de familia male head of household
partido portion of silver ore that mine workers were allowed to keep for themselves after fulfilling quotas owed to their employers; also known as *pepena*
peninsular person born in Iberian peninsula (noun or adjective; plural, *peninsulares*)
pepena portion of silver ore that mine workers were allowed to keep for themselves after fulfilling quotas owed to their employers; also known as *partido*
presidio military fort or garrison
Provincias Internas term used to describe northern frontier of New Spain

pueblo small village, usually of Indians; when used as proper noun, indigenous sedentary inhabitants of northern New Mexico
ranchería dispersed settlement of indigenous peoples
real unit of currency, one-eighth of a peso (plural, *reales*); also used to denote a mining camp
regidor permanent member of town council (plural, *regidores*)
repartimiento grant of Indian draft laborers
rescatador petty entrepreneurs who scavenged silver ore for themselves or purchased it from others
Semana Santa Holy Week, the week before Easter
sirviente literally, servant; in practice a generic term applied to most employees
sociedad de castas term used to describe multiethnic society of colonial Mexico
soltera woman who had never married
tenatero mine worker who carried sacks of ore to the surface
teniente lieutenant; refers to lieutenant of alcalde mayor
tienda store or shop
vecino householder
villa official category of municipal organization; usually conferred right to establish cabildo; applied to towns too small to qualify as *ciudades* (cities)

Notes

The principal sources for this book can be found in the Archivo del Ayuntamiento de Chihuahua. Most notes cite the microfilm copy at the University of Texas at El Paso Library. This microfilm consists of a main collection, hereinafter cited as AACh, UTEP 491, and two supplements, cited as AACh, UTEP 501 and AACh, UTEP 502.

There is no guide to these microfilmed collections, other than a rough index that I compiled while working with them; a copy of it can be consulted in the Special Collections Department of the UTEP Library. I have assigned *expediente* (file) numbers to the documents according to the order in which they appear on each reel of film. On some occasions, several contiguous but unrelated loose documents have been grouped into a single expediente. Citations below give the reel number first, followed by a hyphen and the expediente number.

Archivists in Chihuahua have recently arranged the original documents in topical and chronological order and compiled a thorough index to the collection. In those cases in which I have used the originals, I have indicated their locations.

Other frequently cited sources are the microfilm copy of the Archivo Municipal de Parral (abbreviated AMP), and the microfilm collections of the Genealogical Society of Utah (abbreviated GSU).

INTRODUCTION

1. Hadley, pp. 27–28.
2. AACh, UTEP 491, 93-20. A portion of a sugar hacienda in the central Mexican state of Morelos was known as "*las tierras de Chihuahua*" (the lands of Chihuahua), presumably because it seemed as far from the estate's

headquarters as the distant mines of Chihuahua. See Archivo General de la Nación, Mexico City, Ramo Tierras, vol. 2047, exp. 1, fols. 59v-60.

3. AACh, UTEP 491, 20-7.

4. AACh, UTEP 491, 25-11.

5. Darnton, pp. 3–4.

6. See, for example, the extensive references to Chihuahua in Bannon, *The Spanish Borderlands Frontier.*

7. Lockhart and Schwartz, pp. 253–304, 337.

8. On the Pueblo Revolt and associated northern unrest, see A. Chávez, pp. 85–126; Gutiérrez, pp. 130–40; Forbes, pp. 177–224; Hackett, *Revolt of the Pueblo Indians*; Griffen, pp. 9–13.

9. On the disturbances of the 1690s and on measures undertaken by Mexico City authorities to guarantee greater stability in the wake of the 1692 riot, see Cope, pp. 125–60; Guthrie, pp. 243–58; Robles, vol. 2, pp. 250–58; Yoma Medina and Martos López, pp. 24–37.

10. Cope, pp. 42–44.

11. Ibid., p. 148.

12. On the economic, political, social, and cultural evolution of Indian communities in central and southern Mexico, see Gibson; Taylor, *Landlord and Peasant* and *Drinking, Homicide, and Rebellion*; Van Young, "Conflict and Solidarity"; Wood; Martin, *Rural Society*; Cline; García Martínez; Haskett, *Indigenous Rulers*; Lockhart, *Nahuas After the Conquest.*

13. For a discussion of the extent of migration in colonial Mexico, see Swann, *Migrants in the Mexican North*; Stern and Jackson.

14. For concise summaries of the literature relating to social passing in colonial Mexico, see Anderson's opening remarks; Kicza. See also Gutiérrez, pp. 198–206.

15. Cope, p. 165.

16. See, for example, Ladd; Taylor, *Drinking, Homicide, and Rebellion.*

17. The most notable recent study to emphasize the limitations of the so-called Bourbon Reforms is Deans-Smith.

18. See Hadley.

19. The most comprehensive of Francisco Almada's many works are *Diccionario de historia, geografía y biografía chihuahuenses* and *Resumen de la historia del estado de Chihuahua.*

20. J. C. Scott, p. 67.

21. See Thompson.

22. J. C. Scott.

23. Ibid., p. 199.

24. AACh, UTEP 491, 10-8, 72-15; AACh, UTEP 501, 4-29.

25. AACh, UTEP 501, 6-43.

26. AACh, UTEP 491, 46-18.

27. AACh, UTEP 491, 32-82, 103-12, 109-19; AACh, UTEP 501, 1-33, 4-15.

28. AACh, UTEP 491, 27-15, 94-12, 109-20; AACh, UTEP 501, 6-36.

CHAPTER ONE

1. The classic work on the development of Zacatecas is Bakewell. On hostilities between the Chichimecas and Spanish intruders, see Powell.

2. For the early settlement of Nueva Vizcaya, see Swann, *Tierra Adentro*, pp. 10–31; Jones, *Nueva Vizcaya*, pp. 17–29, 66–67; Mecham; Cramaussel; Porras Muñoz, *La frontera con los indios*, pp. 14–19; Hackett, *Historical Documents*, vol. 2. The province of Nueva Vizcaya eventually encompassed most of the territory that now comprises the states of Durango and Chihuahua; until 1734 it also included much of Sinaloa and Sonora, while the Parras-Saltillo district of present-day Coahuila remained part of Nueva Vizcaya until 1786. On the territorial evolution of Nueva Vizcaya, see Jones, *Nueva Vizcaya*, pp. ix, 3.

3. On founding of New Mexico, see Hammond and Rey; Hackett, *Historical Documents*, vol. 1; Simmons, *The Last Conquistador*; Gutiérrez, pp. 46–94.

4. Swann, *Tierra Adentro*, pp. 4–6; Cramaussel, pp. 54–56; Porras Muñoz, *La frontera con los indios*, pp. 19, 141–62; Griffen, pp. 4–5.

5. For the early history of Parral, see West; Swann, *Tierra Adentro*, pp. 15–31; Jones, *Los Paisanos*, pp. 85–86, and *Nueva Vizcaya*, pp. 84–86; Porras Muñoz, *La frontera con los indios*, pp. 38–39, 68.

6. Swann, *Tierra Adentro*, p. 19; Gerhard, pp. 197–98; Griffen, pp. 5–13; Porras Muñoz, *La frontera con los indios*; Deeds, pp. 425–49; Jones, *Nueva Vizcaya*, pp. 90–115.

7. Almada, *Diccionario*, pp. 136–37.

8. Porras Muñoz, *La frontera con los indios*, pp. 179–86, 203–9, 241–47.

9. Deeds, pp. 439–40.

10. Hadley, pp. 38, 68–69; Almada, "La fundación"; Archivo General de Indias, Seville, Audiencia de Guadalajara, 67-5-15, typescript in the Barker Texas History Collection, University of Texas at Austin, Box 2Q137, Binder 24.

11. Hadley, pp. 35, 70–72; Barri; Almada, "La fundación." Hadley, pp. 52 and 71, reports one version in which a Christianized Indian named Juan de Dios Barba, originally from New Mexico but residing in the mission of Nombre de Dios, started the bonanza after various Tarahumaras in the area showed him the silver deposits. Barba then informed his stepson, Cristóbal Luján, of the presence of silver at Santa Eulalia. They registered claims and worked them for a time, but eventually their claims ended up in the hands of others. Other versions say that a cowboy stumbled on the first silver findings.

12. Hadley, pp. 70–72; Almada, "La fundación"; Bargellini, pp. 13, 63.

13. Hadley, pp. 72–75; Bargellini, p. 13.

14. Some sources give the governor's name as Manuel San Juan de Santa Cruz.

15. Almada, "La fundación"; Hadley, p. 72–80; Bargellini, p. 13; Porras Muñoz, *Iglesia y estado*, p. 156.

16. Hadley, p. 41; AMP, reel 1716a, frames 283, 310.

17. AACh, UTEP 491, 15-5; AACh, UTEP 501, 5-7; Almada, *Diccionario*, pp. 136–38. Most authorities consider the name "Chihuahua" to be of Tarahumara origin; see Almada, *Diccionario*, p. 138.

18. Jones, *Nueva Vizcaya*, p. 120.

19. General works on municipal administration in colonial Latin America include Bayle; Moore, *The Cabildo in Peru under the Hapsburgs* and *The Cabildo in Peru under the Bourbons*; Marzahl; Cruz.

20. Jones, *Nueva Vizcaya*, pp. 119, 139; p. 253, n. 24.

21. AACh, UTEP 491, 83-3.

22. Jones, *Nueva Vizcaya*, p. 123.

23. Bargellini, pp. 21–26.

24. AACh, UTEP 501, 1-17, 1-34, 3-8, 4-4; Hadley, pp. 137–40.

25. AACh, UTEP 491, 27-15; AACh, UTEP 501, 6-40.

26. Hadley, pp. 142, 203; Jones, *Nueva Vizcaya*, pp. 122, 187–88; Moorhead, *New Mexico's Royal Road*, p. 49.

27. AACh, UTEP 491, 8-2; Gerhard, p. 199; Hadley, p. 33.

28. Archivo General de la Nación, Mexico City, Ramo Provincias Internas, vol. 142, exp. 1.

29. Bargellini, p. 19; Cramaussel and Alvarez, p. 49.

30. Cited by Vito Alesio Robles in his edition of Tamarón y Romeral, p. 163, n. 74.

31. Hadley, p. 33.

32. On the technology of mining and refining in Chihuahua and Santa Eulalia, see Hadley, pp. 153–86.

33. See, for example, AACh, UTEP 491, 20-3.

34. There are, however, occasional references to the amalgamation process; see AACh, UTEP 491, 124-9. Even when amalgamation was used, however, it was not the familiar patio process, but a process called "*amalgamación en caliente*," introduced by Andrés Facundo Carbonel in 1706; see Hadley, p. 157.

35. AACh, UTEP 491, 10-19, 10-32; Hadley, pp. 132–33.

36. Deeds, p. 442; AACh, UTEP 491, 18-6.

37. AACh, UTEP 491, 18-14, 68-2.

38. AACh, UTEP 491, 32-72. 39. AACh, UTEP 491, 32-33.

40. AACh, UTEP 491, 41-12. 41. AACh, UTEP 491, 112-37.

42. Chihuahua (El Sagrario) Parish Registers, Burials, GSU reels 0162697, 0162698.

43. AACh, UTEP 491, 63-3, 64-22, 114-12; Jones, *Nueva Vizcaya*, pp. 144–98.

44. Quoted in Jones, *Nueva Vizcaya*, p. 162; on the Rubí expedition, see also Bannon, pp. 172–80.

45. AACh, UTEP 501, 5-4.

46. AACh, UTEP 491, 110-40.

47. AACh, UTEP 491, 126-11; AACh, UTEP 502, 2-5.

48. AACh, UTEP 491, 95-1; for additional information on general demographic trends in Nueva Vizcaya from 1765 to 1810, see Swann, *Tierra Adentro*, pp. 111–60.

49. AACh, UTEP 491, 89-23.

50. Tamarón y Romeral, pp. 152–54.

51. Swann, *Tierra Adentro*, p. 114.

52. Figures for 1779 and 1791 are from Archivo General de la Nación, Mexico City, Ramo Provincias Internas, vol. 142, exp. 1; figures for 1785 are from AACh, UTEP 502, 3-23.

53. AACh, UTEP 491, 139-17. Some published accounts have overestimated the population of San Felipe and Santa Eulalia for the late colonial period. Hadley, pp. 32–33, cites H. G. Ward, *México in 1827*, 2 vols. (London: H. Colburn, 1828), vol. 2, p. 129, who suggests a figure of 6,000 for Santa Eulalia in 1791. It is likely that Ward derived this figure from a report given by leading miners from Chihuahua in 1791 (in Archivo General de la Nación, Ramo Provincias Internas, vol. 142, exp. 1, cited above, note 52), in which they estimated the mining camp's population to have been about 6,000 in 1720. Jones claims that San Felipe had a population of 11,698 in 1793, but this figure must have included the villa's entire jurisdiction, for he quotes a population of 4,895 for San Felipe in 1813; Jones, *Nueva Vizcaya*, pp. 203–4.

54. AACh, UTEP 491, 95-20. For long-term fluctuations in the fortunes of silver mining at Chihuahua, Parral, and other mining centers in Nueva Vizcaya during the seventeenth and eighteenth centuries, see Swann, *Tierra Adentro*, pp. 56–60.

55. Hadley, p. 210.

56. AACh, UTEP 501, 11-6.

57. Archivo General de la Nación, Mexico City, Ramo Provincias Internas, vol. 142, exp. 1.

58. AACh, UTEP 491, 89-7.

59. Tamarón y Romeral, p. 152.

60. Jones, *Nueva Vizcaya*, p. 187.

61. Hadley, p. 211.

62. AACh, UTEP 491, 124-11.

63. Swann, *Tierra Adentro*, pp. 64–65; Hadley, pp. 210–11; Moorhead, *New Mexico's Royal Road*, pp. 50–54; Jones, *Nueva Vizcaya*, pp. 187–88; Gutiérrez, pp. 300–4; Frank.

64. Bannon, pp. 180–89; Moorhead, *The Apache Frontier*, pp. 3–18, 46–48, 119–23, 155–59.

CHAPTER TWO

1. There were probably many others, but I have counted as peninsulares only those explicitly designated as such in reliable documents, including wills, declarations made under oath, parish registers, and census reports.

2. AACh, UTEP 502, 3-23. The 1785 census notes only 21 peninsulares, but other sources confirm that at least another 10 persons listed in the census were in fact born in Spain.

3. Brading, "Los españoles en México."

4. Chihuahua (El Sagrario) Parish Registers, Marriages, GSU reel 0162689, Oct. 1779.

5. Chihuahua (El Sagrario) Parish Registers, Baptisms, GSU reel 0162663, Jan. 1789. Charles Nunn has estimated that at most some 15 percent of the peninsular immigrants in the early eighteenth century were women, while David Brading has calculated that 4 percent of the peninsulares (excluding male clergy) residing in New Spain in the 1790s were female. See Nunn, p. 4; Brading, "Los españoles en México," p. 132.

6. On the preponderance of northerners among late colonial Spanish migrants to the colonies, see Socolow, *The Merchants of Buenos Aires*, pp. 18–19; Brading, *Miners and Merchants*, pp. 106–8, and "Los españoles en México."

7. AACh, UTEP 491, 34-3; Almada, *Diccionario*, p. 72.

8. Personal communications from Anthony Reaza, Dec. 3, 1991; Jan. 27, 1994.

9. AACh, UTEP 491, 30-3, 33-49, 36-18, 42-12. On education in Spain in the seventeenth and eighteenth centuries, see Kagan; Kamen, pp. 311–12.

10. On creole attitudes toward peninsular immigrants, see Van Young, "Parvenues and Popinjays," p. 6.

11. Socolow, *The Merchants of Buenos Aires*, p. 112.

12. AACh, UTEP 491, 43-5.

13. AACh, UTEP 491, 18-5; Chihuahua (El Sagrario) Parish Registers, Burials, GSU reel 0162697, Jan. 1731.

14. AACh, UTEP 491, 59-43.

15. An important exception was Antonio Deza y Ulloa, governor of Nueva Vizcaya at the time of the founding of San Francisco de Cuéllar. He was born in Huejotzingo in the jurisdiction of Puebla de los Angeles. Almada, *Diccionario*, p. 165.

16. For a list of Chihuahua's elected alcaldes and their birthplaces, see Table 1 in the Appendix.

17. AACh, UTEP 491, 8-2.

18. AACh, UTEP 491, 10-16.

19. AMP, reel 1731B, frame 532.

20. AACh, UTEP 491, 99-7.

21. AACh, UTEP 491, 29-5, 29-6, 32-72, 34-4, 36-5, 42-18, 42-25, 47-

15; Chihuahua (El Sagrario) Parish Registers, Marriages, GSU reel 0162689, May 1717, Oct. 1726; Chihuahua (El Sagrario) Parish Registers, Baptisms, GSU reel 0162660, Aug. 1735; GSU reel 0162661, Sept. 1737, Nov. 1738, Apr. 1740; Hadley, p. 43.

22. Chihuahua (El Sagrario) Parish Registers, Marriages, GSU reel 0162689, June 1749; Baptisms, GSU reel 0162661, May 1756, Apr. 1759; AACh, UTEP 491, 100-9; personal communication from Anthony Reaza, Dec. 3, 1991.

23. Hadley, pp. 74, 96; Almada, *Diccionario*, p. 535; personal communication from Anthony Reaza, Jan. 27, 1994.

24. Hadley, p. 37; Chihuahua (El Sagrario) Parish Registers, Marriages, GSU reel 0162689, June 1713; AACh, UTEP 491, 13-19, 25-24.

25. AACh, UTEP 491, 11-26, 36-5, 37-16, 69-19, 80-28; AACh, UTEP 501, 3-16; Chihuahua (El Sagrario) Parish Registers, Marriages, GSU reel 0162689, Jan. 1740.

26. AACh, UTEP 491, 59-43, 61-8, 62-11, 69-11, 84-1, 116-25, 121-2, 121-12, 125-7, 125-16, 125-17, 143-10; AACh, UTEP 501, 5-6; AACh, UTEP 502, 3-23, 4-24; Chihuahua (El Sagrario) Parish Registers, Marriages, GSU reel 0162689, Aug. 1767, Apr. 1774, Feb. 1782; GSU reel 0162691, Sept. 1804; Burials, GSU reel 0162698, Aug. 1779; Almada, "Lista de los alcaldes"; Baquera, p. 43.

27. AACh, UTEP 491, 3-17, 7-16, 57-15, 89-2, 89-4, 89-22, 94-12, 99-7, 100-4, 100-8, 100-13, 100-21, 108-36, 121-4; AACh, UTEP 501, 4-40.

28. Chihuahua (El Sagrario) Parish Registers, Marriages, GSU reel 0162689, Apr. 1730, Sept. 1731; Burials, GSU reel 0162697, June 1738; see also AACh, UTEP 491, 13-10, 15-5, 101-7. Documents refer to Moreno's wife as "*una india comprada*" ("a purchased Indian"); see AACh, UTEP 491, 23-5.

29. AACh, UTEP 491, 12-24, 14-1; AMP, reel 1716a, frame 283; reel 1724a, frame 11.

30. Brading, *Miners and Merchants*, pp. 109–10.

31. AACh, UTEP 491, 76-5.

32. AACh, UTEP 501, 1-20.

33. AACh, UTEP 491, 18-5.

34. AACh, UTEP 501, 4-44.

35. AACh, UTEP 502, 3-5.

36. Chihuahua (El Sagrario) Parish Registers, Burials, GSU reel 0162697, Mar. 1729; GSU reel 0162698, Feb. 1757; Baptisms, GSU reel 0162660, Apr. 1730; AACh, UTEP 491, 27-15.

37. AACh, UTEP 491, 118-24.

38. AACh, UTEP 501, 3-19.

39. AACh, UTEP 501, 4-7.

40. Nunn, pp. 2, 6. Nunn estimates that from 3 to 4 percent of the European-born residents of New Spain during the first half of the eighteenth

century were foreigners, that is, born outside Spain or its American colonies. Non-Spanish subjects of the Spanish crown, including Flemings, Sardinians, Neapolitans, and Milanese, were more readily accepted.

41. AACh, UTEP 491, 10-16, 13-20; AMP, reel 1731B, frame 532; Chihuahua (El Sagrario) Parish Registers, Marriages, GSU reel 0162689, Apr. 1727; Baptisms, GSU reel 0162660, May 1730. Eighteenth-century documents sometimes spell his name "Masjalca."

42. AACh, UTEP 491, 9-19.

43. AACh, UTEP 491, 3-9, 10-32, 25-17, 29-4, 33-11, 42-9; AMP, reel 1725a, frame 264; reel 1731b, frame 532.

44. AACh, UTEP 491, 85-29, 100-21; AACh, UTEP 502, 3-23; Chihuahua (El Sagrario) Parish Registers, Burials, GSU reel 0162698, Nov. 1776.

45. AACh, UTEP 491, 42-15; 93-39; Chihuahua (El Sagrario) Parish Registers, Marriages, GSU reel 0162689, Nov. 1762. José Marioni may be the same person as Claudio Giuseppe Marioni, a Neapolitan who was granted a special royal permission to emigrate to New Spain in 1750. See Nunn, pp. 32, 137.

46. AACh, UTEP 491, 8-2, 8-11, 8-15, 25-11, 60-4, 60-10, 80-28; Chihuahua (El Sagrario) Parish Registers, Marriages, GSU reel 0162689, Aug. 1726.

47. AACh, UTEP 491, 43-5; Hadley, p. 36; Nunn, p. 125.

48. AACh, UTEP 491, 20-7.

49. AACh, UTEP 491, 136-3, 139-6, 143-17; Chihuahua (El Sagrario) Parish Registers, Marriages, GSU reel 0162691, Nov. 1809, Dec. 1813.

50. AACh, UTEP 502, 3-23.

51. For the status of españoles elsewhere in late colonial Mexico, see Anderson.

52. AACh, UTEP 491, 108-26, 108-36, 116-26, 118-11, 118-36.

53. AACh, UTEP 491, 108-36; Chihuahua (El Sagrario) Parish Registers, Baptisms, GSU reel 0162663, July 1779, Nov. 1780; GSU reel 0162664, June 1792; Almada, *Diccionario*, p. 537; Baquera, pp. 64–81.

54. AACh, UTEP 491, 135-2; Hopper.

55. Chihuahua (El Sagrario) Parish Registers, Baptisms, GSU reel 0162663, May 1778; Burials, GSU reel 0162699, Apr. 1788; AACh, UTEP 491, 134-8.

56. AACh, UTEP 491, 10-16; Chihuahua (El Sagrario) Parish Registers, Burials, GSU reel 0162697, Mar. 1750.

57. AACh, UTEP 491, 80-28; Chihuahua (El Sagrario) Parish Registers, Burials, GSU reel 0162697, Mar. 1756.

58. AACh, UTEP 491, 5-16, 8-18, 11-1, 11-9, 22-8, 47-20, 49-14, 72-31, 125-7, 125-33; AMP, reel 1716a, frame 310; Santa Eulalia Parish Registers, Marriages, GSU reel 0162594, June 1717.

59. AMP, reel 1712, frame 101.

60. El Valle de San Bartolomé (Valle de Allende) Parish Registers, Baptisms, GSU reel 0162634, Feb. 1672, Aug. 1677, Oct. 1698, Jan. 1706; Marriages, GSU reel 0162650, Dec. 1695, Feb. 1706, Nov. 1722.

61. For a more complete biographical sketch of Juana de Cobos, see Chapter 7.

62. AACh, UTEP 491, 89-23.

63. AACh, UTEP 491, 105-25.

64. AACh, UTEP 491, 27-15.

65. AACh, UTEP 491, 30-12, 30-13, 30-31, 45-2; Chihuahua (El Sagrario) Parish Registers, Marriages, GSU reel 0162689, Jan. 1719.

66. AACh, UTEP 491, 23-16.

67. Chihuahua (El Sagrario) Parish Registers, Marriages, GSU reel 0162689.

68. Santa Eulalia Parish Registers, Marriages, GSU reel 0162594, Mar. 1720.

69. AACh, UTEP 491, 18-16, 25-26, 35-15, 45-1, 47-1, 47-21, 54-9, 56-6, 69-19, 77-8, 77-23, 82-3, 82-6, 90-11, 90-33, 92-7, 107-24, 110-15, 112-9, 115-33, 127-15, 127-20; AACh, UTEP 501, 5-3; AACh, UTEP 502, 2-5; Deeds. For the use of repartimiento workers in Coahuila, see Cuello.

70. AACh, UTEP 491, 100-15.

71. AACh, UTEP 491, 46-15, 72-29; Deeds, pp. 446-47.

72. AACh, UTEP 491, 76-1; AACh, UTEP 501, 6-43.

73. AACh, UTEP 491, 5-6, 51-19, 117-26, 130-36; AACh, UTEP 501, 4-27.

74. AACh, UTEP 491, 35-15, fol. 226v.

75. AACh, UTEP 502, 3-23.

76. AACh, UTEP 491, 99-2.

77. AACh, UTEP 491, 29-5.

78. Cramaussel and Alvarez, p. 48, n. 10.

79. Tamarón y Romeral, pp. 152–54; AACh, UTEP 501, 4-16.

80. Jones, *Nueva Vizcaya*, p. 162.

81. AACh, UTEP 491, 42-14, 87-6, 91-10.

82. Santa Eulalia Parish Registers, Baptisms, GSU reel 1062596, May 1725.

83. AACh, UTEP 491, 26-40.

84. AACh, UTEP 491, 34-3, 38-19, 59-61.

85. AACh, UTEP 491, 8-3, 20-23, 65-12, 73-4; AACh, UTEP 501, 5-3.

86. AACh, UTEP 491, 23-17, 24-19, 27-15, 105-29; AACh, UTEP 501, 3-16, 3-24, 4-31, 4-43, 5-3.

87. AACh, UTEP 491, 32-38, 101-1.

88. AACh, UTEP 491, 103-12.

89. AACh, UTEP 491, 32-82, 103-12; AACh, UTEP 501, 1-33, 4-15, 6-43. See also the marriage record of the "indios mexicanos" Ramón Francisco

and Nicolasa de la Cruz, Santa Eulalia Parish Registers, Marriages, GSU reel 0162594, Mar. 1720.

90. AACh, UTEP 491, 25-13.
91. AACh, UTEP 491, 32-17.
92. AACh, UTEP 502, 3-23.
93. AACh, UTEP 501, 3-12.
94. AACh, UTEP 491, 27-15.
95. AACh, UTEP 502, 3-23.
96. AACh, UTEP 491, 19-23.
97. AACh, UTEP 491, 66-35.
98. AACh, UTEP 491, 20-7. For a fuller description of the crime and prosecution of Chico and Angolita, see Chapter 6.

CHAPTER THREE

1. Hadley, pp. 184–85.
2. See Deeds. For general treatments on the repartimiento in central Mexico, see Gibson, pp. 224–43; Haskett, " 'Our Suffering with the Taxco Tribute.' "
3. AACh, UTEP 491, 15-5.
4. AACh, UTEP 491, 17-17.
5. AACh, UTEP 491, 26-23, 30-31, 32-73, 36-19.
6. Chihuahua (El Sagrario) Parish Registers, Marriages, GSU reel 0162689.
7. AACh, UTEP 501, 1-28.
8. AACh, UTEP 491, 22-6.
9. AACh, UTEP 491, 1-20.
10. AACh, UTEP 501, 6-40.
11. AACh, UTEP 491, 15-5, 24-1.
12. Hadley, p. 190; del Río, pp. 92–111. The word "*pepena*" derives from a Nahuatl word meaning to choose, glean, pick over; see Lockhart, "Commentary," p. 111–14. On the history of labor relations in other mining communities, see Bakewell, especially pp. 122–28; Ladd.
13. AACh, UTEP 491, 26-15; 29-5, fol. 56.
14. AACh, UTEP 491, 28-7.
15. AACh, UTEP 491, 14-2, 28-7; Hadley, pp. 190–91, 194; Miguel O. de Mendizábal; Bakewell, p. 125.
16. AACh, UTEP 491, 11-26; Hadley, pp. 164–71. Evidently this tactic of forcing workers to sell their partidos to their employers was common in eighteenth-century Zacatecas; see Garner, "Zacatecas," p. 324.
17. AACh, UTEP 491, 11-26.
18. AACh, UTEP 491, 15-5; Porras Muñoz, *Iglesia y estado*, pp. 442–45; Almada, *Resumen*, p. 109, and *Diccionario*, p. 486.
19. On Sánchez Camacho, see AACh, UTEP 491, 12-18, 16-21; AACh, UTEP 501, 5-7, fol. 222; AMP, reel 1731b, frame 955.
20. Unless otherwise specified, all information on the mining regulations of 1730 and the resulting labor unrest comes from AACh, UTEP 491, 15-5, and 15-6. See also AMP, reel 1731b, frame 955; Hadley, p. 168.

21. Bishop Crespo y Monroy was still in Chihuahua in early June; see Porras Muñoz, *Iglesia y Estado*, pp. 135, 463. The bishop inspected the parish registers on April 29; see Chihuahua (El Sagrario) Parish Registers, Marriages, GSU reel 0162689.

22. AACh, UTEP 491, 15-5, 15-6; AMP, reel 1731c, frame 1261.

23. AACh, UTEP 491, 15-5. On Fernando de Urrutia, see Burkholder and Chandler, p. 336. Juan José de Urrutia was married to Nicolasa de Orio y Zubiate, daughter of General José de Orio y Zubiate, and widow of the alférez José de Aguirre; see Chihuahua (El Sagrario) Parish Registers, Marriages, GSU reel 0162689, Feb. 1729; AACh, UTEP 491, 19-23.

24. AMP, reel 1731b, frame 955.

25. AMP, reel 1731b, frame 532; reel 1731c, frame 1261; AACh, UTEP 491, 42-11. In the meantime, Barrutia relinquished the governorship in 1733 and returned to Havana, where he was promoted to the rank of general; see Almada, *Diccionario*, p. 64. He eventually returned to Chihuahua, however. He died there in 1754; see Chihuahua (El Sagrario) Parish Registers, Burials, GSU reel 0162697, Dec. 1754.

26. AACh, UTEP 491, 42-17.

27. AACh, UTEP 491, 29-6, 36-5, 43-23.

28. Unless otherwise specified, information on the uprising of 1735 comes from AACh, UTEP 491, 29-5, 29-6, 29-10, and 31-3.

29. AACh, UTEP 491, 29-5, 29-10, 36-5. San Juan y Santa Cruz's opponent Sebastián de Arrieta spent time in jail over the next several years for his alleged support of the rebellious workers. See AACh, UTEP 491, 46-4, 51-19.

30. Meanwhile, San Juan y Santa Cruz remained a powerful figure in Chihuahua until his death in 1749, although he experienced some financial difficulties toward the end of his life, after having squandered a large sum in an effort to set up a relative in office in Veracruz. Almada, *Diccionario*, p. 486.

31. AACh, UTEP 491, 76-5.

32. AACh, UTEP 491, 11-26.

33. See del Río.

34. Brading and Cross; Mendizábal.

35. AACh, UTEP 491, 24-19, 35-15, 39-9, 39-18, 45-1, 47-21, 54-1, 61-6, 86-3, 87-7.

36. Gibson, pp. 251–52.

37. For Mexico City maize prices during the eighteenth century, see Florescano, pp. 201–24.

38. AACh, UTEP 491, 50-1, 51-22, 97-2, 92-20, 99-19.

39. AACh, UTEP 491, 10-19, 10-32; Hadley, pp. 132–33.

40. AACh, UTEP 491, 51-22.

41. AACh, UTEP 491, 64-30, 97-2.
42. Garner, "Price Trends."
43. AACh, UTEP 491, 70-26.
44. AACh, UTEP 491, 16-15, 23-22, 54-1, 64-30, 69-19; Gibson, p. 311.
45. AACh, UTEP 491, 57-5.
46. AACh, UTEP 501, 5-1.
47. AACh, UTEP 491, 16-15.
48. AACh, UTEP 491, 9-28, 10-26, 21-5, 24-19, 32-37, 35-15, 36-2, 40-3, 45-1, 59-55, 62-44, 64-36.
49. AACh, UTEP 491, 16-19.
50. See, for example, Van Young, *Hacienda and Market*, p. 255.
51. AACh, UTEP 491, 8-16, 10-6, 13-6, 23-8, 24-19, 27-1, 28-7, 37-19, 41-14, 67-6, 72-2.
52. AACh, UTEP 491, 59-3, 60-13, 101-36, 104-49. See also Bakewell, pp. 125–26.
53. AACh, UTEP 491, 9-5, 32-47, 66-16.
54. AACh, UTEP 491, 91-10, 114-25. A similar overlapping of wage labor and slavery existed in Mexico City; see Cope, p. 98.
55. AACh, UTEP 491, 114-25.
56. AACh, UTEP 501, 4-34; AACh, UTEP 491, 10-10, 11-13, 25-51, 65-15, 96-8, 101-36.
57. AACh, UTEP 491, 30-13, 81-4.
58. AACh, UTEP 491, 8-36, 13-37, 96-8, 101-23.
59. AACh, UTEP 491, 24-19, fol. 390; 30-13.
60. AACh, UTEP 491, 96-8.
61. AACh, UTEP 491, 18-14.
62. AACh, UTEP 491, 30-13.
63. AACh, UTEP 491, 61-6.
64. AACh, UTEP 491, 33-43; Chihuahua (El Sagrario) Parish Registers, GSU reel 0162661, Apr. 1739.
65. AACh, UTEP 491, 20-23, 23-22.
66. AACh, UTEP 501, 3-8.
67. AACh, UTEP 491, 29-5.
68. AACh, UTEP 491, 58-7.
69. AACh, UTEP 491, 22-21.
70. AACh, UTEP 491, 101-36.
71. AACh, UTEP 501, 5-5.
72. AACh, UTEP 491, 112-25; AACh, UTEP 501, 3-4.
73. AACh, UTEP 491, 29-5.
74. AACh, UTEP 501, 6-8.
75. AACh, UTEP 491, 101-1. The phrase "domestic enemies" evidently originated in Renaissance Italy and was commonly used to describe household servants in seventeenth- and eighteenth-century France; see Fairchilds, p. xi.
76. AMP, reel 1731b, frame 532.
77. AACh, UTEP 491, 11-36.
78. AACh, UTEP 491, 108-28.
79. AACh, UTEP 491, 50-6; see also AACh, UTEP 491, 24-19, fol. 419.

80. AACh, UTEP 491, 115-26.
81. AACh, UTEP 501, 1-27.
82. AACh, UTEP 491, 112-12.
83. AACh, UTEP 501, 3-13.
84. AACh, UTEP 501, 1-20.
85. AACh, UTEP 501, 4-40.
86. AACh, UTEP 501, 6-23.
87. AACh, UTEP 491, 116-25.
88. AACh, UTEP 491, 23-22.
89. AACh, UTEP 491, 16-33.
90. AACh, UTEP 501, 1-21.
91. Cope, pp. 91–95; quotations from pp. 94 and 91, respectively.
92. AACh, UTEP 491, 11-26.
93. See for example, AACh, UTEP 502, 1-8; AACh, UTEP 491, 43-5, 57-15, 113-23.
94. AACh, UTEP 491, 5-1.
95. AACh, UTEP 491, 105-6.
96. AACh, UTEP 491, 30-12, 81-4.
97. AACh, UTEP 491, 69-6.
98. AACh, UTEP 491, 57-15.
99. AACh, UTEP 491, 131-20.
100. AACh, UTEP 491, 60-24, 65-1, 76-7.
101. AACh, UTEP 401, 101-36. The document reads that providing benefits during a worker's illness was "devido y muy de su obligación, pena de perder la acción, y dominio que en mi pudiera haber y tener."
102. Cope, pp. 94–95.
103. For a discussion of guilds in Chihuahua, see Chapter 5.
104. Thompson, pp. 383–85.
105. AACh, UTEP 491, 131-29.
106. Thompson, p. 384.
107. Ibid., p. 387.
108. Ibid., p. 389.
109. Ibid., pp. 387–88.

CHAPTER FOUR

1. Terrazas.
2. Almada, *Diccionario*, p. 26; Porras Muñoz, *La frontera con los indios*, pp. 204–5; Arras R., p. 83.
3. Hadley, pp. 73, 95–97; AACh, UTEP 491, 28-7; AMP, reel 1716a, frame 283; Almada, *Diccionario*, p. 535, and "La fundación."
4. Hadley, pp. 42, 44, 97; AMP, reel 1731c, frame 1212; AACh, UTEP 491, 13-20, 15-5; Garate; Chihuahua (El Sagrario) Parish Registers, Burials, GSU reel 0162697, June 1723; Almada, *Diccionario*, p. 380; Porras Muñoz, *La frontera con los indios*, p. 207.
5. AACh, UTEP 491, 10-16, 22-20, 22-22, 68-7, 55-2; AACh, UTEP 501, 5-7, fol. 32; Chihuahua (El Sagrario) Parish Registers, Marriages, GSU reel 0162689, Dec. 1723; Hadley, p. 43.
6. AACh, UTEP 501, 5-7; Almada, *Resumen*, p. 112, *Diccionario*, p. 382, and "La fundación"; Hadley, p. 46.
7. AACh, UTEP 491, 18-6.

8. AACh, UTEP 491, 10-16.

9. AACh, UTEP 491, 85-21, 100-13; AACh, UTEP 501, 6-24; AACh, UTEP 502, 9-8; see also AMP, reel 1820, frame 299.

10. AMP, reel 1744, frame 129; reel 1790c, frame 2056; reel 1795, frame 665.

11. Foster, pp. 16, 34; Marc Simmons, "Governor Cuervo"; Marzahl, p. 12; Bayle, pp. 79–80. This preference for urban living also seems to have been rooted in deep-seated psychological needs of settlers in the New World. Numerous scholars have pointed out that English settlers in North America also adopted the grid plan in laying out their towns, even though they were not ordered to do so. As Nancy M. Farriss observes, the creation of an urban setting seemed to suggest order and control in the midst of a human and natural wilderness; see her *Maya Society*, p. 161. On urban planning in Europe and the Americas from the late Middle Ages through the eighteenth century, see Reps, pp. 1–202.

12. On internal migration in Spain, see Kamen, p. 60.

13. Socolow, *The Merchants of Buenos Aires*, p. 19.

14. Kamen, p. 154.

15. Socolow, "Introduction," pp. 3–17; population figures, p. 5.

16. For descriptions of life in colonial Mexico City, see Hoberman and Socolow; Meyer and Sherman, pp. 221–46; Leonard, especially pp. 72–78, 157–60; Romero de Terreros; Robles; Vásquez Mellado.

17. On ceremonial display in colonial Mexico City, see Leonard, pp. 1–17, 117–29; Curcio-Nagy; García Ayluardo; Gonzalbo Aizpuru; Viqueira Albán; "Ceremonial de la novilísima Ciudad de México por lo acaecido el año de 1755," García Collection, folder 135, Benson Latin American Library, University of Texas at Austin.

18. See, for example, AACh, UTEP 491, 42-20.

19. AACh, UTEP 491, 42-15.

20. See, for example, AACh, UTEP 491, 42-15; will of Diego Fernández de Olano, Chihuahua (El Sagrario) Parish Registers, Burials, GSU reel 0162697, Nov. 1723.

21. Almada, *Diccionario*, p. 535.

22. AACh, UTEP 491, 8-2, 13-20, 19-18; see also AACh, UTEP 491, 108-29, 108-36.

23. AACh, UTEP 491, 67-4; 84-30, fol. 70.

24. Van Young, *Hacienda and Market*, pp. 30–31.

25. AACh, UTEP 491, 33-23.

26. AACh, UTEP 491, 67-5.

27. AACh, UTEP 491, 47-15; personal communication from Anthony Reaza, Mar. 17, 1992.

28. See, for example, AACh, UTEP 491, 66-3.

29. AACh, UTEP 491, 8-32; Arellano Schetelig. Wigs were introduced into the Spanish court during the reign of Carlos II; see Kamen, p. 341. Many merchants in late colonial Buenos Aires also wore wigs; see Socolow, *The Merchants of Buenos Aires*, p. 83.

30. AACh, UTEP 491, 19-23, 23-22, 35-15, fol. 266v, 47-15, 55-6, 69-6; AACh, UTEP 501, 1-20, 1-33, 4-25. Carriages were a luxury item in eighteenth-century Buenos Aires; see Socolow, *The Merchants of Buenos Aires*, p. 84.

31. Cramaussel and Alvarez, p. 60, note that the lack of alignment of some side streets in downtown Chihuahua City today resulted from later changes rather than from colonial design.

32. Bargellini, pp. 21–26; quotation, p. 26.

33. Almada, *Diccionario*, p. 11; Cramaussel and Alvarez, pp. 65–67. Jones, *Nueva Vizcaya*, p. 124, notes mistakenly that the aqueduct was constructed "under Jesuit supervision." In reality it was built by Indian repartimiento workers from nearby Jesuit missions who worked under the general supervision of local officials. For a description of the aqueduct in 1846, see Wislizenus, p. 60.

34. AACh, UTEP 491, 99-19; Almada, *Diccionario*, p. 18.

35. AACh, UTEP 491, 95-20.

36. AACh, UTEP 491, 107-17, 117-16, 118-7; AACh, UTEP 501, 5-6.

37. Population figures for various cities in New Spain in the 1790s include: Puebla de los Angeles, 56,859; Guanajuato, 28,963; Oaxaca, 18,000; Durango, 11,027; León, 23,700; see Socolow, "Introduction," p. 5.

38. The distinction between a ciudad and a villa was codified in royal ordinances issued in 1573; see Bayle, p. 24.

39. AACh, UTEP 501, 6-25; Bargellini, pp. 15–16.

40. AACh, UTEP 501, 1-12, 1-15, 1-28, 1-36, 3-15, 4-4, 4-30, 6-12, 6-25, 6-26; AACh, UTEP 491, 10-50, 23-6, 26-7, 60-14, 96-9, 102-19. Prisoners also took refuge in the parish church; see AACh, UTEP 491, 58-28, 96-13; AACh, UTEP 501, 1-34, 4-5, 4-29.

41. AACh, UTEP 491, 55-6.

42. Almada, *Diccionario*, p. 261.

43. Ibid., pp. 31, 398.

44. AACh, UTEP 491, 105-24.

45. Porras Muñoz, *Iglesia y estado*, pp. 229–31.

46. AACh, UTEP 491, 72-13, 89-23. Such loose organization was evidently common among artisan guilds in other parts of colonial Latin America; see Johnson, p. 233.

47. AACh, UTEP 491, 53-4, 83-3, 89-23, 92-10, 104-42, 114-5; Almada, *Diccionario*, p. 256; Jones, *Nueva Vizcaya*, pp. 204, 213, 220.

48. For the uses of this term in Spain and the colonies, see Altman, p. 41; Villamarín and Villamarín, pp. 126–27. See also Schneider, pp. 59, 70.

49. AACh, UTEP 501, 6-49; see also AACh, UTEP 491, 12-18, 24-18, 25-52, 105-25.

50. AMP, reel 1731b, frame 532.

51. AACh, UTEP 491, 41-11, 70-14, 109-17. When peninsular merchant and former alcalde José Fernández de Hinojosa wrote his will in 1748, he left 300 pesos to advance devotion to the mystery of the Immaculate Conception; see AACh, UTEP 491, 67-4. Spaniards were far more devoted to the Immaculate Conception than other people in Catholic Europe; see Kamen, p. 292; Perry, p. 39.

52. AACh, UTEP 491, 83-3.

53. This loose usage of the term "vecino" was evident elsewhere in colonial Latin America; see Marzahl, p. 71.

54. AACh, UTEP 501, 4-30; AACh, UTEP 491, 23-7.

55. See, for example, AACh, UTEP 491, 95-20, 117-17; Baquera, p. 37.

56. AACh, UTEP 491, 99-7. Other cabildos abiertos were held in 1765 (to discuss issues of frontier defense), in 1771 (to consider a refiner's plans to construct a new water mill), and in 1809 (to discuss the raising of funds to help defend Spain against the Napoleonic invasion). See AACh, UTEP 491, 95-20, 117-17; Baquera, p. 37.

57. AACh, UTEP 491, 61-7; AMP, reel 1716a, frame 310.

58. AACh, UTEP 501, 5-7.

59. AACh, UTEP 491, 15-5, 74-5, 108-36; AACh, UTEP 501, 5-7; Almada, *Diccionario*, p. 24.

60. AACh, UTEP 491, 58-27.

61. AACh, UTEP 491, 32-38. See also the numerous petitions in AACh, UTEP 491, 105-25.

62. See citations in Chapter 3.

63. AACh, UTEP 491, 96-2.

64. AACh, UTEP 491, 99-18.

65. AACh, UTEP 491, 9-28, 11-13, 27-7, 30-13, 116-15, 105-25; AACh, UTEP 501, 4-34.

66. AACh, UTEP 501, 6-8.

67. AACh, UTEP 491, 59-24.

68. AACh, UTEP 491, 91-10. For background on Ramírez Calderón, see AACh, UTEP 491, 12-18, 25-24, 25-26, 25-51, 34-20, 35-14, 41-12, 58-6, 66-5, 68-13.

69. AACh, UTEP 491, 42-16. In the previous decade Riaza had had ties to the Zubiate family, having been one of the administrators of the late general's estate. He was married to Catalina de Orio y Zubiate, daughter of the general. AACh, UTEP 491, 16-19.

70. AACh, UTEP 491, 69-11.

71. Moore, *The Cabildo in Peru under the Hapsburgs*, pp. 265–84; Mar-

zahl, p. 86; Garner, "Zacatecas," pp. 144–79; Parry, pp. 33–47; Bayle, pp. 285–300, 420–23; Socolow, *The Merchants of Buenos Aires*, pp. 121–22; Haring, pp. 155, 159, 163.

72. AACh, UTEP 491, 30-15, 38-7, 41-11, 51-17. For a fuller discussion of the concept of calidad, see Chapter 6.

73. AACh, UTEP 491, 15-5, 58-6.

74. AACh, UTEP 491, 15-5, 38-9, 58-6, 101-30; Almada, *Resumen*, p. 110.

75. AACh, UTEP 491, 59-20.

76. AACh, UTEP 491, 57-8, 62-11.

77. AACh, UTEP 491, 96-2.

78. AACh, UTEP 491, 68-1.

79. AACh, UTEP 491, 70-14, 102-5. García de Bustamante had purchased the position of alguacil mayor in 1732; see AACh, UTEP 491, 52-7.

80. AACh, UTEP 491, 100-9.

81. AACh, UTEP 501, 4-21; AACh, UTEP 491, 89-22, 100-3, 100-9, 108-36; Almada, "Lista de los alcaldes."

82. AACh, UTEP 491, 60-3, 85-22, 93-27, 121-20; Almada, "Lista de los alcaldes."

83. AACh, UTEP 491, 32-40, 32-57, 32-65, 37-2, 38-7, 41-11.

84. AACh, UTEP 491, 51-19, 57-1, 59-32, 66-19, 125-7.

85. AACh, UTEP 501, 5-7; Haring, pp. 156–57.

86. AACh, UTEP 491, 58-7.

87. The prosecution of sexual offenses was also a major activity of local authorities in towns in Spain in the late seventeenth century. See Kamen, p. 172.

88. AACh, UTEP 501, 5-7; AACh, UTEP 491, 11-22, 25-24, 25-26, 93-27, 95-17, 101-29, 104-24, 104-42, 107-7, 108-31, 109-17. For an overview of these and other municipal housekeeping functions performed by cabildos in Spanish America, see Marzahl, pp. 75–84; Bayle, pp. 453–85.

89. Porras Muñoz, *Iglesia y estado*, pp. 442–45; AACh, UTEP 491, 15-5.

90. AACh, UTEP 491, 15-5.

91. See, e.g., AACh, UTEP 501, 3-8; AACh, UTEP 491, 15-5.

92. Jones, *Nueva Vizcaya*, p. 121.

93. AACh, UTEP 491, 10-41.

94. AACh, UTEP 491, 10-41, 11-27, 15-5.

95. AACh, UTEP 501, 1-33. For other references to the political turbulence in 1724, see AACh, UTEP 491, 8-6.

96. AACh, UTEP 491, 10-19, 13-20, 15-5, 42-22; AACh, UTEP 501, 6-12.

97. AACh, UTEP 491, 14-6, 16-4.

98. AACh, UTEP 491, 6-13; Archivo del Ayuntamiento de Chihuahua, Sección Justicia, caja 10, exp. 22.

99. AACh, UTEP 501, 5-6; AACh, UTEP 502, 5-3; Chihuahua (El Sagra-

rio) Parish Registers, Marriages, GSU reel 0162689, May 1782; Baptisms, GSU reel 0162663, Apr. 1779.

100. AACh, UTEP 491, 8-32; AACh, UTEP 501, 5-7, fol. 189v; AMP, reel 1724a, frame 11.

101. AACh, UTEP 491, 78-10.

102. AACh, UTEP 491, 42-22.

103. Haring, p. 159.

104. AACh, UTEP 491, 131-20, 133-20, 136-18, 137-25, 138-14, 143-8, 145-23.

105. Haring, p. 159.

CHAPTER FIVE

An earlier version of this chapter appeared as "Public Celebrations, Popular Culture, and Labor Discipline in Eighteenth-Century Chihuahua," in Beezley, Martin, and French, eds. © 1994 by Scholarly Resources Inc. Used by permission of Scholarly Resources Inc.

1. For photographs of varas and mazas, see Bayle, plate opposite p. 60;

2. AACh, UTEP 501, 1-35.

3. AACh, UTEP 501, 3-5.

4. AACh, UTEP 501, 6-42.

5. AACh, UTEP 501, 6-3.

6. AACh, UTEP 502, 5-3.

7. AACh, UTEP 491, 118-2.

8. AACh, UTEP 491, 115-1.

9. AACh, UTEP 501, 5-6.

10. AACh, UTEP 491, 166-25.

11. AACh, UTEP 501, 5-3.

12. AACh, UTEP 501, 3-5.

13. AACh, UTEP 491, 20-7. For another example of a public execution, see AACh, UTEP 491, 117-1.

14. See Arellano Schetelig.

15. AACh, UTEP 501, 5-7.

16. Descriptions of the San Francisco festivities can be found in AACh, UTEP 491, 43-19, 80-28, 87-6, 105-20.

17. AACh, UTEP 491, 56-6; AACh, UTEP 501, 5-6.

18. Almada, *Resumen*, p. 112; AACh, UTEP 491, 109-17.

19. AACh, UTEP 491, 133-15.

20. AMP, reel 1729c, frame 1555; AACh, UTEP 491, 62-47, 100-21.

21. AACh, UTEP 491, 27-13. For Semana Santa observances in Parral, see AMP, reel 1780, frame 226. For these observances in eighteenth-century Spain, see Domínguez Ortiz, pp. 101–3; Callahan, p. 54.

22. AACh, UTEP 491, 56-6, 109-17; AACh, UTEP 501, 5-7, fol. 222.

23. See Moore, *The Cabildo in Peru under the Hapsburgs*, pp. 69, 201; Curcio-Nagy.

24. AACh, UTEP 491, 57-14, 68-1, 72-9, 84-9.

25. AACh, UTEP 491, 59-43.

26. AACh, UTEP 491, 85-22; Almada, *Resumen*, p. 112.

27. AACh, UTEP 491, 103-12, 109-17.
28. See, for example, the reference to the celebration of Día de los Muertos in central Mexico in Cline, p. 25. The visits to cemeteries characteristic of this feast were evidently more popular among Indians than among Europeans; see Viqueira Albán, pp. 156–58.
29. Viqueira Albán, pp. 139–47.
30. AACh, UTEP 491, 42-18.
31. AACh, UTEP 501, 5-3. For a reference to Ash Wednesday, see AACh, UTEP 501, 3-19.
32. For information on these kinds of celebrations in Peru, see Moore, *The Cabildo in Peru under the Hapsburgs*, pp. 201–4, and *The Cabildo in Peru under the Bourbons*, p. 101.
33. AACh, UTEP 501, 5-7.
34. Lynch, pp. 81–84.
35. AACh, UTEP 501, 5-7.
36. Almada, *Resumen*, pp. 99–100; AACh, UTEP 491, 62-11; AACh, UTEP 501, 5-7. For references to the observances honoring King Luis in Parral, see AMP, reel 1724a, frame 212.
37. AACh, UTEP 491, 56-6.
38. AACh, UTEP 491, 94-12.
39. AACh, UTEP 491, 125-7.
40. AACh, UTEP 491, 100-21.
41. AACh, UTEP 491, 142-4.
42. AACh, UTEP 491, 87-6. For a description of these festivities in Seville, see Callahan, p. 55.
43. AACh, UTEP 491, 126-7; AACh, UTEP 502, 5-25.
44. AACh, UTEP 491, 32-5, 56-6.
45. AACh, UTEP 491, 120-5, 128-15.
46. AACh, UTEP 491, 20-7, 42-18, 55-20.
47. AACh, UTEP 491, 68-7.
48. AACh, UTEP 491, 10-53, 109-17.
49. AACh, UTEP 501, 5-7, fol. 195.
50. AACh, UTEP 491, 94-12.
51. AACh, UTEP 491, 84-30, 125-7. For a description of the funeral rites held in San Antonio, Texas, see Cruz, pp. 139–43.
52. AACh, UTEP 491, 125-7.
53. AACh, UTEP 491, 62-11.
54. See Tamarón y Romeral. The bishop was in San Felipe from August 6 through August 17, from September 13 through September 18, and from October 11 through October 27. He was in the villa's immediate environs during the intervening periods.
55. AACh, UTEP 491, 100-9.
56. AACh, UTEP 491, 100-21.
57. AACh, UTEP 491, 100-15.
58. AACh, UTEP 491, 59-43, 80-28, 87-6, 100-15, 109-17.

59. AACh, UTEP 491, 56-6. On the founding of this cofradía, see Bargellini, p. 45. Prominent Spanish-born residents of Chihuahua often remembered the archicofradía in their wills. See, for example, AACh, UTEP 491, 108-36, 109-6.

60. AACh, UTEP 501, 5-7; AACh, UTEP 491, 59-43, 109-17.

61. AACh, UTEP 501, 5-6, 5-7; AACh, UTEP 491, 56-5, 56-6. On similar practices elsewhere in colonial Latin America, see Bayle, pp. 590, 618–19.

62. AACh, UTEP 491, 56-6, 59-43.

63. AACh, UTEP 491, 109-17, 130-38; on customs observed during bullfights in Mexico City, see Viqueira Albán, pp. 30–39, 117–19, 142–43.

64. AACh, UTEP 491, 56-6, 87-6, 109-17; AACh, UTEP 501, 5-7, fol. 222.

65. AACh, UTEP 491, 66-19, 109-17.

66. AACh, UTEP 501, 5-7.

67. Defourneaux, p. 133.

68. Viqueira Albán, p. 57.

69. AACh, UTEP 491, 125-12.

70. AACh, UTEP 491, 94-12.

71. AACh, UTEP 491, 100-21.

72. AACh, UTEP 491, 8-11, 80-28.

73. AACh, UTEP 491, 59-43.

74. AACh, UTEP 491, 110-3.

75. AACh, UTEP 491, 87-6.

76. AACh, UTEP 491, 122-29.

77. AACh, UTEP 491, 80-28; Chihuahua (El Sagrario) Parish Registers, Burials, GSU reel 0162697, Mar. 1756.

78. AACh, UTEP 491, 96-36.

79. See, for example, AACh, UTEP 491, 32-5, 94-12. The reluctance of artisans to participate in local fiestas in eighteenth-century Spain is noted in Callahan, p. 54. For similar developments in France, see Schneider, pp. 302–7.

80. AACh, UTEP 491, 87-6, 100-15.

81. AACh, UTEP 491, 130-38.

82. AACh, UTEP 491, 126-7.

83. AACh, UTEP 491, 62-11. In early modern France, sometimes a delegation of "the poor" marched in ritual processions along with representatives of other social groups. See Schneider, p. 34.

84. On cofradías in colonial Indian communities, see Farriss; Lockhart, *The Nahuas After the Conquest*, pp. 218–29; Gibson, pp. 127–32; Haskett, *Indigenous Rulers*, pp. 121–23.

85. Beezley, pp. 89–93; Gonzalbo Aizpuru.

86. Sergio Rivera Ayala, pp. 27–46.

87. AACh, UTEP 491, 94-12. For a reference to such "ridiculous" disguises elsewhere in colonial Mexico, see Gonzalbo Aizpuru, p. 41.

88. Viqueira Albán, p. 148.

89. See Thompson.

90. AACh, UTEP 491, 89-22.

91. For an introduction to the historical and anthropological literature

on the stabilizing effects of such rituals, see Burke, pp. 199–202; Davis, pp. 107–9, 130–31; Le Roy Ladurie, pp. 191–92, 301–2.

92. Davis, p. 131.

93. On the subversive potential of rituals of inversion, see ibid., pp. 131–51; Le Roy Ladurie; Burke, pp. 202–4; quotation from p. 203.

94. AACh, UTEP 491, 29-10.

95. AACh, UTEP 491, 128-35.

96. For a report on cofradías in Chihuahua, see Archivo del Estado de Durango, microfilm copy at the University of Texas at El Paso Library, film 492, 6-6.

97. AACh, UTEP 491, 72-13, 89-23.

98. AMP, reel 1724a, frame 212; reel 1746, frame 3; reel 1794, frame 105. For the role of pardos in Mexico City observances, see García Collection, Folder 135, Benson Latin American Collection, University of Texas at Austin.

99. On the importance of Basques on the northern frontier of New Spain, see Garate.

100. AACh, UTEP 501, 5-7.

101. Muchembled, pp. 122–48, 171–74, 212; Burke, pp. 207–43; Schneider, p. 353; Garrioch, pp. 197–99.

102. Lynch, pp. 276–78; Burke, pp. 242–43.

103. Domínguez Ortiz, p. 110.

104. Viqueira Albán, especially pp. 152–60, 229–30; Brading, "Tridentine Catholicism." See also W. B. Stephens Collection, Benson Latin American Collection, University of Texas at Austin, exp. 1; Archivo General de la Nación, Mexico City, Ramo Historia, vol. 437, exps. 3, 6, 8.

105. AACh, UTEP 491, 20-7, 42-18, 55-20.

106. AACh, UTEP 491, 30-13.

107. AACh, UTEP 491, 131-29.

108. AACh, UTEP 491, 80-21, 116-21, 118-36; AACh, UTEP 501, 4-44; AACh, UTEP 502, 5-3.

109. Taylor, "Amigos de Sombrero," pp. 52–53.

110. AACh, UTEP 491, 23-15.

111. AACh, UTEP 491, 42-18, 95-19; AACh, UTEP 501, 6-8.

112. AACh, UTEP 491, 69-1. See also AACh, UTEP 491, 62-6, 109-21; AACh, UTEP 501, 3-1.

113. AACh, UTEP 502, 4-14.

114. AACh, UTEP 491, 104-22; AACh, UTEP 501, 4-16.

115. AACh, UTEP 491, 83-3.

116. Deans-Smith, pp. 222–23, 243–45. Hardly anyone used biblical language in formulating petitions in Chihuahua. For an example of one such reference in a petition, in this case made by an employer who objected to the gambling of his employees, see AACh, UTEP 491, 18-14.

CHAPTER SIX

1. On the concepts of hidalguía and limpieza de sangre, see Elliott, p. 112; Liss, pp. 13–14; Gutiérrez, p. 178; Lourie, pp. 54–76.
2. On the encomienda, see Simpson.
3. Nunn, p. 32; Kamen, pp. 226, 303.
4. Seed, *To Love, Honor and Obey.*
5. Villamarín and Villamarín, pp. 127–29, 136.
6. Kamen, pp. 260–62.
7. AACh, UTEP 491, 30-3.
8. AACh, UTEP 491, 46-12, 46-13.
9. AACh, UTEP 491, 33-6.
10. McCaa, pp. 477–501, quotation from p. 477. For a discussion of calidad in colonial New Mexico, see Gutiérrez, pp. 191–94.
11. See, for example, AACh, UTEP 491, 113-33.
12. AACh, UTEP 501, 6-13.
13. AACh, UTEP 491, 25-35.
14. AACh, UTEP 491, 1-20.
15. AACh, UTEP 491, 20-7.
16. AACh, UTEP 491, 23-19, 23-22.
17. AMP, reel 1731b, frame 955.
18. AACh, UTEP 501, 4-40.
19. AACh, UTEP 491, 52-8.
20. AACh, UTEP 491, 143-17.
21. AACh, UTEP 491, 118-14.
22. AACh, UTEP 501, 3-10; see also AACh, UTEP 491, 83-8.
23. See, for example, AACh, UTEP 491, 32-28, 51-19.
24. AACh, UTEP 491, 93-27.
25. Cope, pp. 120–21.
26. Socolow, "Acceptable Partners," pp. 209–46.
27. AACh, UTEP 491, 47-24.
28. AACh, UTEP 491, 32-38, 83-8; AACh, UTEP 501, 4-15, 6-38, 6-43.
29. AACh, UTEP 491, 30-19, 41-12; AACh, UTEP 501, 1-1.
30. AACh, UTEP 491, 23-16.
31. AACh, UTEP 491, 9-28.
32. AACh, UTEP 491, 91-10.
33. AACh, UTEP 491, 30-12, 30-13.
34. AACh, UTEP 501, 1-35.
35. See, for example, AACh, UTEP 491, 87-14.
36. AACh, UTEP 491, 83-8.
37. Thompson, p. 389.
38. AACh, UTEP 501, 6-13.
39. AACh, UTEP 491, 15-5.
40. On the Basque origins of the juego de bolas, see Viqueira Albán, pp. 242–46.
41. AACh, UTEP 501, 1-28.
42. On taverns and pulquerías in Mexico City, see Scardaville; Cope, p. 35; Taylor, *Drinking, Homicide and Rebellion*, pp. 66–67.

43. AACh, UTEP 491, 67-7.
44. AACh, UTEP 501, 4-44.
45. Viqueira Albán, especially pp. 138, 230.
46. AACh, UTEP 491, 62-11.
47. AACh, UTEP 491, 118-36.
48. AACh, UTEP 502, 5-9.
49. AACh, UTEP 491, 147-12.
50. AACh, UTEP 491, 87-14.
51. AACh, UTEP 501, 6-36. Segura was one of those who signed the petition calling for the ouster of Corregidor Juan Sánchez Camacho in 1731; see AMP, reel 1731b, frame 532.
52. AMP, reel 1700, frame 416.
53. Unless otherwise specified, all information on the life and death of Benito Godoy and the trial of his accused killers is taken from AACh, UTEP 491, 20-7; the original documents can be found in Archivo del Ayuntamiento de Chihuahua, Sección Justicia, caja 37, exp. 31.
54. See, for example, AACh, UTEP 491, 10-48, 18-5; AACh, UTEP 501, 4-4.
55. AACh, UTEP 491, 12-9, 12-19; Archivo del Ayuntamiento de Chihuahua, Sección Justicia, caja 4, exp. 13; caja 18, exp. 3; caja 26, exp. 3; caja 27, exp. 8.
56. On the lifestyles of peninsular merchants, see Brading, *Miners and Merchants*, pp. 109–10.
57. AACh, UTEP 491, 11-27.
58. AACh, UTEP 491, 52-8; Chihuahua (El Sagrario) Parish Registers, Baptisms, GSU reel 0162660, May 1731.
59. Archivo del Ayuntamiento de Chihuahua, Sección Justicia, caja 18, exp. 3; caja 24, exp. 21; caja, 26, exps. 4, 41; caja 27, exp. 8; caja 30, exp. 4; AACh, UTEP 491, 2-13, 12-19, 14-5, 14-14.
60. For biographical information on Graciano, see Chapter 2.
61. Thompson, p. 389.
62. AACh, UTEP 491, 32-14.
63. Archivo del Ayuntamiento de Chihuahua, Sección Justicia, caja 19, exp. 14.
64. AACh, UTEP 501, 1-21.
65. AACh, UTEP 491, 113-33, 113-34. Rivas was originally from Mexico City and was able to sign his name fairly well.
66. AACh, UTEP 491, 118-24.
67. AACh, UTEP 501, 3-5.
68. AACh, UTEP 501, 6-10.
69. J. C. Scott, pp. 11, 50; quotation from p. 50.
70. Socolow, *The Merchants of Buenos Aires*, p. 119.
71. AACh, UTEP 491, 62-5.
72. AACh, UTEP 491, 10-49, 23-22, 100-13, 101-1.

73. AACh, UTEP 501, 6-26.
74. AACh, UTEP 491, 22-30.
75. AACh, UTEP 501, 4-41.
76. AACh, UTEP 501, 6-51.
77. AACh, UTEP 501, 6-8.
78. AACh, UTEP 501, 4-35.
79. AACh, UTEP 491, 62-2.
80. AACh, UTEP 501, 6-9.
81. AACh, UTEP 491, 101-36.
82. Quoted in McCaa, pp. 491–92.
83. AACh, UTEP 501, 4-11.
84. AACh, UTEP 491, 109-2.
85. AACh, UTEP 491, 32-38, 101-1.
86. See, for example, AACh, UTEP 491, 28-6.
87. AACh, UTEP 491, 20-7; Archivo del Ayuntamiento de Chihuahua, Sección Justicia, caja 37, exp. 31.
88. AACh, UTEP 491, 66-22.
89. Gutiérrez, p. 226. Other scholars have also pointed out the importance of personal honor for nonelite groups in colonial Mexico. See, for example, Lipsett-Rivera.
90. Cope, pp. 49–67.
91. Cope finds that when asked to select surnames at the time of their marriage, many castas chose names that had nothing to do with their ancestry. Perhaps at the urging of their priests, they frequently selected religious designations, such as "de la Cruz" or "de la Concepción." Over 23 percent of the 187 mestizo and castizo men who married at Mexico City's Sagrario Metropolitano between 1670 and 1672, and over 34 percent of the 203 brides belonging to those groups, had "religious" surnames. Among the 203 mulato men and the 165 mulata females who married during this same interval, religious surnames accounted for 20 percent of the men and nearly 29 percent of the women. See Cope, pp. 58–67. Records of marriages performed at San Francisco de Cuéllar between 1710 and 1718 also show a lack of knowledge or concern over genealogy among mestizos and free mulatos. Men and women listed in the Chihuahua registers were less likely to have "religious" surnames than those who married in Mexico City, however. At San Francisco de Cuéllar, only 7 of the 79 men listed as mestizos or free mulatos bore religious surnames, but another 10 had no last name at all. Thus about 23 percent of these men lacked "Spanish" surnames—a proportion roughly comparable to the mestizos and mulatos who married in Mexico City in the early 1670s. The percentage of women without Spanish names may have been even greater in Chihuahua than in the viceregal capital; over 45 percent of the women who married mestizos or free mulatos had either a religious surname or none at all. In most cases, however, the records omit racial designations for the brides, so it is possible that a significant portion of these women were Indians, who everywhere were less likely to have Spanish names than mestizos or mulatos. Chihuahua (El Sagrario) Parish Registers, Marriages, GSU reel 0162689.

CHAPTER SEVEN

1. J. W. Scott; Davis, pp. 127–28.
2. Lynch, p. 46.
3. Perry, p. 58.
4. See Dillard, especially pp. 12–24, 211–12; quotation from pp. 211–12.
5. Perry; Lavrin, "In Search of the Colonial Woman."
6. Liss, pp. 96–98.
7. See, for example, Clendinnen; Farriss, pp. 169–70.
8. See, for example, AACh, UTEP 491, 9-22.
9. AACh, UTEP 502, 3-7.
10. AACh, UTEP 491, 52-13; AACh, UTEP 501, 5-4.
11. AACh, UTEP 491, 68-19, 105-25.
12. See, for example, AACh, UTEP 491, 103-12; AACh, UTEP 502, 2-12.
13. Archivo del Estado de Durango, UTEP 492, 10-11.
14. AMP, reel 1780, frame 246.
15. AACh, UTEP 491, 101-19, 113-33.
16. See, for example, AACh, UTEP 491, 9-22, 59-26, 68-10. For the use of similar political terms in European definitions of social relations, see Davis, pp. 127–28.
17. AACh, UTEP 501, 1-22; AACh, UTEP 491, 83-8.
18. AACh, UTEP 501, 4-9.
19. AACh, UTEP 491, 9-22.
20. AACh, UTEP 491, 84-16.
21. AACh, UTEP 491, 113-35, 116-1.
22. For a fuller discussion of the use of these insults in eighteenth-century Chihuahua, see Martin, "Popular Speech and Social Order."
23. AACh, UTEP 491, 15-5, 33-6, 66-22.
24. AACh, UTEP 491, 21-6; see also AACh, UTEP 501, 6-40.
25. AACh, UTEP 501, 4-36.
26. AACh, UTEP 501, 3-1; Boyer; Socolow, "Women and Crime"; Arrom, *The Women of Mexico City*, p. 232–38. See also Dillard, p. 92.
27. AACh, UTEP 491, 62-6; 66-25; 78-7; Socolow, "Women and Crime."
28. AACh, UTEP 491, 104-22.
29. AACh, UTEP 491, 55-8, 101-24.
30. See, e.g., AACh, UTEP 491, 103-13.
31. AACh, UTEP 501, 1-10; AACh, UTEP 491, 47-14.
32. AACh, UTEP 491, 114–12.
33. AACh, UTEP 491, 119-25.
34. AACh, UTEP 491, 9-22.
35. AACh, UTEP 491, 76-8.
36. AACh, UTEP 491, 119-25.
37. AACh, UTEP 501, 5-10.
38. AACh, UTEP 491, 105-25.
39. AACh, UTEP 491, 121-41.
40. For a discussion of women's attempts to protect their own reputations for personal honor, see Lipsett-Rivera.

41. Martin, "Popular Speech and Social Order."

42. On charivaris and other rituals mocking traditional gender roles in Europe, see Davis, especially pp. 97–123, 129–43, 200, 301, 307–8.

43. AACh, UTEP 491, 6-13; Archivo del Ayuntamiento de Chihuahua, Sección Justicia, caja 10, exp. 22; Chihuahua (El Sagrario) Parish Registers, Marriages, GSU reel 0162689, Apr. 1712.

44. AMP, reel 1705, frame 647.

45. AACh, UTEP 491, 93-8.

46. AACh, UTEP 491, 116-26; AACh, UTEP 501, 4-10, 6-45.

47. AACh, UTEP 491, 29-5, 47-26, 64-45, 72-1, 79-11, 93-38, 95-19; AACh, UTEP 501, 1-19, 4-23.

48. AACh, UTEP 501, 4-16.

49. AACh, UTEP 501, 6-25.

50. AACh, UTEP 491, 4-9, 13-6, 105-25.

51. AACh, UTEP 491, 105-25, 119-25.

52. See, e.g., AACh, UTEP 491, 26-37, 47-14, 72-11, 83-8, 89-23, 93-8, 96-32, 105-20, 121-44.

53. AACh, UTEP 491, 20-7.

54. AACh, UTEP 491, 62-49.

55. AACh, UTEP 501, 4-21.

56. AACh, UTEP 491, 56-6, fol. 307; 103-12.

57. AACh, UTEP 501, 3-13; AACh, UTEP 491, 101-13.

58. AACh, UTEP 491, 36-10, 66-22, 73-8, 101-1; Archivo del Ayuntamiento de Chihuahua, Sección Justicia, caja 10, exp. 22; J. C. Chávez, "La mulata esclava."

59. AACh, UTEP 491, 67-17.

60. AACh, UTEP 491, 70-25, 109-21, 110-3.

61. AACh, UTEP 491, 21-6.

62. AACh, UTEP 491, 109-21, 110-3.

63. Lavrin, pp. 29–30.

64. Arrom, *The Women of Mexico City*, pp. 105–11; Calvo, pp. 287–312; Swann, *Tierra Adentro*, pp. 209, 327; Anderson, p. 215. On women's economic importance, see Lavrin and Couturier; Leyva.

65. AACh, UTEP 502, 3-23.

66. AACh, UTEP 491, 139-17.

67. Arrom, *The Women of Mexico City*, p. 133.

68. AACh, UTEP 501, 3-13, 81-4.

69. AACh, UTEP 491, 103-12.

70. See, e.g., AACh, UTEP 491, 10-54, 11-1, 31-12, 32-48, 32-64, 32-76, 43-1, 52-15. On the correlations between surnames and social status, see Cope, pp. 58–66.

71. AACh, UTEP 491, 67-9.

72. AACh, UTEP 491, 22-21, 28-7, 30-12, 35-15, 36-2, 60-2, 68-13, 68-17, 80-28; AACh, UTEP 501, 6-53.

73. AACh, UTEP 491, 14-6, 19-23; Chihuahua (El Sagrario) Parish Registers, Marriages, GSU reel 0162689, Feb. 1729; Burials, GSU reel 0162697, Sept. 1728.

74. AACh, UTEP 491, 64-6.

75. AMP, reel 1716a, frame 283. Philip Hadley read this name as "Diego Núñez" (see Hadley, p. 43), but close inspection of the documents reveals the name "Diega"; moreover, servants of this refinery referred to their "ama." See also AACh, UTEP 491, 61-7.

76. AACh, UTEP 491, 21-1.

77. AACh, UTEP 491, 46-12, 106-11. A few other women who owned mines or refineries at various points in Chihuahua's eighteenth-century history are mentioned in Archivo General de la Nación, Mexico City, Ramo Provincias Internas, vol. 142, exp. 1.

78. AACh, UTEP 491, 105-25.

79. AACh, UTEP 491, 25-9, 45-2, 101-1. She died in April of 1739; see Chihuahua (El Sagrario) Parish Registers, Burials, GSU reel 0162697.

80. AACh, UTEP 491, 25-46.

81. AACh, UTEP 491, 10-7.

82. AACh, UTEP 491, 10-39, 71-2, 108-31.

83. AACh, UTEP 491, 33-12, 92-10, 100-21, 104-12, 109-17, 121-2.

84. AACh, UTEP 502, 3-16.

85. AACh, UTEP 491, 58-24, 73-4, 93-39.

86. Juana was baptized on January 17, 1706; her parents, Ignacio de Cobos and Catalina de Olguín, were married three weeks later on February 8. El Valle de San Bartolomé (Valle de Allende) Parish registers, Baptisms, GSU reel 0162634, Jan. 1706; Marriages, GSU reel 0162650, Feb. 1706.

87. El Valle de San Bartolomé (Valle de Allende) Parish Registers, Marriages, GSU reel 0162650, Nov. 1722; Baptisms, GSU reel 0162635, Oct. 1723; Oct. 1725; Nov. 1727; Apr. 1730; July 1732.

88. See, for example, AACh, UTEP 491, 89-23, 97-2.

89. AACh, UTEP 491, 25-46, 90-21, 92-10; Chihuahua (El Sagrario) Parish Registers, Burials, GSU reel 0162697, Feb. 1749, contains a reference to a New Mexican servant of Juana de Cobos.

90. On the bakery business in Chihuahua, see AACh, UTEP 491, 89-23, 108-31.

91. AACh, UTEP 491, 59-3.

92. AACh, UTEP 491, 89-23, 92-10.

93. AACh, UTEP 491, 90-21, 92-10.

94. See, e.g., AACh, UTEP 491, 85-7.

95. AACh, UTEP 491, 67-12.

96. Chihuahua (El Sagrario) Parish Registers, Burials, GSU reel 0162697, June 1755.

97. El Valle de San Bartolomé (Valle de Allende) Parish Registers, Baptisms, GSU reel 0162635, Oct. 1725; Chihuahua (El Sagrario) Parish Registers, Marriages, GSU reel 0162689, Aug. 1746.

98. AACh, UTEP 491, 78-7.

99. Unless otherwise specified, all information on this dispute comes from AACh, UTEP 491, 78-7.

100. AACh, UTEP 491, 71-6; Chihuahua (El Sagrario) Parish Registers, Burials, GSU reel 0162699, Oct. 1790. Miguel Mayor Rico de Cuesta was the nephew of Nicolás Rico de Cuesta, a peninsular immigrant and bachelor shopkeeper who had set up shop in Chihuahua as early as 1722. Rico de Cuesta was evidently another ornery gachupín; over the years he became involved in a number of disputes with his neighbors. See AACh, UTEP 491, 5-6, 8-2, 11-14, 11-27, 15-2, 23-19, 25-10, 33-4, 42-9; AACh, UTEP 501, 6-31; Chihuahua (El Sagrario) Parish Registers, Burials, GSU reel 0162697, Dec. 1751.

101. AACh, UTEP 491, 99-7.

102. Chihuahua (El Sagrario) Parish Registers, Marriages, GSU reel 0162689, Dec. 1752.

103. AACh, UTEP 491, 89-23.

104. AACh, UTEP 491, 121-20.

105. AACh, UTEP 491, 108-31; AACh, UTEP 502, 1-17.

106. AACh, UTEP 502, 3-23, household number 500.

107. AACh, UTEP 491, 142-4; Chihuahua (El Sagrario) Parish Registers, Burials, GSU reel 0162699, Oct. 1790.

108. Chihuahua (El Sagrario) Parish Registers, Burials, GSU reel 0162699, Dec. 1797.

109. AACh, UTEP 491, 105-25.

110. Chihuahua (El Sagrario) Parish Registers, Baptisms, GSU reel 0162661, Mar. 1758.

111. AACh, UTEP 491, 105-25.

112. AACh, UTEP 491, 138-31, 138-32.

113. AACh, UTEP 491, 25-46.

114. AACh, UTEP 491, 80-21.

115. AACh, UTEP 491, 118-36.

116. On the practice of depósito, see Arrom, *The Women of Mexico City*, pp. 212–17; Seed, *To Love, Honor, and Obey*, especially pp. 78–79.

117. On the recogimentos de mujeres, see Muriel.

118. AACh, UTEP 491, 83-8. Although the complaint bears the name of Juana Moreno, whose husband was charged as an accessory to the crime, it

is clear from the rest of the expediente that it was Corral who was held in prison.

119. AACh, UTEP 491, 132-18.

120. AACh, UTEP 491, 33-2, 58-29.

121. AACh, UTEP 501, 4-10.

122. AACh, UTEP 491, 109-2.

123. AACh, UTEP 501, 1-2.

124. AACh, UTEP 491, 10-35.

125. AACh, UTEP 491, 26-12, 26-14.

126. AACh, UTEP 501, 5-4.

127. AACh, UTEP 501, 4-24.

128. On prostitution in early modern Spain, see Perry, especially pp. 137–52.

129. AACh, UTEP 491, 20-7.

130. AACh, UTEP 491, 20-7.

131. AACh, UTEP 491, 81-6.

132. AACh, UTEP 491, 23-16.

133. AACh, UTEP 501, 5-7.

134. AACh, UTEP 491, 83-8.

135. AACh, UTEP 491, 8-15, 42-15.

136. AACh, UTEP 491, 55-4, 56-7.

137. AACh, UTEP 491, 18-17; Archivo del Ayuntamiento de Chihuahua, Sección Justicia, caja 34, exp. 15.

138. AACh, UTEP 491, 27-6, 55-21, 96-2, 60-4, 60-10; Chihuahua (El Sagrario) Parish Registers, Burials, GSU reel 0162697, Mar. 1751; AMP, reel 1731b, frame 532.

139. AACh, UTEP 491, 99-7.

140. AACh, UTEP 491, 113-33.

141. AACh, UTEP 491, 59-26, 104-22; AACh, UTEP 501, 4-36.

142. AACh, UTEP 491, 9-22.

143. AACh, UTEP 491, 13-30.

144. AACh, UTEP 491, 43-17.

145. AACh, UTEP 501, 5-4.

146. AACh, UTEP 491, 68-21.

147. Arrom, *The Women of Mexico City*, pp. 26-29. See also Susan Deans-Smith's discussion of the employment of women in the royal tobacco manufactory of Mexico City; Deans-Smith, pp. 174–215. On the proposal to open a cigar factory in Chihuahua, see AACh, UTEP 491, 132-21.

148. On the growing importance of behavioral norms rooted in commerce in eighteenth-century Mexico, see Seed, "Marriage Promises," and *To Love, Honor and Obey*.

CONCLUSION

1. On the effectiveness of frontier military garrisons, see Moorhead, *The Presidio*.

2. Vásquez Mellado, p. 105.

3. Cope, p. 200, n. 3.

4. AACh, UTEP 491, 128-34.

5. AACh, UTEP 491, 116-21.

6. AACh, UTEP 491, 114-16, 115-27, 116-25.

7. AACh, UTEP 491, 115-10; AACh, UTEP 501, 5-3, 5-5.

8. AACh, UTEP 491, 124-11, 126-11, 128-38, 129-7, 129-18, 129-33, 130-20, 130-21, 131-18, 132-24, 135-21, 136-22, 136-41, 145-6.

9. AACh, UTEP 491, 116-8.

10. AACh, UTEP 491, 132-21.

11. AACh, UTEP 491, 134-13.

12. For a representative but by no means exhaustive sample of the recent literature on economic and social change in late colonial Mexico, see Viqueira Albán; Florescano; Brading, *Miners and Merchants* and *Haciendas and Ranchos*, pp. 174–204; Martin, *Rural Society*, pp. 97–192; Seed, *To Love, Honor, and Obey*, especially pp. 161–225; Van Young, *Hacienda and Market*; Arrom, *The Women of Mexico City*, pp. 26–32; Deans-Smith; Tutino, pp. 41–98; and James Lockhart's discussion of the growth of Spanish linguistic competence among the Indians of central Mexico, in *Nahuas After the Conquest*, pp. 318–23.

13. Gutiérrez, pp. 298–336.

14. For a concise summary of the historigraphical literature on these measures see S. J. Stern, "Feudalism, Capitalism and the World-System," p. 856, nn. 71, 72.

15. Van Young, "Recent Anglophone Scholarship"; quotation on pp. 728–29. For further reflection on the degree of change in the period before 1750, see Martin, "The Dynamics of Clio."

16. Costeloe, pp. 1–30; quotation from Lucas Alamán on p. 17; latter quotation on p. 28.

17. See, e.g., Flores Caballero; Van Young, "Millennium on the Northern Marches."

18. Arrom, "Popular Politics in Mexico City"; quotation on p. 263.

19. Arrom, *The Women of Mexico City*; quotation on p. 268.

Bibliography

Almada, Francisco. *Diccionario de historia, geografía y biografía chihuahuenses*. 2d. ed. Ciudad Juárez: Impresora de Juárez, 1968.

———. "La fundación de la ciudad de Chihuahua." *Boletín de la Sociedad Chihuahuense de Estudios Históricos* 1, no. 1 (May 1938): 6–10.

———. "Lista de los alcaldes de la Villa de San Felipe el Real de Chihuahua, 1718–1823." *Boletín de la Sociedad Chihuahuense de Estudios Históricos* 1, no. 9 (Feb. 1939).

———. *Resumen de la historia del estado de Chihuahua*. Mexico City: Libros Mexicanos, 1955.

Altman, Ida. *Emigrants and Society: Extremadura and Spanish America in the Sixteenth Century*. Berkeley: University of California Press, 1989.

Anderson, Rodney. "Race and Social Stratification: A Comparison of Working-Class Spaniards, Indians, and Castas in Guadalajara, Mexico in 1821." *Hispanic American Historical Review* 68, no. 2 (May 1988): 209–44.

Arellano Schetelig, Lorenzo. "Las elecciones de alcaldes en 1740." *Boletín de la Sociedad Chihuahuense de Estudios Históricos* 2, no. 10–11 (May-June 1940): 352–56.

Arras R., Hector. *Parral Colonial*. Chihuahua: Talleres Gráficos del Gobierno del Estado, 1990.

Arrom, Silvia M. "Popular Politics in Mexico City: The Parián Riot, 1828." *Hispanic American Historical Review* 68, no. 2 (May 1988): 245–68.

———. *The Women of Mexico City, 1790–1857*. Stanford, Calif.: Stanford University Press, 1985.

Bakewell, Peter J. *Silver Mining and Society in Colonial Mexico: Zacatecas, 1546–1700*. Cambridge, Eng.: Cambridge University Press, 1971.

Bannon, John Francis. *The Spanish Borderlands Frontier, 1513–1821*. Albuquerque: University of New Mexico Press, 1974.

Baquera, Richard V. "Paso del Norte and Chihuahua, 1810–1821: Revolution and Constitutionalism." Master's thesis, University of Texas at El Paso, 1978.
Bargellini, Clara. *La catedral de Chihuahua.* Mexico City: Universidad Nacional Autónoma de México, 1984.
Barri, Jr., León. "Descubrimiento de la mina de Santa Eulalia." *Boletín de la Sociedad Chihuahuense de Estudios Históricos* 6, no. 11 (Oct.–Nov. 1949): 319.
Bayle, Constantino. *Los cabildos seculares en la América Española.* Madrid: Sapientia, 1952.
Beezley, William H. *Judas at the Jockey Club and Other Episodes of Porfirian Mexico.* Lincoln: University of Nebraska Press, 1987.
Beezley, William H., Cheryl English Martin, and William E. French, eds. *Rituals of Rule, Rituals of Resistance: Public Celebrations and Popular Culture in Mexico.* Wilmington, Del.: Scholarly Resources, 1994.
Boyer, Richard. "Women, *La Mala Vida*, and the Politics of Marriage." In Lavrin, *Sexuality and Marriage.*
Brading, David A. "Los españoles en México hacia 1792." *Historia Mexicana* 23, no. 1 (July-Sept. 1973): 126–44.
———. *Haciendas and Ranchos in the Mexican Bajío: León, 1700–1860.* Cambridge, Eng.: Cambridge University Press, 1978.
———. *Miners and Merchants in Bourbon Mexico, 1763–1810.* Cambridge, Eng.: Cambridge University Press, 1971.
———. "Tridentine Catholicism and Enlightened Despotism in Bourbon Mexico." *Journal of Latin American Studies* 15, no. 1 (May 1983): 1–22.
Brading, David A., and Harry E. Cross. "Colonial Silver Mining: Mexico and Peru." *Hispanic American Historical Review* 52, no. 4 (Nov. 1972): 545–79.
Burke, Peter. *Popular Culture in Early Modern Europe.* New York: New York University Press, 1978.
Burkholder, Mark A., and D. S. Chandler. *Biographical Dictionary of Audiencia Ministers in the Americas, 1687–1821.* Westport, Conn.: Greenwood Press, 1982.
Callahan, William J. *Church, Politics, and Society in Spain, 1750–1874.* Cambridge, Mass.: Harvard University Press, 1984.
Calvo, Thomas. "The Warmth of the Hearth: Seventeenth-Century Guadalajara Families." In Lavrin, *Sexuality and Marriage.*
Chávez, Angélico. "Pohe-Yemo's Representative and the Pueblo Revolt of 1680." *New Mexico Historical Review* 42, no. 2 (May 1967): 85–126.
Chávez, José Carlos. "La mulata esclava." *Boletín de la Sociedad Chihuahuense de Estudios Históricos* 7, no. 2 (Mar.–Apr. 1950): 394–400.
Clendinnen, Inga. "Yucatec Maya Women and the Spanish Conquest: Role

and Ritual in Historical Reconstruction." *Journal of Social History* 15, no. 3 (Spring 1982): 427–42.

Cline, S. L. *Colonial Culhuacan, 1580–1600: A Social History of an Aztec Town*. Albuquerque: University of New Mexico Press, 1986.

Cope, R. Douglas. *The Limits of Racial Domination: Plebeian Society in Colonial Mexico City, 1660–1720*. Madison: University of Wisconsin Press, 1994.

Costeloe, Michael P. *The Central Republic in Mexico, 1835–1846: Hombres de Bien in the Age of Santa Anna*. Cambridge, Eng.: Cambridge University Press, 1993.

Cramaussel, Chantal. *La provincia de Santa Bárbara en la Nueva Vizcaya, 1563–1631*. Ciudad Juárez: Universidad Autónoma de Ciudad Juárez, 1990.

Cramaussel, Chantal, and Salvador Alvarez. "El plano de 1722 de la villa de San Felipe el Real de Chihuahua." In *Arte y Coerción: Primer Coloquio del Comité Mexicano de Historia del Arte*, pp. 45–69. Mexico City: Instituto de Investigaciones Estéticas, Universidad Nacional Autónoma de México, 1992.

Cruz, Gilbert R. *Let There Be Towns: Spanish Municipal Origins in the American Southwest, 1610–1810*. College Station: Texas A & M University Press, 1988.

Cuello, José. "The Persistence of Indian Slavery and Encomienda in the Northeast of Colonial Mexico, 1577–1723." *Journal of Social History* 21, no. 4 (Summer 1988): 683–700.

Curcio-Nagy, Linda. "Giants and Gypsies: Corpus Christi in Colonial Mexico City." In Beezley, Martin, and French, *Rituals of Rule*.

Darnton, Robert. *The Great Cat Massacre and Other Episodes in French Cultural History*. New York: Basic Books, 1984.

Davis, Natalie Z. *Society and Culture in Early Modern France*. Stanford, Calif.: Stanford University Press, 1975.

Deans-Smith, Susan. *Bureaucrats, Planters, and Workers: The Making of the Tobacco Monopoly in Bourbon Mexico*. Austin: University of Texas Press, 1992.

Deeds, Susan M. "Rural Work in Nueva Vizcaya: Forms of Labor Coercion on the Periphery." *Hispanic American Historical Review* 69, no. 3 (Aug. 1989): 425–49.

Defourneaux, Marcelin. *Daily Life in Spain in the Golden Age*. Newton Branch, trans. Stanford, Calif.: Stanford University Press, 1970.

Del Río, Ignacio. "Sobre la aparición y desarrollo del trabajo libre asalariado en el norte de Nueva España (siglos XVI–XVII)." In Elsa Cecilia Frost, Michael C. Meyer, and Josefina Zoraida Vázquez, eds., *El trabajo y los trabajadores en la historia de México*. Mexico City: El Colegio de México; Tucson: University of Arizona Press, 1979.

Dillard, Heath. *Daughters of the Reconquest: Women in Castilian Town Society, 1100–1300.* Cambridge, Eng.: Cambridge University Press, 1984.

Domínguez Ortiz, Antonio. *Hechos y figuras del siglo XVIII español.* Madrid: Siglo Veintiuno de España, 1973.

Elliott, J. H. *Imperial Spain, 1469–1716.* New York: St. Martin's Press, 1963.

Fairchilds, Cissie. *Domestic Enemies: Servants and Their Masters in Old Regime France.* Baltimore: Johns Hopkins University Press, 1984.

Farriss, Nancy M. *Maya Society Under Spanish Colonial Rule: The Collective Enterprise of Survival.* Princeton, N.J.: Princeton University Press, 1984.

Flores Caballero, Romeo. *Counterrevolution: The Role of Spaniards in the Independence of Mexico, 1804–1838.* Jaime Rodríguez O., trans. Lincoln: University of Nebraska Press, 1974.

Florescano, Enrique. *Precios del maís y crisis agrícolas in México, 1708–1810.* Mexico City: El Colegio de México, 1969.

Forbes, Jack D. *Apache, Navajo and Spaniard.* Norman: University of Oklahoma Press, 1960.

Foster, George M. *Culture and Conquest: America's Spanish Heritage.* Chicago: Quadrangle Books, 1960.

Frank, Ross. "The Creation of a Vecino Culture in Late Colonial New Mexico, 1780–1820." Paper presented at the 8th Conference of Mexican and North American Historians, San Diego, Calif., Oct. 18–20, 1990.

Garate, Donald T. "Basque Names, Nobility, and Ethnicity on the Spanish Frontier." *Colonial Latin American Historical Review* 2, no. 1 (Winter 1993): 77–104.

García Ayluardo, Clara. "A World of Images: Cult, Ritual and Society in Colonial Mexico City." In Beezley, Martin, and French, *Rituals of Rule.*

García Martínez, Bernardo. *Los pueblos de la sierra: El poder y el espacio entre los indios del norte de Puebla hasta 1700.* Mexico City: El Colegio de México, 1987.

Garner, Richard L. "Price Trends in Eighteenth-Century Mexico." *Hispanic American Historical Review* 65, no. 2 (May 1985), 279–325.

———. "Zacatecas, 1750–1821: A Study of a Late Colonial Mexican City." Ph.D. diss., University of Michigan, 1970.

Garrioch, David. *Neighbourhood and Community in Paris, 1740–1790.* Cambridge, Eng.: Cambridge University Press, 1986.

Gerhard, Peter. *The North Frontier of New Spain.* Princeton, N.J.: Princeton University Press, 1982.

Gibson, Charles. *The Aztecs Under Spanish Rule: A History of the Indians of the Valley of Mexico, 1519–1810.* Stanford, Calif.: Stanford University Press, 1964.

Gonzalbo Aizpuru, Pilar. "Las fiestas hovohispanas: Espectáculo y ejemplo." *Mexican Studies/Estudios Mexicanos* 9, no. 1 (Winter 1993): 19–45.

Griffen, William B. *Indian Assimilation in the Franciscan Area of Nueva Vizcaya.* Tucson: University of Arizona Press, 1979.

Guthrie, Chester. "Riots in Seventeenth-Century Mexico." In Adele Ogden and Engel Sluiter, eds., *Greater America: Essays in Honor of Herbert Eugene Bolton.* Berkeley: University of California Press, 1945.

Gutiérrez, Ramón A. *When Jesus Came, the Corn Mothers Went Away: Marriage, Sexuality, and Power in New Mexico, 1500–1846.* Stanford, Calif.: Stanford University Press, 1991.

Hackett, Charles W., ed. *Historical Documents Relating to New Mexico, Nueva Vizcaya, and Approaches Thereto, to 1773.* 3 vols. Washington, D.C.: Carnegie Institution, 1923–37.

———, ed. and trans. *Revolt of the Pueblo Indians of New Mexico and Otermín's Attempted Reconquest, 1680–1682.* 2 vols. Albuquerque: University of New Mexico Press, 1942.

Hadley, Philip L. *Minería y sociedad en el centro minero de Santa Eulalia, Chihuahua (1709–1750).* Mexico City: Fondo de Cultura Económica, 1979.

Hammond, George P., and Agapito Rey, eds. and trans. *Don Juan de Oñate: Colonizer of New Mexico, 1595–1628.* 2 vols. Albuquerque: University of New Mexico Press, 1953.

Haring, Clarence H. *The Spanish Empire in America.* New York: Harcourt, Brace, & World, 1963.

Haskett, Robert S. *Indigenous Rulers: An Ethnohistory of Town Government in Colonial Cuernavaca.* Albuquerque: University of New Mexico Press, 1991.

———. "'Our Suffering with the Taxco Tribute': Involuntary Mine Labor and Indigenous Society in Central New Spain." *Hispanic American Historical Review* 71, no. 3 (Aug. 1991): 447–75.

Hoberman, Louisa Schell, and Susan Migden Socolow, eds. *Cities and Society in Colonial Latin America.* Albuquerque: University of New Mexico Press, 1986.

Hopper, Jack. "Orcasitas Family Genealogy." Manuscript.

Johnson, Lyman. "Artisans." In Hoberman and Socolow, *Cities and Society.*

Jones, Oakah. *Nueva Vizcaya: Heartland of the Spanish Frontier.* Albuquerque: University of New Mexico Press, 1988.

———. *Los Paisanos: Spanish Settlers on the Northern Frontier of New Spain.* Norman: University of Oklahoma Press, 1979.

Kagan, Richard L. *Students and Society in Early Modern Spain.* Baltimore: Johns Hopkins University Press, 1974.

Kamen, Henry. *Spain in the Later Seventeenth Century, 1665–1700.* London: Longman, 1980.

Kicza, John. "The Social and Ethnic Historiography of Colonial Latin

America: The Last Twenty Years." *William and Mary Quarterly* (3d ser.) 45, no. 3 (July 1988): 453–88.

Ladd, Doris M. *The Making of a Strike: Mexican Silver Workers' Struggles in Real del Monte, 1766–1775*. Lincoln: University of Nebraska Press, 1988.

Lavrin, Asunción. "In Search of the Colonial Woman in Mexico: the Seventeenth and Eighteenth Centuries." In Asunción Lavrin, ed., *Latin American Women: Historical Perspectives*. Westport, Conn.: Greenwood Press, 1978.

———, ed. *Sexuality and Marriage in Colonial Latin America*. Lincoln: University of Nebraska Press, 1989.

Lavrin, Asunción, and Edith Couturier. "Dowries and Wills: A View of Women's Socioeconomic Role in Colonial Guadalajara and Puebla, 1640–1790." *Hispanic American Historical Review* 59, no. 2 (May 1979): 280–304.

Leonard, Irving A. *Baroque Times in Old Mexico: Seventeenth-Century Persons, Places, and Practices*. Ann Arbor: University of Michigan Press, 1959.

Le Roy Ladurie, Emmanuel. *Carnival in Romans*. New York: George Braziller, 1979.

Leyva, Yolanda C. "El Amparo de las Viudas: Widows and Land in Colonial New Mexico." Master's research paper, University of Texas at El Paso, 1989.

Lipsett-Rivera, Sonya. "Women, Honour, and Violence in Late Colonial Mexico." Paper delivered at the Rocky Mountain Council on Latin American Studies, Vancouver, B.C., Apr. 1–3, 1993.

Liss, Peggy K. *Mexico under Spain, 1521–1556: Society and the Origins of Nationality*. Chicago: University of Chicago Press, 1975.

Lockhart, James. "Commentary." In Elsa Cecilia Frost, Michael C. Meyer, and Josefina Zoraida Vázquez, eds., *El trabajo y los trabajadores en la historia de México*. Mexico City: El Colegio de México; Tucson: University of Arizona Press, 1979.

———. *The Nahuas After the Conquest: A Social and Cultural History of the Indians of Central Mexico, Sixteenth Through Eighteenth Centuries*. Stanford, Calif.: Stanford University Press, 1992.

Lockhart, James, and Stuart B. Schwartz. *Early Latin America: A History of Colonial Spanish America and Brazil*. Cambridge, Eng.: Cambridge University Press, 1983.

Lourie, Elena. "A Society Organized for War: Medieval Spain." *Past and Present* 35 (Dec. 1966): 54–76.

Lynch, John. *Bourbon Spain, 1700–1808*. Oxford: Basil Blackwell, 1989.

Martin, Cheryl English. "The Dynamics of Clio: Periodization in the Social History of Colonial Mexico." *Latin American Research Review* 20, no. 1 (1985): 171–75.

———. "Name Index for Eighteenth-Century Chihuahua." Manuscript, Special Collections, University of Texas at El Paso Library.

———. "Popular Speech and Social Order in Northern Mexico, 1650–1830." *Comparative Studies in Society and History* 32, no. 2 (Apr. 1990): 305–24.

———. *Rural Society in Colonial Morelos*. Albuquerque: University of New Mexico Press, 1985.

Marzahl, Peter. *Town in the Empire: Government, Politics, and Society in Seventeenth-Century Popayán*. Austin: University of Texas Press, 1978.

McCaa, Robert. "*Calidad, Clase*, and Marriage in Colonial Mexico: The Case of Parral, 1788–90." *Hispanic American Historical Review* 64, no. 3 (Aug. 1984): 477–501.

Mecham, J. Lloyd. *Francisco de Ibarra and Nueva Vizcaya*. Durham, N.C.: Duke University Press, 1927.

Mendizábal, Miguel O. de. "Los minerales de Pachuca y Real del Monte en la época colonial." *El Trimestre Económico* 8, no. 2 (July–Sep. 1941): 253–309.

Meyer, Michael C., and William L. Sherman. *The Course of Mexican History*. 4th ed. New York: Oxford University Press, 1991.

Moore, John Preston. *The Cabildo in Peru under the Bourbons: A Study in the Decline and Resurgence of Local Government in the Audiencia of Lima, 1700–1824*. Durham, N.C.: Duke University Press, 1966.

———. *The Cabildo in Peru under the Hapsburgs: A Study in the Origins and Powers of the Town Council in the Viceroyalty of Peru, 1530–1700*. Durham, N.C.: Duke University Press, 1954.

Moorhead, Max L. *The Apache Frontier: Jacobo Ugarte and Spanish-Indian Relations in Northern New Spain*. Norman: University of Oklahoma Press, 1968.

———. *New Mexico's Royal Road: Trade and Travel on the Chihuahua Trail*. Norman: University of Oklahoma Press, 1958.

———. *The Presidio: Bastion of the Spanish Borderlands*. Norman: University of Oklahoma Press, 1975.

Muchembled, Robert. *Popular Culture and Elite Culture in France, 1400–1750*. Lydia Cochrane, trans. Baton Rouge: Louisiana State University Press, 1985.

Muriel, Josefina. *Los recogimientos de mujeres: Respuesta a una problemática social novohispana*. Mexico City: Instituto de Investigaciones Históricas, Universidad Nacional Autónoma de México, 1974.

Nunn, Charles F. *Foreign Immigrants in Early Bourbon Mexico, 1700–1760*. Cambridge, Eng.: Cambridge University Press, 1979.

Parry, J. H. *The Sale of Public Office in the Spanish Indies under the Hapsburgs*. Berkeley: University of California Press, 1953.

Perry, Mary Elizabeth. *Gender and Disorder in Early Modern Seville.* Princeton, N.J.: Princeton University Press, 1990.
Porras Muñoz, Guillermo. *La frontera con los indios de la Nueva Vizcaya en el siglo XVII.* Mexico City: Fomento Cultural Banamex, 1980.
———. *Iglesia y estado en Nueva Vizcaya (1562–1821).* Mexico City: Universidad Nacional Autonóma de México, 1980.
Powell, Philip Wayne. *Soldiers, Indians and Silver: The Northward Advance of New Spain, 1550–1600.* Berkeley: University of California Press, 1952.
Reps, John W. *The Making of Urban America: A History of City Planning in the United States.* Princeton, N.J.: Princeton University Press, 1965.
Rivera Ayala, Sergio. "Lewd Songs and Dances from the Streets of Eighteenth-Century New Spain." In Beezley, Martin, and French, *Rituals of Rule.*
Robles, Antonio de. *Diario de sucesos notables (1665–1703).* 3 vols. Mexico City: Editorial Porrua, 1972.
Romero de Terreros, Pedro. *La plaza mayor de México en el siglo XVIII.* Mexico City: Universidad Nacional Autónoma de México, 1946.
Scardaville, Michael C. "Alcohol Abuse and Tavern Reform in Late Colonial Mexico City." *Hispanic American Historical Review* 60, no. 4 (Nov. 1980): 643–71.
Schneider, Robert A. *Public Life in Toulouse, 1463–1789: From Municipal Republic to Cosmopolitan City.* Ithaca, N.Y.: Cornell University Press, 1989.
Scott, James C. *Domination and the Arts of Resistance: Hidden Transcripts.* New Haven, Conn.: Yale University Press, 1990.
Scott, Joan Wallach. "Gender: A Useful Category of Historical Analysis." *American Historical Review* 91, no. 5 (Dec. 1986): 1053–75.
Seed, Patricia. "Marriage Promises and the Value of a Woman's Testimony in Colonial Mexico." *Signs: Journal of Women in Culture and Society* 13, no. 2 (Winter 1988): 253–76.
———. *To Love, Honor and Obey in Colonial Mexico: Conflicts over Marriage Choice, 1574–1821.* Stanford, Calif.: Stanford University Press, 1988.
Simmons, Marc. "Governor Cuervo and the Beginnings of Albuquerque: Another Look." *New Mexico Historical Review* 55, no. 3 (July 1980): 189–204.
———. *The Last Conquistador: Juan de Oñate and the Settling of the Far Southwest.* Norman: University of Oklahoma Press, 1991.
Simpson, Lesley Byrd. *The Encomienda in New Spain: The Beginning of Spanish Mexico.* Berkeley and Los Angeles: University of California Press, 1950.
Socolow, Susan Migden. "Acceptable Partners: Marriage Choice in Colonial Argentina, 1778–1819." In Lavrin, *Sexuality and Marriage.*

———. "Introduction." In Hoberman and Socolow, *Cities and Society.*

———. *The Merchants of Buenos Aires, 1778–1810: Family and Commerce.* Cambridge, Eng.: Cambridge University Press, 1978.

———. "Women and Crime: Buenos Aires, 1757–97." *Journal of Latin American Studies* 12, no. 1 (May 1980): 39–54.

Stern, Peter, and Robert H. Jackson. "Vagabundaje and Settlement in Colonial Northern Sonora." *The Americas* 44, no. 4 (Apr. 1988): 461–81.

Stern, Steve J. "Feudalism, Capitalism and the World-System in the Perspective of Latin America and the Caribbean." *American Historical Review* 93, no. 4 (Oct. 1988): 829–72.

Swann, Michael M. *Migrants in the Mexican North: Mobility, Economy and Society in a Colonial World.* Boulder, Colo.: Westview Press, 1989.

———. *Tierra Adentro: Settlement and Society in Colonial Durango.* Boulder, Colo.: Westview Press, 1982.

Tamarón y Romeral, Pedro. *Demostración del vastísimo obispado de la Nueva Vizcaya, 1765.* Vito Alesio Robles, ed. Mexico City: Editorial Porrua, 1937.

Taylor, William B. "Amigos de Sombrero: The Patterns of Homicide in Rural Central Jalisco, 1784–1820." Manuscript.

———. *Drinking, Homicide, and Rebellion in Colonial Mexican Villages.* Stanford, Calif.: Stanford University Press, 1979.

———. *Landlord and Peasant in Colonial Oaxaca.* Stanford, Calif.: Stanford University Press, 1972.

Terrazas, Silvestre. "Confirmación y juramento de las primeras autoridades habidas en la Villa de San Felipe el Real de Chihuahua, al recibirse el documento real que la autorizó y el costo habido para ello." *Boletín de la Sociedad Chihuahuense de Estudios Históricos* 1, no. 12 (May 1939): 413–16.

Thompson, E. P. "Patrician Society, Plebeian Culture." *Journal of Social History* 7, no. 4 (Summer 1974), 382–405.

Tutino, John. *From Insurrection to Revolution in Mexico: Social Bases of Agrarian Violence, 1750–1940.* Princeton, N.J.: Princeton University Press, 1986.

Van Young, Eric. "Conflict and Solidarity in Indian Village Life: The Guadalajara Region in the Late Colonial Period." *Hispanic American Historical Review* 64, no. 1 (Feb. 1984): 55–79.

———. *Hacienda and Market in Eighteenth-Century Mexico: The Rural Economy of the Guadalajara Region.* Berkeley: University of California Press, 1981.

———. "Millennium on the Northern Marches: The Mad Messiah of Durango and Popular Rebellion in Mexico, 1800–1815." *Comparative Studies in Society and History* 28, no. 3 (July 1986): 385–413.

———. "Parvenues and Popinjays: Spaniards in Eighteenth-Century

Mexico." Paper presented at the South Central Society for Eighteenth-Century Studies, Austin, Texas, Mar. 1981.

———. "Recent Anglophone Scholarship on Mexico and Central America in the Age of Revolution." *Hispanic American Historical Review* 65, no. 4 (Nov. 1985): 725–44.

Vásquez Mellado, Alfonso. *La ciudad de los palacios: Imagenes de cinco siglos*. Mexico City: Editorial Diana, 1990.

Villamarín, Juan A., and Judith E. Villamarín. "The Concept of Nobility in Colonial Santa Fe de Bogotá." In Karen Spalding, ed., *Essays in the Political, Economic, and Social History of Colonial Latin America*. Newark: University of Delaware, 1982.

Viqueira Albán, Juan Pedro. *¿Relajados o reprimidos? Diversiones públicas y vida social en la ciudad de México durante el siglo de las luces*. Mexico City: Fondo de Cultura Económica, 1987.

Ward, Henry G. *Mexico in 1827*. London: H. Colburn, 1828.

West, Robert C. *The Mining Community in Northern New Spain: The Parral Mining District*. Berkeley: University of California Press, 1947.

Wislizenus, Frederick A. *Memoir of a Tour to Northern Mexico, Connected with Col. Doniphan's Expedition, in 1846 and 1847*. Glorieta, N.M.: Rio Grande Press, 1969.

Wood, Stephanie Gail. "Corporate Adjustments in Colonial Mexican Indian Towns: Toluca Region, 1550–1810." Ph.D. diss., University of California, Los Angeles, 1984.

Yoma Medina, María Rebeca, and Luis Alberto Martos López. "El Parián: Un siglo y medio de historia y comercio." *Boletín de Monumentos Históricos* 10 (July-Sept. 1990): 24–37.

Index

In this index an "f" after a number indicates a separate reference on the next page, and an "ff" indicates separate references on the next two pages. A continuous discussion over two or more pages is indicated by a span of page numbers, e.g., "57–59." *Passim* is used for a cluster of references in close but not consecutive sequence.

Library of Congress Cataloging-in-Publication Data

Martin, Cheryl English.
Governance and society in colonial Mexico: Chihuahua in the eighteenth century/Cheryl English Martin.
p. cm.
Includes bibliographical references (p.) and index.
ISBN 0-8047-2547-0 (cloth)
ISBN 0-8047-4168-9 (pbk)
1. Chihuahua (Mexico)—Social life and customs.
2. Mexico—History—Spanish colony, 1540–1810.
3. Chihuahua (Mexico)—Politics and government.
4. Chihuahua (Mexico)—Economic conditions. 5. Social structure—Mexico—Chihuahua. 6. Frontier and pioneer life—Mexico—Chihuahua. 7. Chihuahua (Mexico)—Race relations. I. Title.
F1391.C447M37 1996
972'.1602—dc20 95-16036
CIP

Original printing 1996
Last figure below indicates year of this printing:

15 14 13 12 11 10 09

Printed and bound by CPI Group (UK) Ltd, Croydon, CR0 4YY

09/06/2025

14685746-0002